DIPLOMATIC HISTORY
of the
SOUTHERN CONFEDERACY

AMERICAN CLASSICS

DIPLOMATIC HISTORY
of the
SOUTHERN
CONFEDERACY

James Morton Callahan

FREDERICK UNGAR PUBLISHING CO.
NEW YORK

Republished 1964 in the
AMERICAN CLASSICS SERIES

Reprinted from the first edition, 1901

Printed in the United States of America

Library of Congress Catalog Card No. 64-25546

CONTENTS

PREFACE

This volume is a study of the efforts of the Confederate authorities, in the face of waning hope and diminishing resources, to secure foreign recognition and support. It considers also the forces which controlled the European powers and defeated the attempt to divide the American Union, which, if successful, would have changed the current of political and economic evolution.

It attempts to give a careful and purely historical presentation of the theories, purposes, policies, diplomatic efforts, and difficulties of the Secessionists, as reflected from their official archives and other original records. It traces the inner working of the diplomatic machine during the many variations of the military and political situation, closely observes the attitude, motives, and policy of the great nations with whom the Confederate agents sought to negotiate, and throws light upon international questions arising between the United States and foreign powers.

Though other materials have not been neglected, the work is, in a large measure, based upon the Confederate diplomatic correspondence, which is now in manuscript in the United States Treasury Department. For permission to read this correspondence and to make extracts, I desire to acknowledge the courtesies of Judge Lewis Jordan, Chief of the Miscellaneous Division of the Treasury Department. For permission to examine several of the duplicates of Mr. Mason's despatches and originals of his instructions, I am grateful to his daughter, Miss Virginia Mason. For the narrative of Mr. Kenner, which has been utilized in the preparation of part of Chapter XII, I am under obligations to Brigadier-General J. L. Brent, of Baltimore, and the late Hon. William Wirt Henry, of Richmond. For suggestions of value in obtaining material, or for information upon particular points, my thanks are due to Mrs. Jefferson Davis and Burton N. Harrison, Esq., of New York; Comtesse Roman, of Paris; Brigadier-General Marcus J. Wright, Brigadier-General F. C. Ainsworth, Dr. J. L. M. Curry, Hon. John Goode, and Theodore J. Pickett, Esq., of Washington, D. C.; Colonel William Preston Johnston, Ernest B. Kruttschnitt, and Miss Grace King, of New Orleans; Rev. J. William Jones, of Richmond, and others. For careful and valuable service in the correction of the typewritten manuscript and proof-sheets, acknowledgment is due to Miss Elizabeth R. Daran, Librarian of the Historical Department of the Johns Hopkins University.

I am especially under deep obligations to Professor Herbert B. Adams, who has directed and encouraged me in this and other fields of research.

The materials upon which this volume is based were used in the preparation of a paper on Anglo-Confederate Relations, presented before the American Historical Association, at the New Haven meeting, December, 1898. My investigations resulted later in a course of lectures which were given upon the Albert Shaw foundation in the Johns Hopkins University.

JAMES MORTON CALLAHAN.

WASHINGTON, D. C., *April, 1901.*

CHAPTER I

THE CONFEDERATE DIPLOMATIC ARCHIVES

In a small room on the third floor of the Treasury Department, overlooking the Executive Mansion, are the manuscript archives, sometimes designated as the "Pickett Papers," which relate the story of the unsuccessful diplomatic efforts of the Southern Confederacy to secure admission as an independent member in the family of nations, to obtain the means necessary to the establishment of a navy and the maintenance of an army, and to bring about foreign mediation or intervention.

During the war many valuable despatches were captured while being carried through the blockade, and were afterwards published by United States papers, but the greater part of the Confederate correspondence, copies of which were in the offices at Richmond, were safely kept until the close of the war, and the Confederate Government exercised vigilance to prevent it from falling into the hands of the Federal authorities. For a time in the spring of 1862, locomotives were kept in readiness to remove the treasure and some of the archives. There were preparations for flight from Richmond for several weeks before the evacuation in the spring of 1865. Papers of the Government were revised and marked for destruction, abandonment or preservation.[1] A month before

[1] Pollard: Life of Jefferson Davis, with a Secret History of the Confederacy, Chapter XXX. J. B. Jones: Diary.

the evacuation some of the archives were sent to Lynchburg and others were packed in boxes to send away later. Mr. Benjamin destroyed the secret service papers on April 2, the day the Confederates set fire to Richmond. In the evening of that day trains steamed from the city with the Confederate treasure and archives, including those of the " State Department." The load dwindled until, in Georgia, it was carried in the saddle-bags of individuals. Some of Mr. Davis's papers accidentally fell into the hands of a young man at Richmond, who distributed them as autographs to his friends.[2] Part of his correspondence, including letters from disloyal persons in the North, was carried away and was said to be preserved under seal of personal confidence with Mr. Davis.[3] Many other valuable papers were hidden in the vicinity of Richmond.[4]

The United States captured only the refuse of the archives at the Confederate capital,[5] but soon established a bureau of " Rebel Archives," and added other manuscripts from time to time. On the fall of Charleston the Federal army had found a mass of papers relating to many subjects; some treated of the causes and plans of secession, others related to Southern life before and during the war, while still others were merely the letters and diary of a lady belonging to one of the historic families of South Carolina, whose trembling hand notified an ardent and pleading lover that " men and matters change."

[2] Letter of Mrs. Davis to the author, Jan. 13, 1899.
[3] The volumes of " office copies " of letters written by Mr. Davis, are preserved, and are now in the control of Mrs. Varina J. Davis.
[4] Pollard: Life of Jefferson Davis, etc., p. 368.   [5] Ibid.

Correspondence and records bearing upon the war were obtained in many other places. When General Joseph Johnston surrendered in 1865, he notified General Schofield at Raleigh that he had in his possession at Charlotte, North Carolina, certain records and archives of the Confederacy which he was ready to deliver. A United States officer received them and they were sent to Washington. The United States afterwards claimed all the effects of the Confederacy abroad, including money in the hands of agents and vessels-of-war in foreign ports. Some of the Confederate agents at the close of the war destroyed their papers for fear they might fall into the hands of the Federal Government.[6] Mr. Mason, however, carefully preserved his voluminous correspondence, and while living in Canada guarded against any possibility of its seizure.

While the important Confederate archives were being removed from Richmond, the diplomatic correspondence, consisting of the "State Department" archives, except the secret service vouchers, was taken by a Southern man and hidden in a barn in Virginia. After the excitement had somewhat subsided, the papers were removed to Washington in five separate trunks and, in order to guard against seizure by the Government, were deposited in several places for safe keeping. It appears that the custodian of the papers was in reduced circumstances and that sums of money for his current expenses were advanced by Colonel John T. Pickett, who was employed by him as an agent to dispose of the papers.[7]

[6] Baltimore Sun, July 30, 1872.
[7] Interview with Theodore J. Pickett. It should be stated, however, although Col. Pickett always claimed to be the

Pickett was a well-known Southern man, having been United States Consul at Turk's Island and also at Vera Cruz, Mexico, for a number of years. He had also been commissioned by Louis Kossuth as a general in the Hungarian service. Later he had joined the Lopez expedition to Cuba and was in command against the Spanish regulars at the battle of Cardenas.[8] He was secretary of the Confederate Peace Commission to Washington in 1861, after which he was sent as a commissioner to Mexico, and later served in the Confederate army as chief-of-staff to Gen. John C. Breckinridge.

Pickett, stating that he had found the archives stored away in Canada and had bought a certain control of them, wrote, January 20, 1868, from Toronto, offering them to Seward, who replied that they would have to be brought to Washington and examined before purchase. The proposition was declined. When Grant became President the papers were offered to him in person, and he favored their acquisition, but the consideration of the subject was delayed. Pickett also offered them to Southern men of wealth, to publishers, and to historical associations, but was unable to dispose of them. Knowing that the archives exhibited the fact that Thompson was in Canada with considerable money when the Confederacy fell, Pickett made a long journey to Thompson's home in the summer of 1871, but the latter, feeling that his correspondence had been destroyed by Mr. Benjamin, showed

---

agent of a custodian whom he never named, some of his acquaintances suggested that he, himself, was the custodian.

[8] Many interesting facts relating to Pickett may be found among his private papers now in possession of his son.

no disposition to buy the documents.[9] During the
same summer various persons went to Pickett to investigate the papers, and he, acting as attorney for the
custodian, offered to sell them to the United States
officials, at the same time representing that they were
in Canada. He finally exhibited a copy of the in-
ventory, found with the property, giving indices of
the contents of the trunks. The President, in the
meantime having issued his amnesty proclamation,
and the unknown, needy custodian urging a conclusion, Pickett entered into negotiations with Cabinet
officers and the "Southern Claims" Commissioners.
In April, 1872, the United States agents appointed
to make the purchase went with Pickett to Canada
to examine the contents of the trunks. Pickett, without the knowledge of the agents, carried the trunks
to Canada on the same train, and after crossing the
border they were submitted to a two weeks' examination.[10] He had hoped to obtain $150,000, but accepted
half the sum rather than wait longer. The officers
reported in favor of the purchase, and the custodian
of the papers agreed to deliver them to the Government.

An appropriation to enable the Secretary of War
to examine the Confederate archives was approved
May 8, 1872, but it seems that the diplomatic papers
were purchased by special act of Congress which was
passed a month later.[11] Pickett, having first made
copies of the papers for his own use, transferred them
to the Government. On July 3, 1872, four yellow
trunks were delivered at the White House, where he

[9] The Daily Patriot (Washington), July 19, 1872.
[10] Interview with T. J. Pickett.
[11] See Cong. Globe, Part VI, Appendix, 42-2, p. 711.

was handed $75,000, from which he received stipulated fees and reimbursement for his expenses. Through Mr. Riggs, a Washington banker, a great part of these fees was distributed to needy widows and orphans of Confederate officers, without informing them as to the source of the charity.

The news that the " Pickett Papers " had been purchased soon became public. Among them the report of Jacob Thompson concerning plans to burn Northern cities and commit other depredations was found and soon afterwards published in the newspapers. A great many articles appeared regarding the delivery of the papers to the United States Government, very exaggerated accounts of the character of the papers and the price received were published, and great injustice was done to Colonel Pickett, whose connection with the transaction was that of an agent or attorney of the custodian. Some said that no good could result from the exhibit of long-buried documents, unless they should be in defense of persons maligned; others, including Sanford Conover, said that the papers would prove to be forgeries, and that Secretary Boutwell had wasted $75,000 on four trunks of worthless archives. Some, speaking of them as campaign documents, said that the impending presidential election seemed to have whetted the appetite of the administration to purchase records which, when sifted, might be found to reflect on Judge Davis, who had just been nominated for the presidency. Several prominent Southern men blamed Pickett for delivering the correspondence. Some suggested that it was forged and some that it was stolen.[12]

[12] N. Y. Herald, July 24 and 28, 1872. Daily Patriot, July 22 and 27, 1872.

Colonel Pickett, in a published statement of his agency in the sale of the archives, vindicated his action. To those who feared that prominent men might be injured, he stated that Mr. Benjamin had burned the secret service vouchers, and that under any circumstances he would not have delivered such papers to the Government. Of those delivered he said that the Thompson report was the only one that gave him any pain, and without the consideration of incapacity and blunders, that it was the only one " discreditable to the three or four men who ran the Confederate machine." He admitted that Thompson, Davis and Benjamin might feel uncomfortable for awhile, but stated that Thompson, to whom he had given an opportunity to buy the papers, could not now complain. As to the Thompson report, Pickett declared that he did not know of its presence among the papers until his attention was drawn to it while making the examination in Canada, and that it was then too late to withdraw it. He repudiated the policy of attempting to burn the Northern cities.

Pickett said that the Confederacy yet owed him $50,000, but that, in preserving the documents, he acted only in the interest of his client and of history. " What right had I," inquired he, " to destroy the material by which history is written? The person who spirited the papers away and held them in his possession was getting impatient and swore that he would dispose of them himself. When the papers were sold he received the greater part of the money and took the first train." As to the charge that the documents were stolen, Pickett said that they were rather restored to their rightful owner—the heir-at-law and residuary legatee of the defunct Confederacy. The Baltimore *Sun* asked why Pickett had not delivered them sooner, if they were the rightful property of the United States!

Pickett declared that the archives had no present political significance, and insisted that they should be respected as part of American history. He did not see any wrong in placing them in the hands of the Government so that generations to come might know the truth. He did not think that the Confederate Government should be ashamed of its records, and if by chance their publications should injure some individuals it was simply the fate of war.

Aside from the letters from Confederate agents in Canada, the archives did not contain the material which was expected to make Thompson, Davis, Benjamin and others uncomfortable, and as a campaign weapon the collection was not such a boomerang as had been expected.[13] After the publication of Thompson's report, parties in the South and elsewhere offered to sell other Confederate manuscripts.[14] Pickett had a list of books used by the Confederacy and held by parties in Texas which he proposed to furnish for a remuneration.[15] They contained correspondence or lists relating to subscriptions to the cotton loan, transfers of steamers from English firms to the Confederacy, confiscation of property by the Confederate Government and the exchange of cotton to English

[13] Baltimore Sun, July 30, 1872. Also, the Memphis Appeal.
[14] Baltimore Sun, July 15, 1873.
[15] Pickett also had in his possession the official seal of the Confederacy, but he did not sell it. Electrotype "medals" of it were for awhile on sale by a Washington jeweler. Very few persons know who now has the original seal.

subjects for rifles. Still other papers were offered by other persons, but the Government had decided to make no further purchases. Later, however, some of those who had first been disposed to censure Pickett's conduct sold important military papers to the Government, thus practically sanctioning his action.

In June, 1874, Congress passed an act to enable the Secretary of War to begin the publication of Union and Confederate official records. On July 1, General Marcus J. Wright was appointed agent of the War Department for collecting Confederate military records. He has obtained the originals or copies of many valuable military and executive papers. Persons having correspondence have generally shown a disposition to have it published, though the Government no longer makes purchases.[16] The Naval War Records Office has also gathered much material for publication.

Time has proven that Boutwell did not pay for waste paper. The names in the indexes of the Pickett papers, together with the indexes of the correspondence of the Confederate Treasury and other departments, have proven of great convenience and value to the Government in defeating the payment of fraudulent claims to the amount of many millions of dollars. Hence the transaction has proven a most profitable one from a financial point of view. The indexes are not made according to subjects, but are arranged according to the names of persons, giving their post-office addresses and the subjects of their correspondence opposite. Thus the records of persons making

[16] Marcus J. Wright in Phila. Weekly Times, April 10, 1880.

claims on the Government can be ascertained in a short time by referring to the correspondence itself. In the index the subjects of letters are given by such short titles as are indicated in the following taken from the index of the " Miscellaneous " papers: " Suggestions," " salt-petre," " loud complaints," " abstraction of State-papers," " vents his spleen on his captors," " bustling with joy for the Confederacy."

Outside of the great value which the Pickett archives have had in facilitating the investigation of claims, they have still greater importance as historical material. Embracing the larger part of the diplomatic correspondence of the Confederate Government, they have a far greater value than any of the collections of military papers or records. Pickett said that the archives consisted of all the " State Department " correspondence without the abstraction of a single paper; but it must be remembered that Mr. Benjamin destroyed papers relating to secret missions [17] and that a few despatches from abroad failed to reach Richmond, although second and third duplicates were started across the Atlantic. Of Slidell's despatches, numbered from 1 to 76 inclusive (January, 1862, to December 13, 1864), only " No. 21 " is missing, but several of Mason's failed to reach Richmond. No letters written by Mason and Slidell to Mr. Benjamin, or by Mr.

[17] Mr. Benjamin seems always to have had a desire not to leave behind him any historical material. He also seemed to have an abhorrence of any ransacking of his private papers and correspondence, and a very short time before his death he destroyed all such manuscripts. Some of his correspondence of the period before 1861 may be found *passim* in the archives of the State Department at Washington, but no collection of his private letters is to be found anywhere.

Benjamin to them, after December, 1864, are to be found in the papers purchased from Pickett. It is quite probable that the strict blockade after January, 1865, prevented Benjamin from receiving European correspondence; and his own letters after December 30, 1864, were probably laid aside to be copied in the record books later, and were not packed with the other archives at the time when preparations were made to evacuate Richmond.

The scope of the material included in the Pickett collection may be indicated by the following list:

1. Instructions and despatches of the commission to Washington, 1861.

2. Papers relating to the ratification of the ordinances of secession.

3. Correspondence relating to Fort Sumter.

4. Diplomatic despatches of Yancey, Rost, Mann, Mason, Slidell, Lamar, Lynch, Pickett, Preston, Cripps and Ricken, the Confederate representatives in England, Spain, Belgium, France, Russia, Rome and Mexico.[18]

5. Record books containing the letters of Secretaries Toombs, Hunter and Benjamin to diplomatic, consular and special or confidential agents abroad.

6. Consular correspondence, including that of Hotze, De Leon, McRae, Quintero, Fitzpatrick, La Sere, Avegeno, Bannon, Capston, Dowling, Labor, Walker, Lee, Helm, Heyleger, Thompson, Clay and Holcombe, representing the Confederacy in London, Paris, Mexico, Ireland, the West Indies and Canada.

[18] The larger part of the diplomatic and consular correspondence is in "Trunk B."

7. Record copies and originals of domestic letters from the State Department, and the originals of miscellaneous letters to the department.

8. Applications for appointments to positions, for letters of marque and for passports, and subscription lists for persons to whom passports were issued.

9. Index to testimony concerning property taken or destroyed, etc.

10. Newspapers and clippings.

11. Proclamations, messages, pardons, commissions, appropriations, constitutions, and acts of Congress.

12. Indexes, "Cash Book," ledgers, etc.

Some of the Confederate agents abroad kept copies of their private correspondence. In some cases this is valuable in supplementing the Richmond archives which have been preserved to us through the thoughtfulness of Colonel Pickett. J. M. Mason's complete public and private correspondence, including that with Messrs. Benjamin, Slidell, Mann, and other Confederate officials, is in possession of his daughter, Miss Virginia Mason of Charlottesville, who, after publishing a portion of it, contemplates leaving it with the Virginia Historical Society. Among these papers are several official letters not found in the Richmond archives. John Slidell unfortunately destroyed the bulk of his private correspondence during his residence in Paris.[19]

Colonel Ambrose Dudley Mann wrote from memory an account of his diplomatic career, leaving the task of editing it to Miss Winnie Davis, but owing to

---

[19] Letter of Comtesse Roman to the author.

his death the manuscript was never placed in the hands of Miss Davis and has never been published.[20]

The prominent men, who could have spoken from personal experience and intimate acquaintance regarding the foreign policy and diplomacy of the Confederacy, have passed from the stage of action, and have left no record of personal narratives which might have been drawn from their mines of reminiscences. John H. Reagan, of Austin, Texas, the only surviving member of the Confederate Cabinet, has been so busily engaged with public and private cares since the war that he has had " substantially no opportunity to review and perpetuate the memory of past events." He is now over eighty years of age and can no longer trust his memory on important points unless fortified by the records. He probably had no occasion to know much regarding the department of Mr. Benjamin, who knew how to keep his own secrets.

Mr. L. Q. C. Washington, who was assistant secretary under Benjamin, and now resides in Washington, D. C., is probably the only living man who had opportunity to know the inside motives and plans of Confederate diplomacy. In some cases, he finds himself unable to recall details unless he can refresh his memory by reference to documents. Although he always knew more than anyone else, except Benjamin, regarding the routine work of the office, on some points he has only a vague recollection. Perhaps there were some diplomatic missions, the details of which were not confided to him.

[20] Letter of Mrs. Davis to the author.

Walker Fearn, who was connected with the. missions of Lamar and of Preston as secretary, and was for some time in close relation with Mason and Slidell in Europe, lived until 1899, but was not inclined to write.

In a letter of Colonel Pickett, under date of July 26, 1872, he alludes to a " forthcoming work " on the " diplomacy of the rebellion," but does not name the person who contemplated the preparation of such a work.   J. D. Bullock, an agent of the Confederate navy, in his " Secret Service of the Confederate States in Europe," has given a graphic account of the plans of the Confederacy to secure a navy and of the difficulties which had to be met.   John Bigelow, the United States Consul at Paris and also United States minister at the same place during the Civil War, has treated the same subject in his volume on " France and the Confederate Navy," a work based upon his own observation and upon Mr. Slidell's correspondence.

CHAPTER II

The Confederacy had a *de facto* Government, though it was not formally recognized by any power. For over three years it made its home in Richmond, and the vast armies of the United States unsuccessfully beat against its strongholds. It adopted a flag and a seal of its own.[1] More important than flag or seal, it had an army whose achievements won the admiration of the world; but it had no navy with which to open the blockade and give the Government that probability of permanence which was necessary to secure European recognition.[2]

---

[1] Davis loved the old flag, and many favored keeping it; but the Confederate Congress, in February, 1865, in the face of Federal triumph, decided upon a temporary design, and was debating the adoption of a flag for future generations. The seal was not received at Richmond until near the close of the war. In April, 1863, Congress passed a resolution for the seal and the next month Benjamin authorized Mason to have it executed in England. In July, 1864, after many delays, Mason sent it by Lieutenant Chapman and shipped two boxes containing the iron press necessary for making the impression. [Despatches of Mason, No. 10, July 6, 1864.] The seal reached Richmond in September, but the boxes were lost. [An article on the seal, by J. T. Pickett, appears in the Am. Hist. Record, Vol. III, p. 360.]

[2] In some respects the South had the advantage at the beginning of the war. The United States executive had been left unprepared for war, two-thirds of the serviceable steam vessels were in foreign ports, and many high officials were Southern sympathizers. The Secessionists, from their position, required a less number of troops than the Union-

The organization of a central authority for the seceding states began at Montgomery, Alabama, on February 4, 1861. The conservative leaders, like Stephens, were opposed to secession as " a remedy against anticipated aggressions," and many still hoped for something to occur to prevent permanent dissolution of the Union and at the same time secure terms favorable to the institution of slavery. Stephens had urged that Democratic failure at the polls furnished the South no reason for breaking the Constitution, but he had not been heeded by those of a more impulsive temperament. Cobb, of Georgia, had advised the state legislature to declare for secession without waiting " to hear from the cross-roads and the groceries." Toombs, of Georgia, had demanded that he be given the sword. In December a South Carolina convention had declared for secession, and asked the other slaveholding states to cooperate and to send delegates to form a provisional congress. Other state conventions had soon responded to the invitation.

The Montgomery council of delegates, who had been hastily selected at a time when it was expected that a war resulting from secession could only last a few months, became a provisional congress for one year. Cobb, as the temporary president of the council until the organization of the provisional government, appointed the committees by which the

preservation party. The North, however, had the advantage of resources and factories and more business men. These count in war, and made the North firmer than the South had expected. A navy large enough to blockade the Southern ports was soon created. The North had a population of 23,000,000, while the South only had 9,000,000, of which 3,500,000 were slaves.

organization was effected. The constitution for the provisional government was reported by a committee including two members from each state, and on February 8 it was accepted by the assembled delegates. It was practically the same as the Constitution of the United States. Two new features were introduced, however, by Mr. Stephens.[a] Congress was to have no power to appropriate money unless requested by the executive or the heads of the departments. The clause excluding Cabinet members from Congress was omitted. (Stephens thought it would even be well to choose the Cabinet members from Congress.) The provisional government was to last one year. Davis and Stephens were elected President and Vice-President respectively, the vote being taken by states. Stephens concurred in Toombs's superior qualification for the presidency, but political maneuvering placed it on Davis, who, it seems, did not want it. On February 16, Davis arrived, and at once appointed a Confederate commission to Washington in accordance with a resolution of Congress. He selected Forsyth of Alabama, Crawford of Georgia, and Roman of Louisiana. He desired peace with the United States. Slavery demanded it, and the South was not ready for war. Stephens was greatly bored by the debates of the new Congress; but it was from the people that he expected trouble, for he saw that it would be necessary for them to exercise great patience with the inconveniences of derangements of mails and commerce and the increase of taxes.

The permanent constitution was completed March 9.

Johnston and Browne: Life of Stephens.

Rhett was chairman of the committee that framed it. He, Toombs and Stephens, proposed most of the variations from the Federal Constitution, which was followed as interpreted by Southerners. The central Government was limited and its hands tied. The constitution began: "We, the People of the Confederate States, each State acting in its sovereign and independent character, in order to form a Permanent Federal Government," etc. The " general welfare " clause was omitted. Several new provisions and restrictions were added. Congress was authorized to allow heads of departments to appear in the legislative chambers to explain their recommendations.[*] Appropriations were proposed by the heads of the departments, except in case of a two-thirds vote of both Houses to the contrary. The President, who was given power to convene and adjourn either House at his will, could approve or disapprove an appropriation bill by sections. Bills appropriating money were to relate to but one subject, and that was to be expressed in the title (against the "rider"). The post-office was to be self-sustaining after 1863. Revenue was to be obtained by import duties to pay the debts, to provide for the common defense, and for the expenses of the Government, but no bounties nor pro-

[*] The committee favored the clause in the Federal constitution which prevented the Cabinet from being chosen from Congress, but this view did not carry. The permission to introduce heads of executive departments into Congress was practiced under the provisional government, but after February, 1862, no steps were taken towards putting it into practice, and Congress uttered stinging criticisms against Davis and his cabinet officers, though it yielded to executive need, and its members thereby became men of little influence and initiative.

tective duties were to be placed on imports. The Secretary of the Treasury was required to publish an itemized statement of the receipts and the disbursements of his office. There were to be no general internal improvements to facilitate commerce. Each state was allowed to tax marine commerce in its harbors. In case a harbor was improved by Congress it was necessary to reimburse the Confederate treasury by taxes on the commerce of that harbor. States could unite to improve a river dividing or flowing through them. States were to be admitted by a two-thirds vote of each House, the vote of the Senate being by states. (Stephens had desired the new constitution to be framed so as to admit non-slaveholding states in case they should apply.) Congress could pass no bankruptcy act to discharge debts contracted before such act. Congress could not interfere with the place or the time of electing senators. The African slave trade was forever prohibited, although the Confederate Government had no authority to make treaties upon the subject. Congress could prohibit the introduction of slaves from states not members of the Confederacy. It could take no part in amending the constitution.

The President and Vice-President were to serve for six years and the President was not re-eligible. Provision was made against the dogma " to the victors belong the spoils." If the President removed officials of a lower grade than the Cabinet it was necessary for him to report the cause to Congress, and he could make no appointment if rejected by the Senate.[5]

[5] In the early part of 1865 a conference of the Virginia members of the Confederate Congress advised Davis to reorganize

No supreme court was provided, though it was expected to establish one later. Citizens of one state could not bring suit against citizens of another state in the Federal courts. For constitutional offenses the legislature of a state could not impeach a Federal judge whose duties were confined to that state. The Department of Justice was to be administered under the attorney-general. The states were denied their former privilege of granting franchises to persons not citizens under the general law of naturalization. Provision was made to change the constitution. Three states could demand a convention of states to alter or amend it, but Congress could not suggest alterations. The constitution was ratified by state conventions.[6]

Davis promptly selected a Cabinet. Toombs of Georgia, was appointed Secretary of State; Memminger of South Carolina, Secretary of the Treasury; Mallory of Florida, Secretary of the Navy; Reagan

the cabinet by relieving all the existing members. Davis refused, but on January 18, Mr. Seddon of Virginia, the Secretary of War, handed in his letter of resignation. On February 1, the President finally acquiesced in Seddon's resignation, but he did not admit the power of Congress to control such a matter (as in England). He stated that the Confederate Cabinet members were not members of Congress, did not originate legislation, and were not admitted to the right of debate. Two weeks later the Virginia delegates stated that their advice to Davis had been confidential and had only been given to prevent a collision; that there were many others in Congress who favored a change in the Cabinet, but that they did not assume the power of Congress to compel a resignation of the Cabinet, and had spoken only for public sentiment and safety. [Richmond Dispatch, Feb. 15, 1865.]

[6] On the Confederate Constitution, see articles in the Galaxy for March, 1874, and Frazer's Mag. for Oct., 1862.

of Texas, Postmaster-General, while J. P. Benjamin[7] of Louisiana " full of accomplishments and sophistry, placid and smiling, his brow ever unclouded " was, strangely, not dispatched to European Courts, but made Attorney-General of a government " never destined to have a judiciary." Toombs was chosen Secretary of State only after Barnwell of South Carolina, had refused to accept the place. Chafing under red tape and complaining that too many were seeking bomb-proof positions under a timid administration, he soon resigned and was succeeded by R. M. T. Hunter of Virginia.[8] William Lowndes Yancey was offered the chief place in the European Commission,

[7] Judah P. Benjamin was born in 1811 on the British island of St. Croix in the West Indies. His parents had recently sailed from England with the purpose of settling at New Orleans, but at the close of the war of 1812 they located at Wilmington, N. C. Benjamin located at New Orleans in 1832 to practice law, and in 1852 and again in 1857 he was chosen to represent Louisiana in the United States Senate, where his resolute face, piercing eyes and clear voice helped him in gaining a reputation as an eloquent speaker. He had great influence with the Buchanan administration—much to the discomfort of John Forsyth who was minister to Mexico in 1856-58. During the civil war some spoke of him as " the brains of the Confederacy."

An English journalist said he was the most cordial Confederate he ever met, though " too fond of the card table where cooler heads squeezed his sponge dry."

He was at his office early and late and first suggested many of the measures of the Davis administration, some of which evoked severe criticism from the people and Congress. He had for years been on intimate terms with Slidell, who took steps to secure a Confederate navy in France.

On the fall of Richmond, in 1865, he escaped to England after several romantic adventures, and soon began practice at the English bar, where he won distinction. In 1883 he retired from practice, and died in 1884.

[8] Stovall: Robert Toombs, Chap. XXI.

and although he did not receive the instructions which he considered necessary to his success, he decided to accept.[9]

The provisional congress soon passed laws relating to the tariff, navigation, the slave trade, the establishment of ports, and the issue of money. An act for raising money authorized Mr. Davis to borrow $15,000,000, payable in ten years at 8 per cent, and to impose an export duty on cotton as a means of creating a fund for paying the principal and interest of the loan. At a session held by the call of Mr. Davis at Montgomery on April 29, 1861, Congress recognized the existence of war, authorized letters of marque, and passed a bill for the issue of $50,000,000 in bonds, or, in lieu of these bonds, $20,000,000 of treasury notes of small denomination, without interest.

In June the Government was removed to Richmond for political and military reasons. Davis, expecting to direct the armies, desired to be in Virginia near the seat of war, and Congress decided to follow the executive department.[10] The battle of Bull Run in July gave the Confederacy bright views of the future, and Stephens expected a " reign of terror to develop in the North." But there soon arose a strong opposition party in the South. Many opposed Davis's policy of endeavoring to produce a cotton famine in order to force Europe to recognize his Government.[11] Congress gradually became alienated. As the time approached for the inauguration of the " permanent

[9] Du Bose: Life and Times of Yancey.

[10] Confed. " Dip. Cor.", Vol. I. Instr. to Yancey, Rost and Mann, No. 6, May 24, 1861.

[11] Mrs. Davis: Jefferson Davis.

government," Hunter and Beauregard were mentioned for the presidency, but Davis continued to hold the reins.

In November, 1861, the people at the polls chose presidential electors, and elected members to serve in the new Congress. In the case of states overrun by the enemy, as Missouri and Arkansas, congressmen were elected by a handful of votes in the camps of the army of Virginia. The electors confirmed the provisional choice of Davis and Stephens; and with little ceremony Davis passed from a provisional chief to a president chosen for six years. The permanent government had its birth in a storm on February 22. The skies poured incessantly and Capitol Square was black with umbrellas, but there was an impression that the Confederacy would yet thrive in sunshine. Davis retained his former Cabinet, with the exception of Hunter, who was succeeded by Benjamin as Secretary of State. He admitted that errors had been made in the war policy, but he had abundant faith in the administration for the future.

After February, 1862, Congress was composed of two Houses, the representatives being now chosen by the people instead of by conventions, as in 1861.[12]

[12] The last session of the provisional Confederate Congress began in Richmond on Nov. 18, 1861, and ended Feb. 17, 1862. The first session of the first regular Confederate Congress met on Feb. 18. Hunter, of Virginia, was chosen president of the Senate, and Bocock, of Virginia, speaker of the House. The more prominent members were Wm. L. Yancey of Ala., B. H. Hill of Ga., R. M. T. Hunter and Wm. B. Preston of Va., A. H. Garland of Ark., Julian Hartridge of Ga., H. C. Chambers of Miss., W. H. Smith of N. C., Wm. Porcher Miles of S. C., H. S. Foote of Tenn., and C. W. Russell, J. P. Holcombe and John P. Baldwin of Va. Though Foote

The members were prevented, by law, from holding military commissions in the army, as many had done in the provisional Congress. Some, like Pollard, said that this was unfortunate and that it resulted in making Congress an inane and incompetent assembly, the best men having a passion for military service. Pollard declared that the Congress came at last to be a reflection of Mr. Davis, and was composed of unknown men or broken-down politicians, " who abandoned the whole government to Davis and a few weak creatures around him," though a few distinguished politicians returned from the battle-field before the close of the war. Stephens, on February 26, 1862,

urged aggressive measures, a defensive policy of conducting the war was sustained. The Senate recommended the destruction of all cotton and tobacco that could not safely be removed beyond the reach of Federal forces; and the House advised the planters to devote their attention to the production of provisions instead of cotton and tobacco. Authority was given to impress negroes to work on fortifications. At the second session, which began Aug. 18, 1862, Congress extended the conscript law to persons under 45 years of age, and passed a bill to reduce the interest on the funded debt and to authorize the issue of 6 per cent convertible bonds. At the third session, which began Jan. 12, 1863, it passed an act authorizing the impressment of produce necessary for the use of the army, and discussed a bill for the organization of a Supreme Court, which passed the House (March 18), but died in the judiciary committee of the House, where there was much difference of opinion as to how much power should be conferred upon the court. At the session which began Dec. 7, 1863, a conscript act was passed making persons between the ages of 18 and 55 subject to military duty. The gravity of the situation induced many to favor resolutions for peace. At the last session, which met Nov. 7, 1864, Congress talked more than it worked, but finally adopted the most important of Mr. Davis's recommendations and adjourned *sine die.*

wrote that Congress was not such as he could wish it either in the Senate or in the House. In April, he said: " This is a very poor Congress. There are few men of ability in the House—only two or three in the Senate." Again, in September, when fretting over military orders and the suspension of the writ of habeas corpus, he said: " We have not the men in Congress to act—they have not the knowledge of principles. They are children in politics and statesmanship." [13] There were, however, several remarkable men in the Senate, Yancey of Alabama, and Wigfall of Texas, were the fiercely eloquent orators. Orr of South Carolina, and Hill of Georgia, were also prominent. Barksdale, a friend of Davis, was the leader in the House. [14]

The dispersion of the " fugacious Congress " in

[13] Johnston and Browne: Life of A. H. Stephens.

[14] Hon. John Goode, in response to a query, has named the following persons as the ablest and most active members of the Confederate Congress from 1862 to 1865:

1. Supporters of the policy of the administration—In the House: R. M. T. Hunter of Va., Clement C. Clay of Ala., Benj. H. Hill of Ga., Gustavus Henry of Tenn. In the Senate: J. L. M. Curry of Ala., Garland of Ark., Hartridge of Ga., Conrad of La., Barksdale of Miss., Miles of S. C.

2. Those holding views in opposition to the policy of the administration—In the House: Baldwin of Va., Smith of N. C., Foote of Tenn. In the Senate: Louis T. Wigfall of Texas.

Hon. J. L. M. Curry names as the most prominent members of the second Congress: Jemison, Walker, Hill, Johnson, Semmes, Graham, Orr, Barnwell, Wigfall and Hunter.

Probably not more than ten or twelve members of that Congress lived to see the last year of the nineteenth century. Goode, Curry, Pugh, Breckinridge, Barksdale, Miles, Atkins, Wright, Pryor, Lester, Bell, Bruce and one or two others have been mentioned to the author as late survivors.

April, 1862, when whispered alarms said that McClellan would take Richmond, was a source of much amusement. Members were represented as running to their homes even amidst the contempt of women.[15] Shop-windows were filled with amusing caricatures representing congressmen, with carpetbags, pursued by insects magnified to represent gunboats. Newspapers stated that some of the stampeders left in canal-boats drawn by three sweet-tempered mules (for fear of accidents on railroads), and that a regiment of women were detailed to march in front of the mules "to clear the tow-path of piratical snakes and bull-frogs." [16]

Congress had no commodious quarters in which to hold its sessions. The Senate met in a plain, dingy, third-floor chamber. There were no accommodations for ladies. The House had better chambers, but the chairs were uncushioned and the benches slashed by knives. There was no legislative decorum. Members were described as sitting with their heels in the air. All important business was conducted in secret session. A synopsis of the ordinary debates appeared only in the newspapers and there was no stenographic report.[17] In August, 1862, Yancey desired to check the undemocratic practice of secret sessions so that the people could see how senators voted on the war plans of the Government. A short time

[15] Richmond Examiner, April 21, 1862. Also, the Richmond Whig.

[16] E. A. Pollard in the Galaxy, Dec., 1868. For the temper of the women in the war see G. C. Eggleston's " Recollections " (N. Y., 1875), Chap. III.

[17] Du Bose: Yancey; The Weekly Register (Lynchburg), Vol. I, Feb. 27, 1864.

later a committee of the Senate decided that a reporter of the Richmond *Enquirer* had violated the privileges granted him by the Senate and advised that he be excluded from the bar hereafter. Yancey opposed such action as an infringement of the liberty of the press. Several months before this a report of the judiciary committee of the provisional Government had recommended a law to restrict or restrain the press and speech under certain circumstances, and Wigfall, solemnly rising, simply read the sedition law. On April 13, 1863, Johnson of Arkansas, moved in the Senate that a committee of three be appointed by the chair with leave to sit during vacation, and to investigate and report to the Senate at the next session upon the expediency of providing for regular and perfect reports of the debates of the Senate, and of embracing secret as well as open sessions, and to report the terms for which reporters could be obtained, and other costs incident to publication. The Senate agreed to the resolution, but the debates were never reported, and were more and more concealed from the public eye.[18] Toward the end of the war, when the people were growing more restless, nearly everything was done in secret session.[19]

There were many animated debates and exciting scenes at Richmond which did not find their way into the newspapers, but which leaked out in whispered conversations. In January, 1863, when the Senate was considering the organization of the judiciary, Yancey and others opposed the conferring of appel-

[18] Richmond Whig, April 14, 1863.
[19] N. Y. Times, March 12, 1865.

late jurisdiction on the Confederate supreme court over the state supreme courts, as had been proposed by the judicial committee of the provisional Congress of which Mr. Hill had been chairman. On February 4, Hill, while speaking on the same bill, made some bitter references concerning Yancey, who replied that the statements were false. Shortly afterwards, during a lull in business, Senator Hill, after some remark by Yancey, whizzed a tumbler past his head and broke an inkstand over his cheek bone.[20] Yancey, in a long speech of March 14, was severe on Hill for making violent " assaults from the rear." In a night secret session of the summer of 1863, a row occurred in the House between Foote of Tennessee, and Judge Dargan of Alabama, throwing the whole House into a panic. Dargan drew a bowie-knife and advanced toward Foote, to resent some language which Foote had muttered while Dargan was speaking. Several members pinned Dargan to the floor, and Foote changed passion to laughter by striking a melodramatic attitude and saying: " I defy the steel of the assassin." The following December a lady entered the House of Representatives and cowhided Mr. V.— of Missouri.[21] The Richmond correspondent of the London *Times*, in a letter of March 4, 1865, when the struggle seemed nearing the end, said that the conduct and language of legislative assemblies during the war had brought republican institutions into derision and disrepute.[22]

Toward the end of the war, Congress became very

[20] Du Bose: Yancey, p. 739.
[21] E. A. Pollard in the Galaxy, Dec., 1868.
[22] London Times, March 31, 1865.

lively in its opposition to Davis, the disposition to oppose him being spurred on by such papers as the Richmond *Examiner* and the Charleston *Mercury*. Wigfall returned from the army to speak against him with vehement passion, and the Richmond editors feared to report his bitter, vindictive speeches. There was, in fact, during the last year of the war, serious thought in the South of inaugurating a counter-revolution against Davis's administration.

The Confederacy had all the paraphernalia of a constitutional government, but in reality the executive department wielded powers far beyond those given by the constitution.[23] Laws prepared in the executive offices were sent to a small room where the provisional Congress sat to register them. Later in the war, even Senator Miles of South Carolina, when he prepared a bill, sent it to the executive department for approval. In the stupendous struggle, inevitable exigencies made the executive will the force of law, and Congress bent to the necessity of subordinating law to the emergencies of war.

An act of the Confederate Congress in secret session, March 1, 1862, proclaimed martial law in Richmond and vicinity and declared the suspension of the writ of habeas corpus. A passport system placed restrictions upon the free movement of individuals. " Notorious Unionists " and those suspected of Federal sympathy were arbitrarily arrested. A military police was established under General Winder of Baltimore, and rowdyism, which had recently shown it-

[23] Du Bose: Yancey; The Richmond Examiner (J. M. Daniels), Feb. 24, 1862.

self, disappeared, but the despotic espionage of the Baltimore detective system became a source of much complaint,[24] though it kept watch on the people of Richmond until May, 1864, issuing its "reign of terror passports." In April and September, 1862, Congress passed conscription acts which gave much dissatisfaction.[25] Stephens declared that conscripts would go into battle like a horse starting from home, while volunteers would go like horses returning home. It is said that Davis at first opposed the conscription policy, preferring the voluntary system, but that he yielded to the newspapers and necessity. The September law caused a quarrel in Georgia between the Secessionists and the Unionists. An exemption law was passed about the same time for the benefit of the overseers of slaves.[26]

Stephens feared that the Confederacy tended toward errors which would lead to its overthrow. In 1862 he was disappointed at the President's message and dissatisfied with his appointments. The policy of the Government was against his judgment, and he stated that there was "no energy except such as a turtle with fire on its back." Military orders and the suspension of the writ of habeas corpus were to him the source of the greatest concern. Though he succeeded in inducing the President to request some of the generals to revoke part of their orders, he failed to arouse Congress to opposition. He still clung to the

[24] J. B. Jones: Diary.

[25] For the acts of the Confederate Provisional Government and the first and second Congress, see " Statutes at Large," edited by J. M. Matthews [one volume, 1861-64].

[26] Du Bose: Yancey.

view that government by the people was not a failure; but it seemed to him that the people, though living under a constitution, were indifferent, and yielded to usurpations.[27]

Mr. Davis and his administration have been variously estimated. Pollard has written pages to give his mistakes, and General Thomas Jordon says of him: " The longer he held power the narrower grew his conceptions, the more imperious his will, until to differ from or cross the orbit of his fancies, or even to run counter to the plans or wishes of his favorites, became a personal affront. . . . He and his ministerial clerks . . . were always anticipating success in a preposterous manner, always displaying little practical industry, and quite as little judgment in preparing for contingencies." [28] Mr. Alfriend, on the other hand, has written a volume to praise him.

Mr. Davis, like all who accept offices in exciting times, probably had to suffer from much censure that was unjust. He was as sensitive to disapprobation as Thomas Jefferson, the man of peace. He grew cold under the criticism of his qualities as a military organizer, and his appointments to civil and military positions, but he seldom changed his opinion or his policy. The pressure of public opinion could not induce him to change his Cabinet or to dismiss Dr. Northrop from the Commissary Bureau. His disposition to have his own way, and his attitude toward those who sought to interfere with what seemed to him was a part of his own prerogative, swelled the

---

[27] Johnston and Browne: Life of A. H. Stephens.
[28] Atlantic Monthly, Vol. XXXI, p. 610. Oct., 1865.

opposition and made him very unpopular. His im-
prisonment at the close of the war drew to him the
sympathies of the South, but during the closing
months of the conflict, when the Confederacy was
gasping for breath, he was rapidly losing the influence which his magnetic personality had been able
to command. Much of the dislike for Davis arose
from the fact that he did not meet the people oftener
in social intercourse. He was a sufferer from nervous
dyspepsia; and with the arduous labors of his office
—examining as he did into the minutest details—he
found it necessary to be careful of his diet and to
economize his time. Soon after going to Richmond,
he resolved to administer the Government instead of
giving entertainments, and the people soon said he
was hoarding his wealth.[29] Tuesday evening receptions were begun later in the war, but were discon-
tinued after a month. Davis received a salary of
$25,000 in Confederate money. Richmond had offered
to make him a present of his house, but he declined
it.[30] Toward the close of the struggle his salary was
insufficient to meet the household expenses, though
there were very few receptions and levees. In April,
1864, it was reported that Davis intended to move
the Government to Montgomery, because of the
scarcity and high price of supplies. In June, 1864,
Congress doubled the salaries of its own members
so that they received $5500, and debated a measure
for the increase of the President's salary, but took
no action upon the latter.

[29] Mrs. Davis: Jefferson Davis.
[30] J. W. Daniel: Life and Reminiscences of Jefferson Davis
(by distinguished men of his time).

The Confederate Government was much embarrassed by popular opinion, state opposition, and by controversies between officials. At the beginning of the war Union sentiment probably preponderated in several states that seceded. After the Battle of Bull Run the voice of the Unionists was silenced by the shouts of victory, but it was heard again in the train of disaffection and defeat. "Secession from Secessia" was also threatened. In November and December, 1862, when state authorities complained of military usurpations, some of the clerks at Richmond said that patriotism was mainly in the army and among the women, and that the President should change his Cabinet and policy, and cultivate the support of the people, else the Confederacy might split into states. It was feared that Lincoln's message for gradual emancipation would find advocates in the South. A letter to Davis said that Louisiana and a large part of Mississippi, if overrun by Federal troops, would submit to the United States. Davis went to Mississippi a few days later to encourage fighting. In June, 1863, while the Federals thundered at the gates, jealousy was growing between the Confederacy and the state authorities and Davis feared conspiracy. In September, defection was spreading in North Carolina and the United States flag was raised. Davis made a month's tour in the South and it was suspected that he was preparing to take measures for fuller control. In December, collision between the Confederate and Georgia authorities was imminent on the question of "just compensation" for sugar seized by the agents of the commissary. Northrop said that it was necessary to impress food for the soldiers.

Foote was denouncing both Davis and Northrop, and Senator Orr and others asked for the removal of Northrop, but Davis refused, stating that the Commissary-General was one of the greatest geniuses of the South.

In January, 1864, the breach was widening between Congress and Davis, but for the sake of the country, Congress, in February, obediently passed the new conscript act and other laws, greatly increasing the power of the executive.[31] It also passed a bill suspending the writ of habeas corpus for six months, though it refused to pass Judge Campbell's supreme court bill. A revival of the murmurs against Davis followed. Colonel Brown ordered an armed guard to protect him, and it soon became a fixture in front of Mr. Davis's residence.[32] Judge Pearson of North Carolina continued to grant the writ of habeas corpus. In March Stephens said the purpose of the bill to suppress the writ was to muzzle the North Carolina press. In April, in a speech against the suspension of the writ, Stephens said that independence without liberty was of no value to him, and that he would as soon have a Northern as a Southern master. In June, while the Federal guns thundered down the river, there were intermittent "rows" in the Bureau of Conscription, and they continued in

[31] An act approved Feb. 6, 1864, prohibited all exports of cotton, tobacco, etc., except by specific regulations issued by the President, who was thus practically given full power as to the regulation of foreign commerce. In carrying this act into effect, Mr. Davis required that one-half the tonnage of all vessels should be reserved for the use of the Confederate authorities.

[32] J. B. Jones: Diary.

September, November and December. The Government was almost in a state of paralysis. In July the murmurs against Davis grew louder.[33]

The feeling against speculators and class exemptions increased the disaffection against the Government in the autumn of 1864, and there were signs that the curtain would soon rise on the last act of the drama, and that the disturbed and divided nation would " cease to float upon a sea of blood." Both Seward and McClellan, in the North, were making promises, and in the hour of dulness many reflected on the repose once enjoyed in the Union. Many favored a revolution in the South. Governor Vance of North Carolina *showed his teeth*, and said that he would not allow the Confederate Government to interfere with his furnishing clothes to his troops. From the attitude of Governors Brown, Toombs, Stephens and others it appeared that Georgia was in danger of making peace with the United States. Davis went South to make speeches. Governor Brown refused to respond to his call for the Georgia militia. He held to states rights, and said that Davis must send reinforcements if he demanded the return of the Georgia troops. Notwithstanding Davis's speeches in Georgia and Alabama to reanimate the people, the states seemed determined to control their own men not in the regular army, and the Union party was increasing. There was danger of losing North Carolina. In November J. T. Leach of that state offered submission resolutions in the Confederate Congress, and two of his colleagues voted for them. A

[33] J. B. Jones: Diary, June 1, Sept. 6, Nov. 9 and Dec. 4.

few days later peace resolutions were offered in the North Carolina legislature. General Lee's correspondence indicated that the conscription officers were not doing their duty—that the rich, the slaveholders and the speculators, were buying their way out of service. He complained that rich young men were elected magistrates in order to escape field service. The law exempting large slaveholders was creating an anti-slavery party. In September, a clerk in the War Department said that over 100,000 landed proprietors, and the majority of the slave-owners, were out of the ranks—and that some wanted to keep the horses that had been lent them by the Government, while the poor were thrust into the trenches. Military officers were impressing men into the army, while state governors were granting exemptions. In October many men with exemptions were being forced into the army—some while getting medicine for their sick wives, and many became indifferent as to which side should prevail.[34] New and strong farmer soldiers murmured, and many hoped that the soldiers in both armies would desert and go home, and that the guns would " cease to shoot *sine die*." Some who once held the idea that "beauty and booty" were the aim of the Northern troops, said that "Beast" Butler was proving himself very generous before Richmond, and they declared that the press had "long misrepresented the conduct of the enemy and tried to keep animosity alive." They complained that they were put in the trenches as "volunteers" under threat of dismission, while able-bodied men escaped the army

[34] J. B. Jones: Diary.

and rode through the streets on sleek horses.   Clerks supposed that they were exempted from military service by the constitution, but in November, Attorney-General George Davis said that though the constitution exempted certain civil officers, the recent impressment act of Congress must be executed.   A few weeks later the clerks favored revolution.

As the year 1864 drew to a close, Congress was sitting most of the time in secret session, and while Mr. Davis was suffering from neuralgia or busy with appointments, promotions or the details of the administration, a strong party was preparing to transfer the military powers of the executive to General Lee, in order to prevent Georgia from reentering the Union, and to strengthen the confidence of the people.   The Federal cannon kept up their monotonous noise, Lee's army was being depleted by desertions, incessant rains made gloom gloomier, and the hungry people complained that they were at the mercy of the quartermasters, commissaries, railroads and the Southern Express Company.   Foote, in the House of Representatives on December 17, announced his intention to withdraw from the Confederate Congress rather than to legislate under a despotism, and said that there was a land of freedom yet left that would receive to its bosom a poor refugee.[85]   At the beginning of the new year the Government, in a voluminous correspondence, was planning for the arrest of men who should attempt to cross the Potomac.   To the south " mountains were looming up everywhere." States were evading the Confederate law and ignoring

[85] Richmond Examiner, Dec. 19, 1864.

Confederate authorities, while the Confederate Government was preparing the way for negro enlistment and emancipation. North Carolina was swarming with deserters and Georgia was favorable to the Union. The people desired peace. Mr. Collier, in the Virginia legislature, on February 25, said that the chief characteristic of the Confederate administration was that it had separated the Government from the people.[36] Future events were casting their shadows before.

The breach between Davis and Congress grew wider as the alarm tocsin sounded and the end drew nearer. While the Federal artillery thundered at the gates, the politicians quarrelled. Congressional committees of five or six would visit Davis in a private way to remonstrate or to ask the removal of Commissary Northrop, " the pepper-corn doctor from North Carolina," but it was breath wasted. Members of Congress asked the dismissal of members of the Cabinet. On some questions Vice-President Stephens used all his influence against the administration.[37] In March, 1864, he had objected to the act of Congress to suspend the writ of habeas corpus which he heard had for one of its objects the control of the elections and the assemblages in North Carolina and to muzzle certain presses in that state. He declared that the act was unconstitutional, and that the denial of constitutional liberty could only hasten the departure of states. " I want to see no Maryland this side of the Potomac," said he.[38] In January, 1865, there was a tie vote in

[36] Richmond Sentinel.

[37] Cleveland: A. H. Stephens, p. 761.

[38] H. S. Foote made a speech in favor of repealing the act for suspending the writ of *habeas corpus*. He was not afraid

the Senate on a bill to re-suspend the writ of habeas corpus, and Stephens was on the point of giving his deciding vote in opposition to the bill when he was prevented by a senator who changed his vote to the affirmative. Stephens declared that the senator had no right to change his vote after the result had been announced. But the Senate overruled him. Stephens, considering this as an indignity, told Senator Hunter that he would resign. Hunter urged him not to do so. The next day the Senate succeeded in conciliating him by unanimously passing a resolution requesting him to address them in secret session upon the situation of public affairs. The bill to suspend the writ of habeas corpus ultimately failed to pass.

After long secret debates, in which policy oscillated between " not yet " and " too late," Congress finally passed the bill for negro enlistments and decided to adjourn March 10, 1865. But Mr. Davis requested its members to remain a short time, as further legislation would be required. There was much anxiety as to the kind of communication that he was preparing to lay before Congress. Some supposed that it related to foreign complications. Rumor said that a treaty with France for alliance was about to be consummated. On Sunday, March 12, Davis was closeted with Benjamin and the Secretary of War nearly all day.[39] The next day he sent a message to Congress stating that he considered the measures already passed to be insufficient, and that only by the prompt

of newspaper criticism of the Government. " Paper bullets are harmless " said he. [The Weekly Register (Lynchburg), May 28, 1864.]

[39] J. B. Jones: Diary.

devotion of the entire resources of men and money in the Confederacy could independence be achieved. He said that Congress had so long debated and delayed his recommendation of the preceding November as to the enlistment of negroes, etc., that much of their value was now lost. He asked that restrictions on the power to impress supplies be removed on account of the condition of the Confederate finances; he again recommended a diminution of exempts and the abolition of class exemptions; and he said that the suspension of the writ of habeas corpus was indispensable.[40] Davis and Benjamin were said to be already rejoicing over their triumph over Congress. But on March 16, the Senate committee or Congress presented their reply which stated that if the President had urged the *necessity* of the negro bill legislation might have been quickened—but that he had seemed to dissent from the general policy of arming them as soldiers and had not even responded to calls for information by the Senate. The committee defiantly declared that all measures recommended by Mr. Davis to promote the efficiency of the army had been adopted " except the entire repeal of class exemptions." (Exemption of overseers between 18 and 45 had been repealed.) Mr. Davis was informed that on account of executive abuse of the power of detail Congress had revoked details and limited their power. When the members of the committee waited upon Mr. Davis he fired a parting broadside into them. Congress adjourned *sine die*, March 18, without passing Davis's last recommendations, but also

[40] Richmond Dispatch, March 15, 1865.

without succeeding in ousting Mr. Benjamin from the cabinet.[41]

The Confederacy while embarrassed by political conditions was also handicapped by lack of resources and of communication with the world. The want of skilled labor was a source of weakness. In April, 1863, Mallory asked Captain Bullock to send out English mechanics capable of manufacturing Bessemer steel but he met with difficulties in obtaining and sending them. In the South there were no great iron manufacturing establishments for furnishing materials for ships and railways. Mason, in 1863, sent a model of a wooden railway which was supposed to have some advantages over the iron roads but the Government appears to have had less confidence in it than did Mr. Mason.[42] Frequently the Government was unable to obtain even reference books in the library at Richmond.[43] Benjamin, anxious to keep posted on the British debates on the blockade, etc., had to wait months for a copy of " Hansard."

There was no direct communication with Europe, though several plans were proposed before the close of 1862. There were Government vessels most of the time from Nassau and Bermuda to Charleston and Wilmington, but supplies and dispatches were often sent by private blockade runners which charged enormous freight. Agents carrying despatches were in-

[41] Richmond Dispatch, March 20, 1865. J. B. Jones: Diary. C. A. Evans (Ed.): Confederate Military History (Atlanta, 1899), Vol. I, Chap. 24, p. 538, et seq.

[42] Despatches of Mason, No. 35, April 30, 1863. Ibid., No. 13, Paris, Sept. 29, 1864.

[43] Instr. to Mason, No. 27, June 22, 1863.

structed to destroy them in case they were in danger of capture, but in several instances United States cruisers apprehended correspondence containing important plans or damaging statements.

On July 19, 1862, Mr. Benjamin had for weeks had no opportunity to send Mason instructions with any reasonable hope of his getting them. Mr. Ward, recently United States minister to China, had just brought Mason's despatches of May 6 and 15, which were the first received since his despatch of February 7. Wetler and Ficklin had been entrusted with despatches of a later date than February 7, and they had arrived safely, but found it necessary to throw their despatches overboard.[44] In November, 1862, Mason had heard nothing from Benjamin since his letter of the preceding April. In January, 1863, after the capture of Reid Sanders, the Northern papers were full of "intercepted correspondence"[45] of Benjamin and others, berating Russell and charging Napoleon's consuls with occult designs to seize Mexico as a colony, detach Texas and recognize it separately. The correspondence also revealed the Confederate plans to obtain money and vessels in Europe.

The Northern papers were often the only means of obtaining news from Europe. They also seem to have been correctly advised of what happened at

[44] Instr. to Mason No. 6, July 19, 1862. Also, see Instr. to Mason No. 20, April 14, 1863.

[45] Richmond Examiner, Jan. 24, 1863. J. B. Jones: Diary, Jan. 23, 1863. Benjamin advised that no more despatches should be entrusted to Mr. Sanders. Instr. to Mason, No. 15, Feb. 7, 1863.

Richmond. Perhaps in some cases persons with regular passports carried information, but there were other means.[46] Dr. McClure, an embalmer, was detected taking live men through the lines in his coffins. In December, 1864, a "Yankee" mail line was discovered between Federal gunboats and the city with a lady at one end of the line.

The Confederate Government resorted to all possible expedients in financial measures, and its hands sometimes largely controlled Southern resources. By an act of May 16, 1861, and by subsequent laws, Confederate treasury notes, payable six months after the war, were provided. In June, 1861, a bureau of printing and engraving was established and soon began "to make money." A loan was provided in April, 1861, and was met by a double subscription. Another of $100,000,000 was provided in August, and still others followed. The Government received loans of cotton from planters who promised to accept 8 per cent bonds for a portion of it when sold. This "produce loan" was conceived with the idea that cotton could be made a basis for security. Within a short time the whole amount of the loan was taken. By an order of the Treasury Department no vessel was granted a clearance unless one-half her cargo was shipped on Government account from the accumulated Government stores. The Confederacy also paid for direct purchases from planters [47] in 8 per

[46] Secret service agents often furnished the U. S. Government with valuable information as to the plans of the Confederates. See an interesting article, by Allan Forman of Baltimore, on "A Bit of Secret History," in the Magazine of American History, Vol. XII, Oct., 1884.

[47] H. D. Capers: Life and Times of C. G. Memminger, Richmond, 1893.

cent bonds. When it was seen that the blockade and war would continue, arrangements were made to use cotton as a basis of a foreign loan negotiated by Erlanger, of Paris. The states in undertaking to support their quotas issued paper money and, in some cases, seized supplies for the army, paying for them state certificates of indebtedness. The property of all alien enemies was sequestered.

Supplies were impressed by the Confederate Government where the depreciated currency failed to command them. In order to secure cotton as a basis on the foreign loan it was sometimes found necessary to enforce a tax in kind. In the early part of 1863 there was a bill before the Confederate Senate to regulate the impressment of private property. It was strongly opposed, especially by Yancey who had for several months been making long speeches in Congress protesting against the usurpations of the Government and insisting that the war power was not superior to the civil power. The administrative officials called Yancey a professional alarmist, but the Richmond *Whig* declared that he was the guardian of public liberty. Yancey favored the exercise of stern war powers by Congress and claimed to oppose only extra-constitutional measures. At the close of 1863, Commissary Northrop found it necessary to impress food for the army. At the close of 1864 and the beginning of 1865 Mr. Benjamin favored the seizure of cotton for the purchase of ships in Europe, and, in a speech of February 9, he said that all persons having tobacco, corn, meat, and other supplies must give them to the Government. Mr. Collier of the Virginia legislature a few days later protested against Benjamin's declaration that everything the people had belonged to the Government in the hour of its adversity.

The treasury notes, simple in appearance, uncertain in promise, resting only on the scriptural faith, "the substance of things hoped for, the evidence of things unseen," nevertheless fell but little below par until after the summer of 1861. When the blockade of the Southern ports shut off all communication with Europe they depreciated more and more, and prices in the Confederacy became higher and higher after 1862. Many suffered for the want of food. Davis, speaking from a dray, quelled the threatened bread riot at Richmond, and later advised the people to raise food instead of cotton. Farmers, losing confidence in the currency, refused to sell grain, stating they had all the currency that they desired. Many suffered in the midst of plenty because they had not the means to purchase. A Richmond lady being told by a merchant the price of flour said: "I have seven children; what shall I do?" "I don't know, madam," replied he, "unless you eat your children." From October, 1863, to March, 1865, flour rose from $70 to $1500 per barrel. In September, 1863, quinine was $100 per ounce, and calico $10 a yard. In July, 1864, a saucer of ice-cream cost $6, a pound of sugar $10, and coffee $1 per cup. In August, $33 in Confederate money were worth only $1 in gold. In March, 1865, the Government was paying $1 in gold for $60 of its currency. In October, 1864, the physicians charged $30 per visit. The Richmond *Dispatch* cost $.50 per copy or $100 per year. Some believed that prices could be regulated and that jugglery could save the Confederate currency. It was as possible for one to lift himself by his boot straps. The Government could not live always on credit. Some believed that a new issue of currency would defeat the schemes of the speculators, but the prices of food would not diminish. The majority of the people lived on limited rations. Rats ceased to appear; cats staggered and died. It cost $200 a year to keep a cat. Wives made their petticoats into undershirts for their husbands. Legislatures threatened to suppress theatrical amusements during the war. In some cases the Government lent horses to the plantation owners.

The scarcity of food and the depreciation of the currency were not the only causes of the high prices.[48] They were often due to the lack of transportation. Crops were abundant but the means of transportation were poor. Railroads were not kept in repair, and, in some cases, there were complaints that the Government monopolized the roads for military purposes. In January, 1863, the Governor transmitted to the Virginia legislature a copy of a joint resolution of the Alabama legislature protesting against the continued exclusive military control of the railroads and favoring their being kept open for private business and transportation. Later complaints in Virginia stated that the speculators occupied too much space in the cars. Sometimes there was not sufficient transportation for food for the troops in the field. In February, 1865, Lee's armies suffered for

[48] An article on the " History of Prices in the Confederacy," by J. C. Schwab, appears in the Report of the Am. Hist. Ass'n for 1898.

want of soap, though there was plenty at Charlotte, North Carolina.

Government regulation of prices and transportation was several times the subject of consideration. In 1863 Congress authorized the seizure of food supply at rates of payment fixed by state commissioners who were to assess prices every sixty days.[49] In October of the same year some favored the Government control of prices and transportation in order to break up the speculators and to get the food to places where it was most needed. Some favored martial law as a step toward the equal distribution of food. In May, 1864, the Government was selling meal to private individuals. The following July, it caused an increase in the price of food by fixing a high price upon the goods which it seized. In November following, Senator Sparrows, of Louisiana, offered a resolution providing that no prices should be higher than those assessed by the army. In January, 1865, Mr. Seddon, the Secretary of War, was requested to impress and distribute the coffee and sugar which was " cornered " when Wilmington was threatened. In some cases there was a state distribution of cloth.

The depreciation of the currency and the lack of transportation made it very difficult for the Confederate armies to get living rations during the last few months of the war. Trenholm, the Secretary of the Treasury, tried to mend the currency by purchasing

[49] In September, 1864, the commissioners of prices for N. C., Ga., Ala., Fla., Miss., and Tenn., met at Montgomery, Ala., with a view to securing uniformity of prices (under the impressment law). [Weekly Register (Lynchburg), Oct. 22, 1864, pp. 248-50.]

all the cotton and tobacco, selling it to foreign merchants and buying treasury notes with the proceeds.
In February the preachers offered to take the stump
to raise subscriptions. President Davis, marking
their proposal " special," sent it to the War Department. " Humbugged to the end," said Jones, a
clerk in the department. In that hour the ministers
could not stem the ebbing tide of Confederate for-
tune. On March 22, Congress deemed it hopeless
to adopt any plan to reduce the currency. Depreciation continued, and the operations of the Federals
made it impossible to collect the taxes.

Until 1863, Fraser, Trenholm and Company were
the only European bankers or " depositories " of the
Confederate Treasury. They paid the drafts of the
Confederate purchasing agents in Europe and the
bills drawn by the heads of departments at Richmond.
Thus, when Congress made appropriations for building naval vessels in Europe, the navy made a requisi-
tion on the treasury for the amount and received
treasury notes which could be converted only by buying cotton and shipping through the blockade to
Fraser, Trenholm and Company, who placed the
proceeds to the Confederate navy.[50] In this way,
Mallory, in 1862, placed $1,000,000 to the credit of
Captain Bullock, the naval agent in Europe. Soon
after that date the Confederate finances were much
depressed. On July 4, Bullock stated that the credit
of the Navy Department was thus far sound, but he
hoped for more money to settle the outstanding con-

[50] Bullock: Secret Service of the Confederate States in
Europe, Vol. II, p. 416.

tracts which amounted to £390,000. Congress appropriated very much larger sums for the navy, but Mallory wrote in September that the exchange of the country was nearly exhausted and that cotton went out in very small lots.[51] It was found necessary to resort to other means of finance for it was seen that the blockade and the war would continue. Mallory stated that if the agent of the treasury could dispose of the Confederate bonds even at fifty cents he would do so in order to pay the requisitions in Europe, and he suggested that Bullock himself might possibly be able to get advances by an agreement to repay with 8 per cent interest in cotton, and that he might agree to have the amount expended at Richmond by the Treasury Department for cotton, which could be stored and transported to the sea-ports by the treasury—regarding it as the property of British creditors.

In May, Mason had enclosed a letter of Mr. Spence, a Liverpool banker, whom he considered sagacious and friendly, suggesting the importance of a Confederate financial agency in Europe. Benjamin replied that the subject was considered premature. "It is by no means certain that we shall require a loan in Europe."[52] In September, Mason suggested that money might be commanded in England by the use of cotton bonds or obligations for the delivery of cotton at any Confederate port upon the thirty days' demand of the holder of the bond, or within three months after peace."[53] In November he wrote again

[51] H. D. Capers: C. G. Memminger.
[52] Instr. to Mason, No. 6, July 19, 1862.
[53] Despatches of Mason to Benjamin, No. 16, Sept. 18, 1862.

enclosing views upon a "cotton bond" mode of finance.[54] Bonds for the delivery to the amount of £60,000 had been negotiated through the house of Lindsay. Erlanger, whose son was engaged to Mr. Slidell's daughter, made a proposal to float a Confederate loan of £5,000,000. Mason said that the cotton bond plan seemed to offer the best scheme of finance, but that political advantages might follow the Paris (Erlanger) plan.

When Mason wrote, the subject of a loan based on cotton certificates had already been considered. Benjamin wrote Mason, October 28, that the Government had confided the matter to Mr. Spence as Mason had suggested. Memminger's cotton certificates represented cotton stored on the plantation and accepted by the Government. These certificates gave the European purchaser an absolute right to the particular lot of cotton with the privilege of shipping the same. Spence was also appointed as agent for the sale of $5,000,000 of 8 per cent bonds if he could realize 50 per cent on them and he was directed to negotiate for the application of $2,500,000 of coin in the Confederate treasury for supplies—by transfer to British owners who could transport it from a Confederate port as British property.

Mr. Spence received the cotton certificates but it was thought best to withhold them from the market until the result of Erlanger's proposals for a direct loan were known. Later they were withheld for fear they would prejudice the proposed loan which was considered of great political importance. The certificate money bonds were also received by Spence; but they could not be used at better rates than 50 cents on the dollar, and they too were withheld until after the floating of the Erlanger loan.

In January, 1863, Benjamin, in informing Mason that the cotton bonds had been forwarded to Spence, said that there was no desire to effect a loan in Europe during the war, and that the Confederacy only wanted moderate sums for the purpose of supplies.[55] The Confederate loan based on cotton and negotiated by Erlanger had, however, been decided on. The cotton was to be delivered at certain ports within six months after the close of the war—or before the end of the war if possible. The agents of Erlanger had recently gone to Richmond to offer to float a loan of $25,000,000, but Memminger would agree to make it only $15,000,000. Erlanger took the 7 per cent bonds at 77 per cent, and said that Davis privately favored increasing the loan. Memminger also seems to have contemplated an extension of the amount in case Congress would amend the loan act so as to relieve all doubt as to his authority to do so; and in January, 1863, he recommended to the Speaker of the House of Representatives that the act be so amended that the bonds provided for might be used for largely increasing the Confederate specie credit in Europe.[56]

The Confederate loan was placed upon the European market March 18, 1863, and, Mason rejoicing that it was a brilliant success, wrote Benjamin the

[55] Instr. to Mason, No. 12, Jan. 15, 1863.
[56] Capers: Memminger.

next day that over £5,000,000 were subscribed at once and that it reached a premium of 4½ per cent before night. "Mr. Erlanger worked it with great diligence," said he, "and has conferred with me freely and frankly." In two days and a half the subscription to the loan reached £16,000,000. The premium fluctuated, being 1¾ to 2 per cent by March 30. Erlanger did not expect it to touch par. "I congratulate you," wrote Mason "on the triumphant success of our infant credit; it shows *malgré* all detraction and calumny that cotton is king at last."[57]   On April 9, however, Mason wrote that the loan had shown a tendency to fall below par more and more. Erlanger told him that the agents of the United States were trying to discredit the loan by large purchases at low rates and that they might cause the subscribers to forfeit the instalment of 15 per cent already paid and abandon future subscriptions. To prevent a panic Erlanger desired the Confederacy to give authority for the purchase of £1,000,000 to bring it back to par.[58]   The bears were bringing down the stock and it was necessary to bull the market to keep it up till April 24, when the second intalment on subscriptions was to be paid.

Mason, by the advice of Slidell and others took the responsibility of authorizing Erlanger and Company to sustain the loan by secret purchases on Confederate account—and from April 9, to April 24, £1,388,500 worth were bought, carrying the price from 4½ per cent discount gradually to about 1½ per cent pre-

[57] Despatches of Mason to Benjamin, No. 32.
[58] Despatches of Mason to Benjamin, Unofficial, April 9, 1863.

mium. Mason acted under the advice and guidance of Mr. Spence, who was attending to the operations in London.[59] A second effort was made to bull the market till May 1. After that, they hoped that with the mass of stock "in certain hands," and with favorable news from the South, the stock would keep at par and enable the government to sell what it had bought. "Our purchase of the stock may yet turn out to be a money-making affair," wrote Mason.

The loan dropped somewhat when the news arrived that United States ships had run the batteries at Vicksburg. Mason found that the conditions were far different from what he had expected, but he said that the press was confident of news from Fredericksburg that would "make our loan buoyant." On June 12, he wrote that the loan seemed solidly placed at last. After the news from Gettysburg and Vicksburg, however, it soon fell to 30 per cent discount and Mason saw that the Confederacy could not expect another loan, and that the Government should arrange to ship cotton to Nassau and Bermuda by fast steamers running the blockade and under Government control.

In May all the Confederate disbursing officers in Europe were in arrears and there was no authority to make the proceeds of the loan available to them. C. J. McRae, who was sent to Europe as special agent of the Treasury Department to regulate the disbursement of the Erlanger loan and to negotiate the sale of treasury bonds arrived about June 1.[60] At first

[59] Ibid., Unofficial, and No. 34, of April 27, 1863.
[60] Bullock: Vol. II.

he had no orders to supply Confederate agents in Europe, but later the heads of departments sent drafts on him to meet the wants of purchasing agents and he was authorized to keep the bankers in funds. At the beginning of August he found only £700,000 on hand while the Government engagements for the army and navy required much more.

A short time later, the financial programme in Europe was changed. Both the Navy and Treasury Departments had sent out large amounts of Confederate bonds to different persons who practically became competitors of each other in negotiating for their sale. This was unsatisfactory and in September, 1863, Benjamin drew up a scheme which provided for a special fiscal agent with power to deal exclusively with all bonds. All who had been entrusted with the sale of bonds were asked to surrender them to McRae who was to negotiate them and distribute the proceeds among the purchasing agents.[61] Mr. Spence was thus superseded. He had been dissatisfied when Erlanger was selected to effect the Confederate loan. His retention was strongly opposed by the Richmond *Examiner*. He was well paid for his services but while speaking and writing in favor of the Confederacy he had also promised that it would abolish slavery as soon as it became independent. For this reason Mr. Benjamin afterwards wrote him that he could not officially recognize him as an agent.

Before the end of 1864, the net proceeds of the Erlanger loan were exhausted, and after the fall of

[61] J. B. Jones: Diary, Sept. 16, 1863.

Fort Fisher the small supply of funds from the sale of bonds ceased, the intercourse with the Confederacy being cut off by one or two shoal bays on the coast of Texas. The financial agents of the Confederacy saw that transmission of supplies must cease and stopped their purchases and shipment. To get money for urgent wants, McRae sold several ships and transferred the funds to the Treasury Department. When the war closed, the Confederate agents abroad had no large sums of money to turn over to the United States.

CHAPTER III

The Confederate Foreign Policy

James L. Orr, chairman of the Confederate House Committee on Foreign Relations, once said that the Confederacy never had a foreign policy, and never attempted any high diplomacy. Whatever may be thought of this statement, the failure of the Confederacy was certainly not due to any deficiency in the number of its agents abroad. Jefferson Davis commissioned many diplomatic consular and secret agents to watch every opportunity to negotiate treaties or to press Confederate interests.[1]

An attempt to open diplomatic negotiations with the United States Government in February, 1861, was made with the hope of securing a peaceful disruption of the Union. The leaders of secession were, no doubt, influenced by the belief that there would be a strong Northern sentiment opposed to coercive measures and in favor of the early establishment of trade and diplomatic relations with the South. They favored peaceful secession, and some desired alliance. They proposed to win the good-will of the West by maintaining the free navigation of the Mississippi.[2] In March, while some thought it impracticable to go on without further accession of territory, many ex-

[1] Confed. Dip. and Consular Commissions. Pickett Papers, "Trunk C."

[2] Proceedings of the Confederate Congress, Feb. 25, 1861.

pected the size and strength of the Confederacy to increase rapidly. Stephens hoped and expected that the border states would join, though the South could get along without them until they should decide to follow.[3] Looking at the distant future, he said that even the states of the Northwest might gravitate toward the Southern door, which he considered was wide enough to receive them " if they assimilate with us in principle."

It has been said that if Andrew Jackson had been President during the term before Lincoln's inauguration he would have discouraged secession in its incipiency and thus prevented the civil war. Buchanan sympathized with the South on the slavery question and took no decided position to prevent preparations for the dissolution of the Union. He did not believe that the states had a constitutional right to secede, but neither did he think the United States Government could constitutionally prevent them.

The seceding states made several unsuccessful attempts to obtain recognition at Washington, and to arrange for a peaceful secession. South Carolina after its resolution to secede sent three commissioners to state its reasons to Buchanan, and to arrange terms of separation, but they were not received. They then prepared a memorial to the Secretary of State but no answer was received. In February, 1861, South Carolina sent its Attorney-General to Washington, but he received no official recognition. When the Confederate Provisional Government was established it sent three commissioners[4] to Wash-

[3] Cleveland: A. H. Stephens, p. 723.
[4] Commission to Washington Record Book. (Pickett Papers, " Trunk B," Nos. 28 and 29.) The three commis-

ington to arrange a peaceable settlement. The latter were instructed to consult upon "matters of interest to both nations," and were authorized to conclude treaties. They arrived March 5, and one week later, through Judge Campbell, they communicated their mission to Seward, who, after delaying his reply until April 8, refused to receive them. The commissioners believed that the United States would evacuate Fort Sumter. Seward and others in Lincoln's Cabinet seem to have thought that Sumter amounted to little as a strategetical point, and were waiting for an expression of public opinion on the subject.[5] Davis believed that Seward's views would prevail at Washington. But as the war party at the North grew, public opinion opposed the evacuation of Government property, and the hope of peaceable secession was lost. Seward was hoping that by waiting and making no attempt to precipitate war, the Union element at the South would assert itself.[6] But in this he was mistaken.

In the history of the mission, which Davis published on April 29, he stated that Seward had induced the commissioners to forbear pressing for an answer and had said that Fort Sumter would be evacuated,[7] but that in the meanwhile preparations were being made for its defense. Lincoln, however, had ex-

sioners were M. G. Crawford, John Forsyth and A. B. Roman. Their credentials were dated Feb. 27, 1861. J. T. Pickett was secretary of the commission.

[5] Stovall: Toombs, p. 222, et seq.

[6] Some favored a foreign war as a means of "reunion," but this project was smothered by Lincoln and Sumner.

[7] Correspondence relating to Fort Sumter. Confederate Archives (Pickett Papers), "Trunk A," Package No. 35.

pressed his views in no uncertain tone. In a speech to the Indiana legislature February 12, referring to some of the "lovers of the Union" who resisted coercion and seemed to "think the Union no regular marriage, but rather a free-love sort of arrangement to be maintained only on passionate attraction," he said it was no coercion or invasion to hold United States forts and collect duties, or even to withhold mails. Abraham of old said to Lot, "Is not the whole land before thee. Separate thyself, I pray thee from me; let there be no strife between me and thee, for we are brethren." But Abraham Lincoln said no such thing to Jefferson Davis. To settle questions by avoiding them was not so easy as in the days of the patriarchs.

President Lincoln remained firm in his purpose to defend Sumter, Davis (in opposition to Toombs in a Cabinet meeting) resolved to attack it, and soon "the hornet's nest" was opened by a bloodless conflict in which no one was hurt. On April 12, the newsboys ran through the streets of Richmond shouting "The storming of Fort Sumter."[8] The *coup d'état*, which some said should have been struck before the inauguration of Lincoln, had started the dogs of war, and it was too late to dream of peaceable separation. On April 15, there was a strong secession demonstration at Richmond. Fiery speeches were made by Tyler, Wise and others. On April 23, Alexander H. Stephens met the state convention in a closed door session to arrange a treaty of alliance with the Confederate states.[9] For two days he waited in suspense while

[8] J. B. Jones: Diary.
[9] Johnston and Browne: Life of A. H. Stephens.

the Virginians debated, but on April 25, the treaty was ratified. The Virginia convention which had strongly declared against secession at last resolved to secede and join the Confederacy. North Carolina and Tennessee followed, and, for the succeeding four years, the Confederate *de facto* Government was independent of Washington and a civil war disturbed the repose of Europe, as well as of America, until the instruments of battle proved, notwithstanding the prophecies of great statesmen, that secession was inadmissible. The devotion and constancy of the South for its principles of government and economics in the face of a waning hope and diminishing resources have, perhaps, no parallel in history, but at the end of the war it accepted the historical situation, and the constitutional interpretation of the majority.

A commission appointed by Davis in January, 1865, when many were anxious to take some step to end the fraternal contest, was directed to proceed to Washington for an informal conference as to the issues of the war and terms of peace. Its members [10] met Lincoln and Seward at Hampton Roads where a friendly interview occurred, but they failed to agree upon the subject of reunion. Compelled by force of circumstances, however the Confederate authorities finally ceased the contest.

No agents were sent to Canada until 1864, when it appeared that the British Government, unless induced by new circumstances or complications, would continue to refuse to favor either recognition, mediation or intervention. Agents were then sent to that

[10] J. A. Campbell, A. H. Stephens, and R. M. T. Hunter.

country to encourage the peace party in the North and disaffection in the Northwest, and to make the Canadian border a base for hostile expeditions into United States territory.[11]

Mexico was a near neighbor whose territory, ever since the purchase of the Mesilla valley in 1853, had been looked upon by many as a field for the future extension of the institution of slavery and its accompanying agricultural system, and very early in 1861 the Confederates desired to open friendly relations with the people of that country and take steps to prevent the United States from securing any treaty advantages in that direction. On May 17, Toombs instructed J. T. Pickett as a special agent to sound the Mexican Government on the subject of alliance, to feel the pulse of merchants and ship owners on the subject of privateering, and authorized him to grant commissions of marque and reprisal or to employ agents in Mexico for the same purpose.[12] Looking for arguments which might induce Mexico to form an alliance with the Confederacy, Toombs said: " The institution of domestic slavery in one country, and that of peonage in the other, establishes between them such a similarity of labor as to prevent any tendency on either side to disregard feelings and interests of the other." Mexico was to be informed that in case the Confederate States were to guarantee her against foreign invasion " they could do so more promptly and effectually than any other nation." [13]

[11] Jacob Thompson and C. C. Clay were appointed Special Agents to Canada, on April 27, 1864, to carry out instructions received orally.

[12] Confed. Dip. Cor., Vol. I, Instr. 1.

[13] Confed. Dip. Cor., Vol. I.

Pickett remained in Mexico until December, writing many letters, most of which Toombs failed to receive. On his arrival at Vera Cruz, which he called "the South Carolina of Mexico," he sent to Mata (who had recently been Secretary of State for Foreign Affairs) an unofficial note, looking toward recognition. He also took steps to open negotiations with the Governor of the province, which he suggested might again resolve to resume its sovereignty as it had done in the past. While awaiting the arrival of a "friend," he wrote: "Let the United States Minister [Corwin] fire at random and waste his ammunition, and then I will go to Mexico City." Learning that the United States had probably made overtures for the passage of her troops through Mexico, in order to reach Arizona, he caused the insinuation to be made (to various persons connected with the Government) that the granting of such a privilege would be "a breach of neutrality, attaining the gravity of a *casus belli*— that it would be a step not only hostile to the Confederacy, but also suicidal to Mexico." At the city of Mexico, he found that the Government was not disposed to give attention to his communications. Negotiations with the United States, however, were "diligently pressed." Corwin wrote Seward, on July 29, that well-informed Mexicans seemed to be aware that the independence of the Confederacy would be a signal for a war of conquest to establish slavery in each of the states of Mexico.

Pickett, on learning that the Mexican Congress had acceded to the American request for the privilege to pass troops through Mexican territory, said privately: "If this decree is not annulled, Mexico will lose the state of Tamaulipas in 60 days." He unofficially informed the Mexican Government that invasion of the northern states of Mexico by Confederate forces would probably result. In October, while threatening retaliation, he proposed to re-cede California and New Mexico in order to secure a treaty of free trade between the Confederate States and Mexico. He also gave notification that the Confederacy could not consent to the sale or hypothecation of the Mexican public lands to any government not in amity with the Confederate Government. On October 29, in a despatch (No. 12) to Toombs, suggesting that the proposed treaty of the United States with Mexico probably had for its basis the hypothecation of Mexican lands and the establishment of a line of United States military posts through Mexican territory, he said: " Under these circumstances does it not become the policy of the Confederate States to take military possession of Monterey and declare their purpose of holding all of that region until all questions with the United States be brought to an amicable adjustment? Such an occupation, under the direction of wise military and civil chiefs would ensure to us the permanent possession of that beautiful country." Mentioning the information that the privilege granted by Mexico as to the passage of troops would probably not be used by the United States, he said: " I have entered no formal protest against that extremely offensive permission; for it affords a golden opportunity to the people of the Confederate States of fulfilling speedily a portion of that inevitable destiny which impels them southward."

On October 30, Pickett received a telegram announcing Confederate victories and the safe arrival of Mason and Slidell at Havana, and proceeded to celebrate the occasion by jollification with his friends. Learning that an American " pill vendor," named Bennett, had doubted the authenticity of the news, and had intimated it to be an invention, he went to his place of business, called him a " liar," slapped him, and inflicted " severe punishment " with his hands and feet. On the following night he was arrested, but was allowed to remain at his hotel. He pleaded his diplomatic character, which the Government refused to recognize. On November 14, he was " thrust into a filthy guard room," to await trial or the payment of an indemnity to Bennett. After his release he wrote: " To preserve my liberty, and perhaps my life, I have had no alternative but to resort to bribery." He was convinced that the Confederacy had few friends in Mexico—" at least among the Mexicans themselves of the dominant party."

In a despatch [from " near Mexico "], on November 29, Pickett informed Toombs that, having no reply from Mexico, and no further instructions from the Confederacy, he considered his mission virtually ended. As early as the middle of October he had so notified the Mexican Government, stating that the chief reason was the persistent violation of neutrality by Mexico. Commenting upon the internal condition of Mexico, the desire of Conservatives for the restoration of Spanish rule, and the effects of his own mission, he said: " My enterprise has afforded the Government of the Confederate States an opportunity which may never present itself again. . . . My approaches to the Conservatives was with the double hope of making them our friends, and of having myself sent out of the country as a pernicious intriguer, and when first arrested I really supposed that to have been the cause. . . . Mexico has placed herself in the wrong in the eyes of all civilized nations . . . and thus have I cut the Gordian knot of our infant diplomacy in this quarter. If the Confederate States improve the golden opportunity, I will not have suffered in vain. . . . . Our people must have an outlet on the Pacific. . . .

" The part for the Confederate States to play in this crisis is clear to my mind. Our revolution has emasculated the Monroe doctrine in so far as we are concerned. The Spaniards are now become our natural allies, and jointly with them we may own the Gulf of Mexico and effect a partition of this magnificent country. I little thought a few years ago ever to counsel a Spanish alliance, but revolutions bring us into strange company, and I am now prepared to advocate an alliance which may tend to check the expansion of the North."

Pickett reached Vera Cruz in December, in time to witness its occupation by Spanish forces. He soon returned to the Confederacy by request from Richmond.[14] After September, 1863, some hoped for recognition by Mexico, and Preston,[15] being appointed envoy extraordinary and minister plenipotentiary, on

[14] Confed. Dip. Cor., Mexico. (Pickett Papers, " Trunk B," Record 5; Pickett's Despatches, June 15 (No. 1), June 17 (No. 2), Oct. 29 (No. 12), Nov. 29 (No. 13) and Dec. 24 (No. 14), 1861; also Corwin's Despatches to Seward, July 29 (No. 3), Aug. 28 (No. 4), Sept. 7 (No. 5) and Oct. 29 (No. 7), 1861.

[15] Walker Fearn was also appointed as secretary.

January 7, 1864, soon left the Confederacy for Cuba with " secret service " money, but receiving no intimation that he would be received by Maximilian he never reached the Mexican capital.[16]

At the opening of the civil war the northern provinces of Mexico were in a state of revolution, and on May 22, Toombs sent J. A. Quintero on a mission to New Leon to inform Governor Vidaurri that the Confederacy wished to maintain friendly relations and to prevent border raids between Mexico and Texas, but that if the Governor failed to stop the raids the Confederacy would be compelled to punish the invaders and to guard against the recurrence of such disturbing inconveniences.[17] Vidaurri impressed Quintero with his friendliness, and confidentially proposed a political union of the northern provinces of Mexico with the Confederacy. Quintero, after returning to report the success of his mission was again sent as confidential agent to northeast Mexico (September 3, 1861) to reside at Monterey, with instructions to declare his official character only to the Governor and such others as he might deem prudent. He was authorized to say that Mr. Davis reciprocated Vidaurri's expressions of friendship and good-will for himself and his people, and that he desired to serve mutual interests by intimate social and commercial relations; but, although the Confederates felt sympathy for the revolutionists, he believed " it would be imprudent and impolitic in the interests of both parties to take any steps at present in regard to the proposition made by Governor Vidaurri in his

[16] Confed. Dip. Cor., Mexico. Ibid., Package 15.
[17] Confed. Dip. Cor., Vol. I.

confidential communication . . . in reference to the future political relations of the Confederate States and the northern provinces of Mexico." Quintero was instructed to send statistics concerning that country, to report on the prospects of getting powder, lead and other war supplies through Matamoras, and, in case Mexico had given the United States permission to transport troops across her territory for war against the Confederacy, to induce Vidaurri to use his influence to prevent it. On November 4, Quintero reported that Vidaurri would oppose the passage of the United States troops through New Leon.[18]

Naturally the Confederacy early sent a special agent to the West Indies, where it was desired to obtain a point of vantage for communication with Europe. On July 22, 1861, Toombs instructed C. J. Helm to perform this office, giving him a letter of introduction to the Captain-General of Cuba to whom it was desired that he should present reasons for friendly relations between Cuba and the Confederacy, leaving no efforts untried to remove apprehensions as to Confederate designs to acquire that island.[19] The Confederate authorities, by sparing no pains to in-

[18] Consular Corres., New Leon and Coahuila—Quintero (Pickett Papers, "Trunk B," Package 17). Also, Dip. Mex. 8 and 9—J. L. Cripps and Charles Ricken; Misc. Cor. and Records, Mexico; Consular, Matamoras—Fitzpatrick; Consular; Vera Cruz—Matamoras, La Sere and Avegno.

Richard Fitzpatrick was appointed commercial agent at Matamoras on Nov. 15, 1862. Bernard Avegno was appointed on Dec. 18, 1862, to act in the same capacity at Vera Cruz. Emile La Sere received credentials on May 30, 1864, to perform the same functions at Vera Cruz.

[19] Confed. Dip. Cor., Vol. I.

form Spain that the South no longer desired Cuba, by urging mutual interests in the institution of slavery, by suggesting probable aggressive expansive designs of the United States, and by proposing a defensive alliance, made strong efforts to secure the friendship of that once powerful people; but Spain remained neutral. In Cuba there was considerable local sympathy with the Confederates; and, during the blockade, the Richmond authorities hoped to make the island an entrepot from which to obtain European supplies, and a base for forwarding despatches between the Confederacy and Europe. Seward, while denying any desire for conquest, informed Spain that the United States could not look with favor upon any policy that would make that island the fulcrum of the lever for overthrowing the Union.[20] The Confederacy several times tried to secure recognition by Spain, but was always disappointed, though it took fresh hope from complications. The Confederate steamer, *General Rusk*, had been used to get Confederate supplies at Havana, and while there, it was supplied with British papers and had its name changed to *Blanche*. After one successful voyage the vessel sailed for Havana with a cargo of cotton, in the latter part of 1862, but, while off the coast of Cuba in the neutral jurisdiction of Spain, was destroyed by a United States steamer. For this act the United States paid Spain $200,000,

[20] James Morton Callahan: Cuba and International Relations, Chap. 11, *passim*; 15 Instr. Sp., p. 263, Seward to Schurz, No. 2, April 27, 1862. [Also, October 28, 1861]; Confed. " Dip. Cor.", Hunter to Yancey, Rost and Mann, Aug. 24, 1861, and Benjamin to Slidell (No. 16), May 9, 1863.

and Benjamin instructed Slidell (March 22, 1863) to urge Spain to pay all of the amount over to the Confederacy, instead of to the individuals who temporarily had the loan of the vessel, but the Confederacy did not press its claim.

Agents in Nassau and the Bermudas, in addition to Helm in Cuba, performed valuable service for the Confederacy during the whole period of the war.[21]

It was to Europe that the Confederate leaders principally looked for sympathy and assistance. Their policy of secession had been greatly influenced by the expectation of foreign aid. Naturally, in presenting their case to Europe they urged the advantages of free trade and avoided a discussion of the slavery question. They desired especially to enlist English sympathy. Benjamin, in a letter to the English consul in New York said that conditions might arise which would even induce Southern states to resume their former allegiance to England.[22] There was a strong belief that in case of war England would not permit the United States to interfere with English trade through the Southern ports. On January 28, Mr. Iverson, of Georgia, in his farewell speech to the United States Senate, referring to the possibility of a blockade, said: " We can live, if need be, without commerce. But when you shut out our cot-

---

[21] The name of Heyleger, who acted as agent at Nassau, and obtained concessions favorable to blockade running, does not appear among those whose credentials (from Mr. Davis) are recorded in the " Diplomatic and Consular Commissions " book of the Confederate State Department. Norman S. Walker was appointed commercial agent at Bermuda on July 7, 1864.

[22] Life of Thurlow Weed, Vol. II, pp. 313-14.

ton from the looms of Europe we shall see whether
other nations will not have something to do on that
subject. Cotton is king and it will find means to
raise your blockade and disperse your ships."

The new American tariff gave the Confederate
leaders further hope of English sympathy, and an
opportunity to urge their opposition to the tariff
with greater effect.[23] Buchanan, in his message of
December, 1858, had recommended a revision of the
tariff in order to increase the revenue, but the administration leader in the House could not get the necessary two-thirds vote for the proposition. In April,
1860, Morrill introduced his tariff bill in the House.
Its principal object was stated to be revenue. It
passed the House by 105 to 64, but its consideration
by the Senate was postponed. On February 20, 1861,
however, it passed the Senate with some amendments
by a vote of 25 to 14—after the senators from seven
seceding states had withdrawn. Some felt that its
passage made England much more liable to recognize
the Confederacy, and Clingman said that it contributed
to the secession of Virginia, North Carolina and Tennessee.

On general principles the Democrats of both
North and South since 1825 had leaned towards a
tariff for revenue only, but since 1832 there had
been no signs that the integrity of the Union was
endangered by tariff legislation. In the farewell
speeches of Southern leaders in Congress there had
been scarcely an allusion to the tariff. The burden
of the grievances expressed were concerning South-

[23] See Hunter's remarks in the Cong. Globe, Feb. 27, 1861.

ern rights as to slavery. Many in the Alabama secession convention desired to induce the United
States to treat with the South as an independent
power and as an ally, and they were willing to agree
to a tariff equal to that of the United States but allowing free trade with the United States in order to
dispense with frontier custom houses, border
troubles and war debts.[24]

The Confederate constitution declared in favor of
a tariff for revenue only, and the commissioners who
were sent to England with instructions (of March 16)
to make a treaty [25] practically providing for free trade
were told to inform the English Government that
dissolution was the result of long and mature deliberation to escape the persistent efforts to compel the
South to pay bounties to the North in the shape of
high protective tariffs. It was soon discovered that
Seward had taken prompt steps to meet their arguments abroad. The nature of Seward's arguments
may be seen in his instructions to Carl Schurz April
27, in which he said: "The interest which now
raises the flag of disunion has directed the Government since the first murmur of discontent was heard.
The United States . . . for forty years has especially
accommodated that interest (slavery) and construct-
ed all defenses required for that section."

[24] Rost to Yancey, April 7, 1862.
[25] The Confederacy offered to continue all the United States
treaties except the clause providing for the maintenance of
a naval squadron on the coast of Africa. The Confederate
constitution had a clause against the slave trade, but if England had asked for a treaty clause against it, she would have
been informed that the constitution gave the Government no
power relating to that subject. " It is not wise to impose
restraints on the future" said Benjamin in January, 1863.
[Instr. to Mason, Nos. 13 and 14, Jan. 15, 1863.]

The instructions of the Confederate commissioners did not mention any of the expressed grievances relating to slavery. But later, the agents in England endeavored through the press and otherwise to leave the impression that the North desired the continuance of the institution of slavery. This policy was based upon the fact that England and France were opposed to slavery but desired commercial intercourse with the South. Palmerston, in July, 1861, said to August Belmont of New York, " We do not like slavery but we want cotton and we dislike very much your Morrill tariff."

There was a strong party in England led by Bright, Cobden and Forster, who had pronounced sympathies with the United States and would have been glad if they could have informed their constituencies that the Lincoln administration was fighting for emancipation as well as for the integrity of the Union. But, notwithstanding the fears which had been expressed in the speeches of the Southern leaders, the Lincoln party proposed only to restrict slavery in the territories and had no emancipation policy until it came as a military exigency during the war. Lincoln in his inaugural address said: " I have no purpose, directly or indirectly, to interfere with the institution of slavery in the states where it exists." The Confederate agents in Europe quoted this as a means of decreasing sympathy with the North. The Confederate arguments were presented to the British Parliament by Lindsay, Gregory, Roebuck and other members who sympathized with the South. Lindsay, in explaining these positions in July, 1862, said that the cry against slavery in the North was only a political cry—else England could sympathize with the North. He declared that taxation without representation was the real cause of the war, stating that the North and West had increased their representation in Congress while the South had fallen behind and had to pay the protective tariffs.[26] Forster, in reply, stated that slavery was the real cause of the war, and that the tariff had scarcely been mentioned in the elections and during the period of secession.[27]

Mr. Davis and his followers at first expected to produce a cotton famine which would induce England and France to break the blockade and recognize the Confederacy. Later, they were willing to offer special commercial advantages to secure the same end, and proposed to give Napoleon a large amount of cotton for the loan of a squadron. They also favored French and Spanish designs in America and, in order to obtain a treaty of alliance, intimated their readiness to guarantee the possessions of those powers. They made England and France a base for secret attempts to fit out vessels. They endeavored to disturb internal affairs and create complications which would serve the interests of the Confederacy. Finally, in a paroxysm of desperation, they proposed to secure emancipation for recognition, and in negotiations with London syndicates agreed to guarantee cotton for money to secure ships to break the blockade.

[26] 168 Parlia. Debates, p 511 et seq. July 18, 1862.
[27] See " Appendix." Also, see F. W. Sargent: England, the United States, and the Confederate States, London, 1864. Also, an article on the changes in tariff legislation since 1789, by W. G. Cutler, in Mag. Am. Hist., Vol. XII (1884), p. 519.

R. B. Rhett, who had made some study of commerce and revenues, had discussed in the secession convention of South Carolina a policy of commercial agreements with the important states of Europe. At Montgomery, he was chosen chairman of the committee of foreign relations, and before the inauguration of Davis had brought in a report authorizing the latter to send a commission to Europe to secure recognition and make treaties, offensive and defensive. As a plan of diplomacy he proposed: (1) A treaty of commercial alliance involving reciprocal obligations offensive and defensive for twenty years or more, during which the Confederacy would impose no import duty higher than 20 per cent ad valorem, no tonnage except for maintaining harbors and rivers, and would permit European parties to the treaty to enjoy the privileges of the coasting trade free, subject only to the police regulations of the states. (2) A discriminating duty of 10 per cent on all goods of all nations refusing to accept the treaty. (3) The commissioners to have power (as Franklin in 1778) to form alliances with European powers and guarantee their North American possessions.[28] This policy was discussed in Congress in the presence of Toombs, who, as Secretary of State, hoped to be allowed to give the commissioners instructions based upon this policy of overcoming European feeling against slavery by offering liberal commercial advantages, but Davis did not embrace these points in his later conversation with Toombs. The commission had already been appointed to go to Wash-

[28] Du Bose: Life and Times of Yancey.

ington; but Toombs, Rhett, and Yancey, expecting nothing from that source to justify a delay in foreign diplomacy, said that the friendship of Europe should first be secured, and that the policy toward the United States should depend upon circumstances. There was a strong feeling, however, in the Confederate Congress, and especially in Alabama, in favor of giving the first advantages of diplomacy to the United States. Some expected that the desire for cotton would induce the Government at Washington to favor a treaty of peace with the Confederacy.

Yancey, the champion leader in " firing the Southern heart " at the beginning of the secession movement, who had been spoken of for the presidency, was asked by Davis to head the commission to Europe, and P. A. Rost and Dudley Mann were named as his colleagues. Yancey was born in 1814 and elected to Congress in 1844. He had opposed the Clay compromise of 1850, anticipated the coming conflict, and prepared schemes for secession as early as 1858. In January, 1860, he advocated the secession of the Southern members from the Charleston convention, if their demands were denied, and he became the chief manager in that convention and in laying the program for secession from the Union. P. A. Rost, born in France, 1797, had gone to Louisiana in 1816, served in the Mississippi legislature in 1826, and a few years later removed to Louisiana where he became judge in the Supreme Court. Mann, born in 1801, had been sent as United States consul to Bremen in 1842, commissioner to Hungary in 1849, and minister to Switzerland in 1850, after which he was appointed Assistant Secretary of State (March 23, 1853).

Yancey found that Davis did not favor the policy of negotiating commercial treaties, but expected to base his diplomacy on the importance of the cotton crop (much of the previous year's crop being still on hand) and the legality of secession. When Yancey informed Rhett of Davis's instructions, Rhett, feeling that the United States had already warned Europe, and that it would be necessary to compensate the latter for the risk of recognition, said: "You have no business in Europe, you carry no argument that Europe cares to hear. My counsel is . . . to stay at home, or to go prepared to conciliate Europe by irresistible proffers of trade." B. C. Yancey, who had recently been in England, and had "studiously sought information touching the feeling of the Government there toward a probable Southern Confederacy, and, also had applied himself to ascertain the feeling of the laboring classes and their leaders, Cobden and Bright," whom he found would oppose the recognition of a slaveholders' confederacy, advised his brother not to undertake the mission, stating that the English Government, however well disposed, could not run counter to the Exeter Hall anti-slavery influence.[29]

Before the commission sailed, Congress and the executive were urged to adopt a foreign policy similar to that by which Franklin, Deane and Lee secured money and supplies during the American Revolution, but the commissioners only received power to encourage practical reciprocity to aid them over a crisis. The opposition afterwards complained that

[29] Du Bose: Life and Times of Yancey, pp. 588-89.

though the ports were open for a year, cotton was left on the plantations " while waiting for the United States to fall into bankruptcy." [30]

Yancey, though he failed to receive the instructions which he considered necessary to success, accepted the mission. The instructions to the commission directed them to inform Europe that secession violated no allegiance, that opposition by the United States was not expected, and that the South, with abundant resources, was able to win, and was willing to accept the treaties between the United States and foreign powers and to make a treaty practically providing for free trade. The commissioners were later authorized to issue commissions to privateers. They sailed March 31, and were in mid-ocean when news arrived from Washington that an armed fleet had been sent to relieve Fort Sumter. A call for troops by Lincoln followed, and Virginia seceded.

Rhett soon appealed to the Confederate Congress to direct Mr. Davis to instruct the commissioners in favor of a more liberal treaty, granting commercial privileges for a period of twenty years. Perkins, fearing that so long a period would extinguish the infant manufactures of the South, proposed to make it six years, stating that England was compelled to have cotton anyhow. Rhett replied that Europe, for a treaty securing vital relief for the Confederacy, would require a twenty years' guarantee, and that

[30] It is said that six iron ships built for the East India trade were, early in the war, offered to the Confederacy by a Liverpool firm for ten million dollars, but that Mallory, knowing the inefficiency of Memminger's department, omitted to communicate this offer to President Davis. [Du Bose: Life and Times of Yancey.]

during this period the Confederacy would have time to recuperate from the sacrifices of the war, which might not end for six years. To those who suggested that goods could be smuggled into the United States, he said that in case of such an event the manufactures of the United States would be injured more than those of the Confederacy. He did not think that a currency based on the cotton deposited in the South as good as a treaty that would make a cotton deposit in Europe the basis of a currency; and he declared that if the cotton ports be closed, England would engage in attempts to cultivate cotton in India and her other possessions, and would thus be led to discourage trade with the Confederacy. The Perkins amendment carried, but on the motion of Rhett the whole subject was laid on the table.

Davis expected to get Europe to recognize his Government and receive its ambassadors on grounds of international duty. Memminger, also, feared to sell the cotton on account of possible political effects at home, stating that the United States would make the blockade more effective if an attempt should be made to take cotton out of Confederate ports and that there was little probability that Europe would send vessels to get the product even if it should be stored in seaports. He said, that cotton stored by the Government on the plantations was the best basis for currency and European diplomacy. Soon after this many began to say that it should all be destroyed by the Government,[31] and that notice

---

[31] J. M. Daniels: Writings in the Richmond Examiner during the Civil War (N. Y., 1868), Feb. 26, 1862.

should be given to England that no more would be raised until that power was willing to grant recognition. The Confederate Government soon placed a tax on cotton production.

Stephens had been strongly in favor of shipping the cotton to Europe to pay for vessels to injure the United States commerce and to hold at least one Confederate port open while other Confederate vessels convoyed cotton to Europe where it could be stored more safely than in the United States. He was strongly opposed to the policy of Mr. Davis. Many others preferred the exportation policy, and strongly tried to convince Davis that his "cotton famine policy" was wrong.[82] Some urged him to sell to persons in the United States. Toombs, who had desired the Confederate Government to take the responsibility of rapidly exporting all the cotton to Europe, chafed under red tape, and resigned because he thought the administration was too timid. He said that if he had been president he would have mortgaged every pound of cotton to France and England at a price sufficient to remunerate the planters as well as to get the aid of the navies of England and France.[83] It is doubtless true that the shipment of 200,000 bales of cotton to Liverpool during the first year of the war would have strengthened the Confederate chances of securing a navy, but there were, probably, insurmountable obstacles to this policy. The Government was new and untried, and the sudden blockade of Southern ports had not been expected. Many merchant vessels made haste to load and get away in March, 1861, but Bullock says

[82] Mrs. Davis: Jefferson Davis.　　　　[83] Bullock.

there were not enough vessels to carry out the cotton even if it had been bought. General J. E. Johnston stating that the blockade was not effective until the end of the winter of 1862, declared that the Confederate Government could easily have shipped 4,000,000 bales to England and received the money for it. Memminger pronounced Johnston's views impracticable and visionary, stating that the blockade was instituted in May, 1861, and that it would have required 4000 ships to get the cotton out before that time. He said that private enterprise shipped as much as the Government could have shipped; that the Government had no funds with which to make purchases; that, even if there had been enough treasury notes and bonds for that purpose, it would have been a bad policy to use them to meet the necessities of the planters; that the Government could not have secured donations of cotton and did not desire to seize it; and, with the expectation that the blockade would last for less than a year, the Government had no motive to store cotton as a basis of credit.[34]

Stephens, who was never very confident of recognition by European powers, always said that it was a serious mistake at the beginning of the war to consider cotton as a political instead of a commercial power.[35] He strongly opposed the recommendations which some made to cease cotton culture[36] and destroy the stock on hand in order to compel England

[34] H. D. Capers: Memminger.

[35] Johnston and Browne: Life of A. H. Stephens.

[36] The Confederate House, on March 3, 1862, passed a resolution advising all growers of cotton and tobacco to stop the cultivation of those products. [C. E. Evans (Ed.): Confederate Military History, Vol. I, p. 436.]

to raise the blockade. He had been in favor of the Government paying ten cents a pound for all the cotton that persons were willing to subscribe for eight per cent bonds, and after the harbor system of the South had been closed, Memminger adopted his views as to the constitutionality of the Government purchasing cotton, but Stephens said it was then too late.

Yancey, Rost and Mann, on reaching Europe, soon saw that the action of France and other powers depended upon the policy of England who, though opposed to slavery, desired commercial intercourse with the South. They were encouraged by the British neutrality act, recognizing the Confederacy as a neutral, and later by the victory of Bull Run, and hoped that the British Government would take offense at the harsh protests of Seward (who at that time would have been willing to unite the North and South in a war against England), but independence was different from belligerency, and Adams, anxiously keeping his hand on the British pulse and watching every indication of variation, presented all of Seward's protests in courteous language and thus avoided an Anglo-American rupture. By their active operations, the Confederates gave rise to important legal and diplomatic questions, and to acrimonious correspondence between England and the United States, and, at the time of the *Trent* affair they anticipated complications which would induce the British Government to take a stand favorable to the Confederacy, but their hopes were disappointed.[37]

[37] On Aug. 24, 1861, Messrs. Yancey, Rost and Mann were also appointed special commissioners to Spain with full powers.

Yancey's commission was embarrassed by lack of funds [38] and secret agents, by Seward's vigorous diplomacy, and by the fact that Europe read the news from Northern papers, but soon after sending Mason and Slidell to Europe the Confederacy decided to spend more money abroad. Agents with secret service money were sent to influence public sympathy. The *Index*, a Confederate organ, was established at London, editorials and other articles were prepared for insertion in the prominent English and French newspapers. About the latter part of 1862 Benjamin, in writing to De Leon, expressed a desire for him to extend his operations to the press of Austria, Prussia and other parts of central Europe. Henry Hotze, the confidential agent at London,[39] in addition to his press duties, also kept Mr. Benjamin informed on European public opinion, forwarding him the London papers and the principal quarterly reviews.[40] Mason and Slidell each received a salary of $12,000 with an allowance of $3000 for contingent expenditures for limited objects. In January, 1864, Mason wrote Benjamin that Slidell and himself both

[38]When Yancey left London on the arrival of Mason he borrowed money for his expenses. His salary had not been remitted.

[39] Hotze was born in Zurich, Switzerland in 1834. In 1858 he was provisionally appointed secretary of the U. S. Legation at Brussels. In 1859 he became associated with John Forsyth in editing the Mobile Register. In April, 1861, he enlisted in the Confederate army. On Aug. 31, he was appointed, by the Confederate war department, to proceed to Europe to purchase supplies of war. On Nov. 14, he was appointed commercial agent at London, where he founded the Index. [The Mobile Register, May 11, 1887.]

[40] Instr. to Mason, No. 35, April 18, 1864.

agreed that there "are objects of expenditure for political ends, occasionally presenting themselves, when it would be well that the commissioners in Europe could have larger discretion." [41] "This character of expenditure might not generally admit of a regular voucher but must be submitted to the integrity of the commissioners." On April 18, Benjamin sent him £500 as a secret service fund.

When Mason and Slidell reached Europe the first of February, 1862, Davis and Hunter were contemplating the possibility that France and England, acting both from commercial and political motives, would end the blockade by intervention, and, on February 8, prepared instructions urging that to prevent the danger of future war or reunion, the area of the Confederacy should be enlarged so as to include the Chesapeake bay, the border states, and New Mexico and Arizona. [42] Mason, while unsuccessfully urging the British Government to adopt the policy of recognizing the Confederacy and breaking the blockade to secure cotton, also directed his efforts to mould public opinion through the press and social channels, and took an active part in arranging for the construction of Confederate vessels in British ports. Though he always exaggerated the chances of success, public opinion in favor of recognizing the Confederacy was increasing in 1862. The battle of Fredericksburg seemed to silence Southern opposition to the Confederate Government, and Gladstone said

[41] Despatches of Mason to Benjamin, No. 1, Paris, Jan. 25, 1864.

[42] Confed. "Dip. Cor., Great Brit." Hunter to Mason, No. 4, Feb. 8, 1862.

that Davis had "created a nation." When the British Government awaited future developments and refused to join France in a policy of mediation, the Confederate leaders were disappointed, and pronounced English neutrality a farce and an irony managed to the advantage of the United States.[43] The Richmond *Enquirer* said that the English policy was to let the war continue long enough to destroy the strength of both North and South.

In November, 1862, Mason having been able "to see and hear nothing from the British Government officially or unofficially," suggested that a termination of his mission might preserve the dignity of the Confederate Government; but, in the same letter he stated that his presence in London was really important.[44] As early as July, seeing that Russell would neither receive him nor recognize the Confederacy he had given a similar intimation, and, on September 26, Benjamin wrote him that Mr. Davis, though desiring him to avoid being placed in the attitude of a suppliant, thought that he should await contingencies. In the last week of October, expecting Sanders to secure the construction of vessels in England,

[43] Alfriend: Jefferson Davis, Chap. 14.

[44] Commander Sinclair arrived at London with an order of the Confederate Navy for money to pay for building a ship; but Bullock's funds were needed to meet contracts already made, and, in order to avoid delay, Mason, as an agent of the Confederacy, agreed to an arrangement with Lindsay and Co. [Despatches of Mason, No. 16, Sept. 18, 1862.] In October, after a murder had occurred on the *Sumter* at Gibraltar, Mason authorized Bullock to sell the vessel and endeavored to induce the English authorities to deliver the murderer at some Confederate port. The government at Richmond afterwards approved his action in these matters.

Davis, notwithstanding Russell's scant courtesy, "offensive arrogance and rude incivility," decided that Mason had better remain waiting for public opinion to force the British Government to change its policy. But, in a speech to the Mississippi legislature in December, after referring to former expectations of recognition and intervention by foreign nations, he said "put not your trust in princes . . . this war is ours; we must fight it out ourselves." [45] The probability that Russia, like England and France, would postpone the question of recognition until the question of might was made clear, caused Benjamin to hesitate in approaching Alexander II., but on November 19 he instructed L. Q. C. Lamar to go to St. Petersburgh and assure the Czar of the Confederate desire for friendly and commercial intercourse. [46] Russia was friendly toward the United States and refused to receive the Confederate commissioner. [47]

Stephens, considering that France and England while jealous of the growth of the United States were also opposed to slavery, had "never looked to foreign intervention or recognition," and on September 1, 1862, in a letter to R. M. Johnston he said that Davis should recall all commissioners. [48] Others held the same views by the close of the year. In January, 1863, Foote in the House urged this measure. On January 15, the Richmond *Examiner*, commenting

[45] Alfriend: Jefferson Davis.
[46] Walker Fearn was appointed as secretary.
[47] Despatches from U. S. Legation, Russia: Bayard Taylor to Seward, No. 30, March 3, 1863 (encloses intercepted communication of Benjamin to L. Q. C. Lamar). Also, 14 Instr. Russia, Seward to C. M. Clay, No. 2, March 31, 1863.
[48] Cleveland: A. H. Stephens, p. 761.

upon Davis's policy to avoid a conclusion upon this subject, also favored a withdrawal, and said that the European powers as soon as they saw the end of the struggle approaching would then have to send ambassadors to Richmond instead of calling up Southern commissioners "now waiting in servants' halls and on the back stairs." New York papers of March 30 published the Mason-Russell correspondence which had been brought before the public by a resolution of Parliament, and the Richmond *Whig* of April 6, republishing part of it, berated Russell for his terror of Seward and his "perversion" of the provisions of 1856 to which the Confederacy had been induced to agree. In the Confederate House on April 6, 1863, Mr. Swan of Tennessee, moved a suspension of the rules to enable him to introduce a joint resolution suggesting that Congress would approve the removal of Mason from London.[49] The vote stood 39 yeas to 39 nays, but as a two-thirds vote was necessary Swan's motion failed. On April 13, the *Sentinel* abused Congress for differing with the President as to the retention of the diplomatic agents.[50] De Leon wrote Benjamin from Paris on

[49] Richmond Dispatch, April 7, 1863.

[50] On March 16, Mr. Davis sent to the Senate the name of L. Q. C. Lamar as commissioner to Russia. The Senate referred the nomination to the committee of foreign affairs. The committee and the Senate did not think it expedient to send a commissioner to Russia, and on April 13, in secret session, requested Mr. Davis to state his reasons for making such an appointment. Davis replied on April 20, but the Senate adjourned May 1 without confirming the nomination, and Lamar's commission thereby expired. Davis, while regretting the action of the Senate, deemed it his duty to yield. [Confed. "Dip. Cor., Russia," Instr. to Lamar, June 11, 1863, with enclosure of Burton N. Harrison to Benjamin.]

June 19, that by reason of the prejudice against slavery no further attempts to get recognition should be made, and renewed suggestions which he had previously made that the commissioners should be recalled from Europe. Slidell, considering De Leon as a spy on his actions and his despatches, soon complained to Benjamin,[51] and, after some annoyance caused by the interception and publication of objectionable correspondence, De Leon's agency was ended.

The Confederacy had felt inconvenienced and handicapped by the slowness of communication with Europe, and was anxious to secure a sure and swift transportation of despatches and news. George N. Sanders had early tried to get the privilege to establish a line of communication.[52] Benjamin would not engage him in that capacity, but agreed to give him a certain sum for the delivery of despatches from abroad.[53] In October, 1862, Benjamin wrote Mason that Mr. Fearn had arranged a plan for facilitating intercourse, but Sanders continued to act as despatch bearer until the beginning of 1863 when his son Reid Sanders, while attempting to run the blockade from Charleston, allowed important despatches to be seized on his person, and caused Benjamin to advise Mason to risk no more letters through that agency. Despatches and supplies were afterwards sent through L. Heyleger, at Nassau or via Bermuda. In November, 1862, Mr. Lindsay proposed a plan for establishing a direct line of French steamers, with a

---

[51] Despatches of Slidell to Benjamin, No. 50.
[52] Instr. to Mason, No. 8, Oct. 28, 1862.
[53] Instr. to Mason, Feb. 7, 1863.

view of diverting the trade of the West, and as far as possible that of the North, through Norfolk and other Confederate ports, but this line was not expected to operate before the close of the war.[54] Davis and Benjamin replied that the Confederate constitution did not allow a grant of postal subsidies as proposed by Lindsay's plan, but suggested that Virginia as a state might grant such a subsidy.[55] About the same time George McHenry made a proposition for the establishment of an Atlantic mail line by Confederate aid, but Davis, on the grounds that the Post Office Department must sustain itself, and that the terms of transportation might be cheaper later, refused to accept the proposition.[56] Despatches continued to be sent by British vessels via Halifax and through the Confederate agents at Bermuda and Nassau.

In the early part of 1863, Benjamin seeing little hope of action by England and suspecting Napoleon's designs in Texas, Louisiana and Florida, asked Slidell to open communication with Spain by suggesting the advantage of alliance and offering to join in a disclaimer as to designs on Cuba.[57] President Davis refused to recognize any longer the British consuls unless they obtained exequaturs from the Confederate Government.

In the middle of 1863 Napoleon with the United

---

[54] Despatches of Mason, Nov. 4, 1862, and March 19, 1863.

[55] Instr. to Mason, No. 12, Jan. 15, 1863. Despatches of Mason, Jan. 16, 1863.

[56] Instr. to Mason, No. 19, March 31, 1863.

[57] An attempt was also made to influence public opinion in Ireland. On March 7, 1863, Robert Dowling was appointed as commercial agent at Cork.

States map before him said he was only waiting for England to act, and the Confederates believed they had two advocates in the British cabinet and expected to get others to support a resolution for recognition, but it was in vain that they hoped to overcome the influence of the British Liberals and of Seward, who with an eye to the future, was watchfully making record of every case where he thought the British Government had favored the Confederates. When they turned secretly to secure the construction of vessels in British ports they found Seward's consular agents watching the dockyards, and securing evidence by which to emphasize protests to the British Government.[58] In the autumn of 1863 Mason withdrew from London to Paris, and soon received duplicate full powers addressed in blank so he could fill them out himself and go to any English capital,[59] but contingencies not arising to call for his services on the continent he alternated between Paris and London until the close of the war, drawing his salary as a commissioner but having no diplomatic duties to perform.[60] At London, however, he aided certain members of Parliament in attempts to embarrass the Government and force it to recognize the Confederacy.

[58] Bullock, Vol. I.

[59] Instr. to Mason, No. 34, Jan. 25, 1864.

[60] On September 24, 1863, Mann was instructed, by Benjamin, to go to the Pope, who had expressed sorrow as to the ruin and devastation of the war, and to assure him that the Southern people were desirous that the war should cease. [Record 1, Instr., p. 21.] On April 4, 1864, Rt. Rev. P. A. Lynch, Bishop of Charleston, was appointed Special Commissioner to the States of the Church, with full powers.

On October 26, 1864, Benjamin published a copy of a despatch,[61] which he prepared for publication in Europe, with the purpose of showing that if the United States continued the war she would be unable to pay her debts abroad, and that the foreigners, in order to escape ruin, ought not to lend her more money.[62] He also tried to impress Spain, England and France with the statement that their American possessions would be in danger from the desire of the United States for empire.

There was considerable English sympathy for the secession movement, but the condition of parties, the sentiment against slavery, the active efforts of English friends of the Union, together with the diplomacy of Seward and Adams, prevented the success of Confederate efforts to secure recognition or intervention.

Earl Russell in his " Recollections and Suggestions " says that the only grave error of his official acts toward America was his neglect to detain the *Alabama*. The British cabinet, while Napoleon was intriguing and Anglo-American relations were strained, was, as a rule, discreet and fair in its policy of neutrality. Benjamin, Mason and Slidell all considered that Earl Russell was cold, distant and unfriendly to their cause, and after 1862 their only hope was for a change of cabinet or complications, but many members of the Lords and Commons were in frequent conference with Mason and openly expressed the desire to embarrass the government and force

[61] Instr. to Mann (circular), Oct. 10, 1864.
[62] Weekly Register (Lynchburg), Dec. 24, 1864. J. B. Jones: Diary, Oct. 26, 1864. The Index, Jan. 5, 1865.

it to recognize the Confederacy. It has been said that the dress suit and digestive apparatus of England were hostile to the United States, but that the cerebro-centres, heart and muscle were friendly.

Napoleon was held back by England and the people. He held many conversations with Slidell and was eagerly planning in the Tuileries to recognize the South and break the blockade, but the capture of New Orleans prevented any step he may have contemplated without the cooperation of England. He afterwards seemed to favor the construction of Confederate vessels in French ports and it was principally the vigilance of Mr. Dayton, the American minister, which prevented these vessels from reaching the sea, but the Confederate agents asserted that the Emperor had wilfully tricked them.

The Confederacy was disappointed in the power of cotton to secure foreign influence. A report to the Richmond congress in December, 1864,[63] said that England, at the beginning of the war, possessed large stocks of cotton and cotton goods which the owners sold for exorbitant prices, doing a smaller business in quantity but a larger one in value and leaving their unemployed operators to be supported by others. Besides, from 1862 there was a steady flow of cotton to both Europe and the Northern states. The report to Congress stated that England had received indirectly from the Confederacy since September, 1863, 4000 bales per week; that United States merchants also had the benefit of exports in Confederate cotton through the trade with Mexico and the West

[63] Geo. McHenry: Cotton Crisis, Dec. 18, 1864.

Indies, and had not drawn from Europe; that King Cotton had been captured by United States vessels while running the blockade, and had thus assisted the finances of the United States. In February, 1862, the Richmond *Examiner* proposed that the Government should burn the cotton to prevent it falling into the hands of citizens of the North.[64] In October, 1862, Benjamin, desiring to secure army stores, gave Mr. Dunnock permission to sell cotton on the coast. Randolph, the Secretary of War, urged the acceptance of offers by others to trade it for meat and bread in ports held by the United States. Davis hesitated, but on November 8, he consented to allow Governor Pettus of Mississippi to trade it for salt at New Orleans which was under the jurisdiction of Butler. In 1863, there were complaints that while the Confederates could not place enough money in Europe to pay for needed supplies, the United States was receiving both cotton and information through the blockade runners and the Southern Express Company was monopolizing the railroads to deliver cotton to speculators who sent it into the North. In April, 1863, it was said that importation by British adventurers was contrived by Northern merchants with the sanction of the United States Government and that war supplies were therefore usually captured. In March, 1864, J. B. Lamar of Savannah, who had command of five steamers, wrote that he could easily arrange with the Federal commanders

[64] Bunch, the British consul at Charleston, wrote Lord Russell on August 15, 1862, that 1,000,000 bales of cotton had been destroyed by the South. By the end of the year very little was taken to the coast.

to permit them to pass out with cotton by paying one-half for freight.[65]   On April 2, General Lee made regulations to prevent cotton from passing to the North unless allowed by the Richmond Government. A month later Memminger favored a proposition of Mr. Bond for the Government to give him a bill of sale of ten thousand bales of cotton in exposed places in the West "to be shipped via New Orleans to Antwerp." In June, one of the commissary officers in the West proposed to the Government to sell cotton on the Mississippi river for London exchange and indicated that he had large sums to his credit by such transactions.

George McHenry, in a pamphlet on the approaching "Cotton Crisis" published at Richmond, in December, 1864, said that under the acts of the United States Congress of July 2, by which the Secretary of the Treasury was directed to authorize purchases of products of the Confederate States, the North had been getting cheap cotton, and the South receiving dear bacon; that the trade had been winked at on the part of some of the Confederate authorities; that frauds had been practiced to a shameful degree; and that there had been a constant drain of cotton from Arkansas, Louisiana and Texas. On September 27, 1864, the Confederate cotton agent in Mississippi was authorized by the Government at Richmond to sell cotton in exposed situations to United States agents for specie. In October, Beverly Tucker who was in Canada made a contract by authority of the Secretary of War to exchange cotton for bacon pound for

[65] J. B. Jones: Diary.

pound. The Secretary of the Treasury was not pleased with the arrangement.

In January, 1865, Trenholm, Secretary of the Treasury, authorized an agent to go to Augusta to buy all the cotton for the Government, and then sell it for the London exchange to parties who were to be allowed to remove it within the Federal lines or abroad. A month later speculators at Wilmington seemed to want their cotton to fall into United States hands.

There had been a considerable loss on the cotton exchanged in Europe for supplies. The rate for blockade running was extravagant and the cotton was usually sold at less than the market price. Some said it would have been far better to pay gold for supplies and retain the cotton; others that the Government should have assumed complete control of all cotton and the regulation of the price. When the Richmond Government saw that the war and the blockade would continue, it arranged to use cotton as the basis of a loan negotiated in Europe by Erlanger,[66] but its power to control the cotton was restricted by a large amount in the hands of those who would not sell, and it did not desire to seize the crops of those who refused to receive a depreciated currency in payment. The first efforts to ship cotton on Government account met with difficulty and delay. Ships engaged in the blockade trade were owned by private firms who wanted all their space and the ships owned by the Government were wanted for other purposes. On December 29, 1863, Mallory wrote Bullock that

[66] Capers: Memminger.

3100 bales had been shipped from Charleston and Wilmington via Bermuda and Nassau to go to Fraser, Trenholm & Co.   Later he said that 1200 bales had been purchased by the State Department and would go forward as rapidly as possible.[67]   At the beginning of 1863, Bullock had suggested that the Government should own its packets in order to avoid heavy freights.   In September, when Mason saw no prospect of another European loan, he wrote Benjamin that the Confederacy in order to cheapen goods, strengthen the Confederate credit and prevent the United States from sharing in the profits of running the blockade should take entire control of exportation of cotton and the importation of supplies.[68]   Bullock suggested the same to Mallory in October, stating that the Confederacy should accumulate in Europe a large supply of cotton by which to rule the market and perhaps exert political influence.   Again, in November, he urged the building of special vessels for shipments by the Government.   In December Benjamin prepared a project for a " Bureau of Export and Import," and early in 1864 he recommended a Government monopoly in the export of cotton and the import of necessary supplies.   Congress adopted the measure; and McRae, who had written from Paris urging this plan, during the following summer contracted with Fraser, Trenholm & Co. for eight steel-clad steamers, six of which reached the Confederate coasts and made one or more trips before the close of the war.   Other vessels were begun but not com-

[67] Bullock, Vol. II.
[68] Despatches of Mason to Benjamin, No. 45, Sept. 5, 1863.

pleted. Notwithstanding the tone of unofficial speeches in England, the British Government refused to allow unarmed ships to escape when they were clearly intended for use by the Confederates.

One of the principal factors in forcing the Confederacy to end the war was the lack of supplies which cotton could have purchased if it could have been shipped to Europe. The blockade by sea and by land was the principal cause of the Confederate failure. If the vessels at Liverpool and Bordeaux had been allowed to go to sea in 1864 the South might have opened some of her ports. George McHenry in his report on "the approaching cotton crisis" in December, 1864, said that if the Confederates could have withheld their cotton from the outer world the powers by that time would have been forced into a policy of recognition, but that a large share of it had absolutely been dissipated away; that most of the Confederate legislation had operated to favor a few speculators who had neither social nor political influence across the Atlantic, and who, so long as they had contracts giving them the monopoly of the trade at 700 per cent profit did not care to see peace brought about.[69] Mr. McHenry said that the cotton operators in England who were over employed before the war had invested money in the savings banks and had been using it during the period of under-employment since the war began, but that they had now expended all their former earnings, and sold their furniture, and must soon have work. He held that England was in error in expecting an increased supply

[69] Geo. McHenry: Approaching Cotton Crisis, Dec. 31, 1864.

of cotton from countries which had hitherto produced little, and stated that the stoppage of the Confederate cotton leak would certainly produce a cotton crisis in England some time during the year 1865 and cause Manchester to force the ministry to recognize the Confederacy.

At the beginning of 1865 Mr. Davis and Mr. Benjamin had resolved not only to offer emancipation for recognition or intervention by England and France, but to contract with syndicates at London and Paris agreeing to seize cotton and furnish it to them in payment for funds necessary to procure a navy. At that time, however, no policy could have secured the success of secession.

CHAPTER IV

MISSION OF YANCEY, ROST AND MANN

In 1860 the Prince of Wales visited the northern portion of the United States, going as far south as Virginia. He slept at the White House, planted a tree at the tomb of Washington, and was given a reception indicating that Anglo-American relations were more cordial than they had been for years. When the storm of the "irrepressible conflict" burst forth in torrents of fury the next year, the sympathy of Queen Victoria, Prince Albert, the Prince of Wales and the majority of the people of England was with the Union cause. Slavery in the South had been a source of much annoyance to England, and the Northern people hoped that the secession movement would receive no support, but in this they were disappointed. Many of the aristocracy of England stood for the South. London club life was Southern in its sympathies and prominent English papers endeavored to mould England in favor of the Southern Confederacy. Prominent statesmen considered that the Union was "shooting the Niagara Falls." Lord Russell spoke of the "*late* United States." The Earl of Shrewsbury spoke of the trial and failure of democracy and prophesied the establishment of an aristocracy in America. In October, 1862, Gladstone said that Jefferson Davis had made an army, a navy and a nation.

On the day of Mr. Lincoln's inauguration Mr. Gregory, in the House of Commons, gave notice of a motion to recognize the independence of the Confederate States; and, soon after, by a public letter, urged this policy as a means of breaking up the slave trade, and as a retaliation against the American tariff. Many of the leaders of the Confederacy already had strong expectations of securing early recognition by both England and France, especially for commercial reasons. On March 16, 1861, while Confederate commissioners were at Washington trying to open peace negotiations with Secretary Seward, Mr. Toombs directed Yancey, Rost and Mann to go to London "as soon as possible" (and then to other European capitals) to press claims for recognition.[1] The instructions recite that dissolution was the result of long and mature deliberation to escape the persistent efforts to compel the agricultural South to pay bounties to the North in the shape of high protective tariffs; that secession violated no allegiance or rights; that the Washington Government was not in a condition to offer opposition; that a large party of Northern people would not favor resistance to secession; that there was no unusual reason to fear war; and that the South had abundant means and determination, would be joined by the border states, and would win. Power was given the commissioners to make a treaty practically providing for free trade. A willingness was expressed to continue all the United States treaties except the clause providing for the maintenance of a naval squadron on the coast of Africa. Though

[1] Confed. " Dip. Cor.," Vol. I.

the Confederacy had prohibited the slave trade, she could not help the rest of the world to end it. With the South controlling the Gulf coast, and one-half of the Atlantic coast, and with her large exports of cotton and her *laissez faire* policy in commerce, it was expected that England would be ready to oppose any measure by the United States Government that would interfere with trade.[2] After Sumter fell, Toombs wrote (April 24) to the commissioners stating that war was unavoidable but that unrestricted intercourse with friendly nations was desired,[3] and he soon authorized them (May 18) to issue commissions for privateers. In 1856 the powers of Europe had endeavored to persuade all nations to abandon privateering, but the United States having no large navy had refused to join such an arrangement. Toombs now stated that the large navy of the United States made it necessary for the Confederacy to adopt this

[2] W. H. Russell, an English journalist, who spent May of 1861 in the South, and had a seat on the floor of the legislative assembly at Montgomery when it was not in secret session, says in his diary (May 6th) that the press was fanning the flames, and that Browne, Assistant Secretary of State, had informed him that 400 letters applying for letters of marque and reprisal had been received by the Confederate government. Russell visited the plain office of Mr. Davis, and also that of the cordial Mr. Benjamin, whom he said was "not afraid of anything." Benjamin stated that if England declared privateers to be pirates the Confederacy would consider it as a declaration of war, and meet it. He was certain that if the United States claimed the Confederate ports as United States ports, that the British law officers would advise the British government not to recognize the blockades. W. H. Russell: Diary, North and South.

[3] Confed. "Dip. Cor.", Vol. I, Instr. to Y., R. and M., No. 2. Ibid., No. 5.

method of warfare. He had made no allusion to slavery in the first instructions, but he now stated that it was evidently the intention of Lincoln to overthrow domestic institutions and to sweep away the rights of the minority. The right of each state to judge what are infractions of the constitution, and the remedy for such infractions, was declared. Assurance of the enthusiasm and unanimity of the South was given, and the commissioners were instructed to present to England the prejudicial results of the blockade. At the same time Captain Bullock was sent to secure war vessels in Europe.

Before the last instructions had been received the three commissioners had reached London, and, on May 3, through the good offices of Mr. Gregory of the House of Commons, had obtained a formal interview with Lord Russell. They stated that a new government in America had been formed without shedding a drop of blood and was prepared to maintain its independence—and they emphasized especially the unrestricted commercial advantages which England would obtain by recognition.[4] They said that the tariff was the principal cause of secession, and pointed to the new Morrill tariff as a means of nearly excluding English manufactures from the North. Earl Russell informed the commissioners that the whole matter would be a subject of Cabinet consideration, but he expressed no opinion. Mr. Rost received more encouragement in Paris, where he had an interview with Count De Morny, a confidential friend of the Emperor Napoleon. The Count said that

[4] Russell to Lord Lyons, May 11, 1861.

France and England had agreed to pursue the same course, and that recognition was a mere matter of time, but that it would be a fatal mistake to urge immediate action. He stated that France would be ready to receive suggestions from the Confederates unofficially and secretly, and that so long as cotton was for sale both France and England would see that their vessels reached the Confederate ports. In a despatch to Secretary Toombs, the commissioners expressed confidence that neither England nor France were averse to the disintegration of the United States, but they feared that public opinion against the Confederacy on the question of slavery would embarrass the governments in dealing with the question of recognition.[5]

In April the British Government had concluded not to intrude its counsels unsolicited to avert war.[6] On May 2, Russell referred to the war as a bad one and said: "For God's sake, let us, if possible, keep out of it."[7] Though war had been declared by neither party, Russell, in reply to Gregory, on May 6, announced the decision of the law officers of the Crown that the Southern Confederacy must be treated as a belligerent as Greece had been in 1825, but he anticipated no disagreement with the United States as to the blockade. On the same day he wrote to the British ambassador at Paris inviting the Emperor to cooperate in a joint endeavor to obtain from each of the belligerents certain concessions in favor of neu-

[5] Confed. "Dip. Cor.," Vol. I, p. 105. Despatches of Yancey and Mann, No. 1, London, May 21, 1861.

[6] 162 Parl. Debates, Lords, April 29, 1861.

[7] Sen. Rp. 1160, 54-2.

trals. The French minister concurred.[8] British statesmen saw the necessity of warning British seamen that privateering was against the foreign enlistment act, and on May 13 the government issued a proclamation of neutrality between the United States and " certain states styling themselves the Confederate States of America." Earl Russell based his action on the " size and population of the seceding states." He soon gave orders to interdict the entrance of all ships of war or privateers with prizes, into any of the British ports.[9] Some believed that Russell felt that recognition of the independence of the Confederacy was only a question of time, and thought that he hurried his proclamation in order to avoid the remonstrance of C. F. Adams, the new American minister who was on his way to London. W. H. Russell, the English journalist who was travelling in the United States, found people in the North very indignant against England on account of the British policy.[10] They pointed out that the United States had taken no such unfriendly course during the Canadian rebellion.

The British proclamation of neutrality, practically recognizing the Confederacy as a belligerent, was given at a time when the United States claimed that no state of war existed, and that this action would

[8] In March, 1861, Mercier at Washington seems to have advised France to recognize the Confederacy. In May he advised his government to intervene by raising the blockade. About May 21 he was at Richmond and held prolonged interviews with Benjamin—probably for the purpose of rescuing tobacco which had been purchased by French citizens.

[9] 163 Parl. Debates, June 7, 1861.

[10] W. H. Russell: Diary, p. 133.

be a means of aiding the secessionists in the establishment of their power.   Complaints were made that
the British Government had not given the new
American administration time to develop its policy of
ending the "demoralization" which had been growing since the November election.   The United States
did not recognize the Confederacy as a belligerent
until President Lincoln under the act of Congress of
July 13, issued his proclamation of August 16, 1861.   It
was stated that England knew the Confederacy had
no navy, and was aware that the United States considered secession unconstitutional.   Secretary Fish in
1869, in referring to the matter, said "the assumed
belligerency of the insurgents was a fiction . . . the
anticipation of supposed belligerency to come, but
which might never have come if not thus anticipated
and encouraged."   English writers, on the other
hand, said that President Lincoln's proclamation of
a blockade to suppress local insurrection practically
recognized belligerency, and that it had become necessary for Great Britain to protect the interests of
her citizens which would be affected by the war.

A few hours after the British Government issued
its proclamation Charles Francis Adams arrived in
London to replace Dallas as United States minister,
and to oppose decidedly any wavering policy of the
British Government which might give the Confederates hope of recognition.   "You alone will represent
your country at London" said Seward in his instructions to Adams, "and you will represent the whole of
it there.   When you are asked to divide that duty
with others, diplomatic relations between the Government of Great Britain and this Government will

be suspended." Before Adams arrived, Dallas had informed Seward of Russell's unofficial interview with the Confederate agents on May 3. Seward had also learned that England and France had decided to act together. He had not expected such an alliance, and resolved to take no notice of it, but he was determined to take a decided stand against European interference in the war. On May 21, in a letter bristling with references to the danger of a war with European nations, and stating that the United States was ready to meet such a war with confidence and success, he wrote Adams that the United States after long forbearance had a right to adopt a blockade as a means of suppressing insurrection, and that the treatment to be administered to Confederate privateers was a matter for the United States alone to decide.[11] He also stated that even unofficial intercourse with the Confederates was hurtful to the United States and he

[11] This letter had several of its teeth drawn by Lincoln before it was sent. In the original draft Seward said, " We intend to have a clear and simple record of whatever issue may arise between us and Great Britain," but Lincoln struck out this phrase, as well as others. W. H. Russell, in his diary said that the relations of the United States with England probably were considerably affected by Seward's failure in his prophecies as to the early suppression of secession. He said that Seward, becoming more exacting and defiant, and assuming higher ground as the Confederacy gained power, had been " fretful, irritable and acrimonious," but that Sumner was useful in allaying irritation. On July 4, Seward told Mr. Russell that if any European power provoked a war the United States would not shrink from it, and had nothing to fear from a foreign war, though it should wrap the world in fire. Russell could not but admire his confidence and coolness. It appeared that he, like Benjamin, was " not afraid of anything."

added "You will . . . . desist from all intercourse whatever, official or unofficial, with the British Government so long as it shall continue intercourse of either kind with the domestic enemies of this country." On June 14, Adams replied that Russell declared he had "no intention of seeing them again."

Seward, by his constant vigilance, embarrassed the Confederate commissioners at every corner. After the passage of the Morrill tariff he expected that the Confederates would ask for recognition as a retaliation and gave Adams his instructions to thwart the arguments of the Confederates. He said that to seek to destroy the Union as a retaliatory measure would be far more injurious to the United States than the temporary disadvantage of a revenue law could be to England; he intimated that England should not assume that the Confederacy would offer more liberal terms of trade than the North could offer; he stated that the Confederates might in case of war find themselves tempted to levy import duties, or be forced to discontinue their offer of practically free trade; he urged that most of the imports from Europe to the United States were consumed in the North, and that the Morrill tariff probably would not decrease the amount; he declared that recognition would mean intervention and war, and that permanent disunion would mean perpetual civil war and Confederate aggression for expansion, which might be fraught with grave consequences to other nations and to the peace of the world; he reminded England that recognition would be a dangerous precedent to be set by a nation whose bonds to her colonies might be put to a severe test by future insurrections.

By June the Confederate commissioners found that the general opinion at London was that the North was too strong for the South.[12]   Seeing no immediate hope of recognition by England and France they suggested that communication should be opened with Spain.   Gregory had proposed to make a move in the Commons on June 7, looking toward recognition, but he postponed his motion at the request of Earl Russell, who said it was opposed to public interests to raise such a question.   The commissioners were hopeful, however, that the Confederacy would win favor by the failure of Seward's pledges to restore the Union in ninety days.   In a recent interview with the Confederate commissioners, Earl Russell had seemed to be interested in their narrative of the conduct of the United States toward the Confederate Peace Commissioners at Washington, but he only said that Great Britain desired to communicate with both the United States and the Confederate States as to the Declaration of Paris and the rights of neutrals, and that the cabinet would consider all the questions that arose—but he could give no promise in regard to recognition.[13]

[12] Despatches of Yancey, Rost and Mann, No. 2, June 1, 1861.

[13] On June 15 Lord Lyons and Mercier in an interview with Seward proposed to read their instructions as to the neutral attitude of their respective governments, and ascertain the position of the United States as to the Declaration of Paris, but Seward already having been informed of the substance of the instructions, and feeling that foreign powers had no right (by assuming the attitude of a neutral) to decide that the United States was divided into two belligerent parties, declined to hear them read, and a few days later instructed Dayton at Paris and Adams at London, that the insurrection in the South did not constitute a war.

In 1856 representatives from the different European governments met at Paris and agreed upon the following declarations:

"(1) Privateering is and remains abolished.

"(2) The neutral flag covers enemies' goods with the exception of contraband of war.

"(3) Neutral goods, with the exception of contraband of war are not liable to capture under the enemies' flag.

"(4) Blockades in order to be binding must be effective, that is to say, maintained by a force sufficient really to prevent access to the coast of the enemy."

At that time the United States, having a small navy as compared to the nations of Europe with whom there was a possibility of a contest in the future, felt that it was inexpedient to agree to a declaration against privateering unless private property should be exempted from capture by sea.[14]

Having practically recognized the Confederacy as a belligerent, Lord Russell, on May 18, instructed Lord Lyons at Washington to take steps to secure the assent of the officials of the Confederacy to the rules of 1856 in regard to a neutral flag, neutral goods and blockades, and authorized him to confide the negotiation to Robert Bunch, the British Consul at Charleston.   On July 5, Lord Lyons directed Bunch to proceed in the negotiations with the Richmond authorities, using caution so as to avoid raising the question of recognition.   Mr. Bunch secured Mr. W. H. Trescot as an agent to lay the matter before Mr. Davis, and the latter, after a cabinet meeting, obtained

[14] Exec. Docs., 24-3, Vol. I, p. 33.

the passage by the Confederate Congress of a resolution maintaining the right of privateering, but acceding to the Declaration of Paris on all other subjects. This resolution was approved August 13, and England practically agreed not to interfere with privateering by the Confederacy.

As soon as Seward heard of the negotiations with the Confederacy he asked the removal of Bunch, but Lord Russell accepted the responsibility of his acts and refused to remove him, whereupon his *exequatur* was revoked by President Lincoln on the ground that his communication invited the insurgents to exercise power belonging to a sovereign state—to become a party to an international agreement which was similar to a treaty. The United States was willing to accept the entire declaration of Paris, but England did not desire her to accept the article against privateering.[15]

The Confederate commissioners abroad were still watching the popular pulse. By July 15, Rost had held an informal interview with M. Thouvenel the French minister of foreign affairs. He found that while France was ready to join the other powers in an effort for peace it was necessary for her to look first to her interests in Europe. Yancey had joined Rost in Paris, and he reported that the Emperor had no feeling hostile to the Confederacy but only waited for England. The commissioners were of the opinion that Spain, Belgium and Denmark were friendly and ready to extend recognition as soon as England and France should do so. In a letter complaining of the

[15] J. B. Moore: International Arbitrations, Vol. I, pp. 564-65.

neglect of the Confederacy to keep the commissioners well informed as to vessels entering and clearing Confederate ports, and urging the establishment of a secret line of communication by way of Canada, he said that opinion was becoming reconciled to secession as a *fact* though it had been opposed to it as a theory. In a letter to Toombs (July 15) the commissioners stated that relations between Mr. Adams and the British Cabinet were neither amicable nor satisfactory. It was seen that complications might arise to the advantage of the Confederacy. But Adams was successful in breaking off the personal interviews between Russell and the commissioners, and this caused a difference of opinion in the commission. Yancey thought that Russell's concession to Adams's demand was a violation of British neutrality. He said that the cause of the Confederacy could not be adequately explained in writing, nor the temper of the British Government be discovered, and urged that a firm but moderate protest should be made, but Rost and Mann objected to the protest and the subject was referred to Richmond.[16]

After the Confederate victory at Manassas (Bull Run), in July, the commissioners were encouraged to renew their efforts and to furnish Russell with a long communication giving reasons for immediate recognition. R. M. T. Hunter, who had replaced Toombs, informed the commissioners that Union sentiment in the South had been silenced, and that Maryland and Missouri were kept in the Union only by Federal troops.[17] Even in the United States some said that

[16] Du Bose: Yancey.
[17] Confed. "Dip. Cor.," Vol. I. Instr. to Y., R. and M., No. 7, July 29, 1861.

the Union was as dead as the Achean League.[18]   Earl Russell in a note of August 7 intimated a desire to have a written explanation of the alleged right of the Confederate States to recognition by England. Yancey and Mann replied on August 8, promising to prepare the document.   Rost came from Paris, the document was prepared the next week, and on August 14 it was presented.   It reviewed the two previous interviews, and the instructions of the Confederate Government, and urged that the secession violated no principles of allegiance, but was sustained by the principles of the American Declaration of Independence in favor of self-government.

The commissioners had already expatiated upon the extent, products and population of the Confederacy, offering arguments to prove that they were not rebels and pirates.   They now explained why it was necessary for the agricultural South to resort to privateering in order to injure American commerce, stating that the English law of neutrality as to ports favored the United States.   They announced that the blockade was ineffective except on the Chesapeake, that Confederate resources were abundant and that reconstruction was impossible.   They then proceeded to show that anti-slavery sentiment could not remain in sympathy with the North.   They were aware of the strength of this sentiment in Europe and of its influence in preventing friendly relation with the Confederacy.   They did not undertake to discuss the morality of the institution; but they stated that the authors of the Declaration of Independence

[18] W. H. Russell: Diary, July 23, 1861.

found the African race in the colonies, in slavery by English law and by the laws of nations, that they left that fact where they found it, and made the declaration of freedom for the white race only and perpetuated slavery in the fundamental theory of the government. As to the wisdom of the fathers, they said that it was not a matter for them to discuss. But they informed Russell that the United States Congress had declared that the war was prosecuted only to maintain the constitution and to preserve the Union. "It was not from fear of liberation of the slaves," they said, "that secession took place. The new party in power has proposed to guarantee slavery forever, if the states of the South will but remain in the Union." Some at this time surmised that the United States might change its policy in regard to slavery. The commissioners met this squarely by stating that the abrupt destruction of a labor system which had given bread to 10,000,000 people engaged in manufacturing, and reared so vast a commerce between America and Europe, "would be disastrous to the world as well as to the master and the slave." In urging the claims of the Confederacy to recognition as a *de facto* Government, Texas and South America were mentioned as precedents, and reference was made to the necessity of British commercial relations with the South in order to preserve great interests in England. As an inducement to break the blockade the commissioners stated that the cotton crop would be delivered at the Southern wharves and ports whenever there was a prospect of the blockade being raised, and not before. An embargo had been laid as an offensive measure against the passage of

cotton across the border into the United States, thus
making it necessary for Europe to seek it at the ports
of the South.[19]   The commissioners closed their communication by saying that they would be surprised if
England left the Confederacy to contend alone for
interests which were as important to the commercial
powers of Europe as to herself without giving even
friendly countenance, but they said that the citizens
of the South would continue their task with vigor
and that when peace should be won they would not
be responsible for all the bloodshed and for the suffering of millions in the eastern as well as the western
hemisphere.[20]

Going to Paris, the commissioners had an interview
with the minister of the marine and colonies, who
gave hopeful intimations.   They also soon received
private information that the letter of August 14 had
made a good impression on Russell; that there was
a strong feeling in the cabinet in favor of recognition;
and that England had suggested to France to take the
initiative in European recognition.   They also learned
that Louis Napoleon had officially asked England to
cooperate with him in recognizing the Confederacy
and breaking the blockade, but that England had refused.   Cotton had gone up 100 per cent; the factories were running on short time and there was a
bread riot in Paris.   But France could not lead in a
policy of intervention or interference.

[19] Raising the blockade by England of course meant war
with the United States.   In order to open the blockade,
Yancey, Rhett and Toombs had desired that the Confederacy
should adopt a policy of offering England a practical monopoly of commerce for twenty years, as well as other stipula-
tions.   [20] See McPherson: Rebellion.

Russell replied on August 24, stating that the British Government did not pretend to pronounce judgment on questions in debate between the United States and her adversaries in North America; that it desired to remain neutral and would perform all the duties required of a neutral; that it could not acknowledge the independence of the Confederacy until arms or some peaceful mode of negotiation should better determine the respective positions of the two belligerents.[21] Yancey soon sent Hunter a letter of resignation.

On August 24, Hunter instructed the commissioners to hurry to Madrid, to inform Spain that since secession the South no longer desired Cuba; to represent that mutual interests seemed to invite a close and mutual alliance; and to ask for recognition. It was stated that both Spain and the Confederacy were interested in the same social system, that the growth of Spanish power and resources could never be a cause for Confederate jealousy, but that in case of reunion the non-slave-holding states would also desire to annex the Spanish colonies. It was suggested that Spain would be justified, even at some risk, in assisting to build up a great friendly power that would prove so advantageous to her.[22]

A short time after Hunter's instructions were written, an act of the Confederate Congress disunited the European commission, and on September 23, Mr. Davis appointed Mason and Slidell[23] as commissioners to England and France respectively with instruc-

[21] 51 Brit. and Foreign State Papers.
[22] Confed. " Dip. Cor.," Vol. I, p. 120.
[23] Instr. to Mann, No. 11, Sept. 23, 1861.

tions to urge that the new " homogeneous " Southern union could serve as no precedent for revolutionary violence, that its existence was of deep commercial and political interest to other nations, and that they should intervene against American intervention and an ineffectual blockade. Of the former commission Mann was sent to Belgium, Rost was expected to go to Spain, and Yancey was asked to remain in Europe until Mason should arrive. Though Mason received his instructions September 23, he did not reach Europe until January 29, 1862.

In the meantime the attitude of the European powers toward the blockade was a disappointment to the Confederacy. Russell, having heard of Mercier's advice to the French Government, to intervene and forcibly raise the blockade, wrote to Palmerston, on October 17, that there was much good sense in Mercier's observations, but that it was not advisable to break a blockade merely for the sake of getting cotton. He intimated that good offices for pacification should first be offered, and that in case they failed, intervention on a large scale might be taken about the end of the year in order to close the war. Palmerston was not ready at that time, and such an aggressive action would have been less popular in England after the American concession in the Trent affair. The English Government knew that the recognition of the Confederacy would place England in the attitude of an ally against the United States, and there was no desire to assume such a position.

Yancey, after a short stay in France, returned to England intending to depart for the Confederate States at an early date. He was still confident of the

ability of the South to resist the superior numbers and
resources of the North. In November, at a dinner of
the Fish-monger's Society, he stated that the South
could live under a blockade. Yancey's return to the
Confederacy was delayed by the capture of Mason
and Slidell on the British steamer *Trent*. Mr.
Hanckel of Charleston, on the arrival of the *Trent* in
England, delivered to Mr. Yancey and his associates
the instructions which had been given Mason and
Slidell.[24] Information of the Trent affair reached
London November 27, and the press was indignant.
Yancey, immediately, while war was menacing, ur-
gently renewed the attempt to get recognition, and,
in order to show the inefficiency of the blockade, presented information (brought by Mr. Hanckel) of a list
of over forty vessels which had passed the blockade in
safety (up to August 7).

In the letter to Russell (November 30) the commissioners, stating that the United States and the Confederacy had both agreed to the Declaration of Paris
on the subject of the blockade, urged that the European powers should enforce it, not only because of the
principles of the Declaration, but also from the interests affected. They declared that a war shutting up
cotton was directed against Europe as well as against
the South, and suggested that since transit routes had
been made neutral, cotton could be made so. They
informed Russell that no blockade would ever sub-
due the South, but that it should be declared ineffective for the interests of mankind as well as for those
of the Confederacy. They insisted that real neu-

[24] U. S. and Confed. Naval Records, Series 1, Vol. I, p. 155.

trality called for a rigid observance of international law on the subject of blockades, and that Europe should not give aid to the United States through considerations of her embarrassed condition.[25]

Russell briefly replied December 7, as follows: "Lord Russell presents his compliments to Mr. Yancey, Mr. Rost and Mr. Mann. He has had the honor to receive their letters and enclosures of the 27th and 30th of November; but in the present state of affairs he must decline to enter into any official communication with them."

The Confederate expectations which arose after the Trent affair were gradually dissipated when the course of the United States Government became known. When Slidell reached Paris in February, 1862, Rost handed him a "Confidential Memorandum" dated "London, 31 Jan., 1862," and indicating a correspondence between the British Cabinet and the maritime powers of Europe concerning the Federal "Stone Fleet," and the blockade, in which the powers alluded to the blockade as ineffectual.[26] But Slidell said that the memorandum was either a hoax played on Rost's credulity, or an invention of his own. Yancey left London upon Mason's arrival, carrying with him Mason's first despatch, which narrated the incidents relating to his eventful journey, and reported that the ministry seemed to "hang fire." Running the blockade at Sabine Pass, Yancey reached New Orleans, where he informed Soule and others that Prince Albert and Queen Victoria were against the seces-

[25] 51 Brit. and Foreign State Papers, pp. 254-57.
[26] Despatches from Mason to Benjamin, No. 25, January 14, 1863.

sionists, and that English feeling was so strong
against slavery that the Government would hardly
dare to give any help that would tend to perpetuate
the institution. On March 29, Mr. Davis accepted
Yancey's resignation with regret.

Rost, after an interview with the French minister in
Paris in the latter part of January,[27] soon went to his
post at Madrid. In March he was informed by
Mr. Calderon Collantes that Spain was not ready to
take the initiative in Europe in a policy recognizing
the Confederacy.[28] There was no encouragement in
this mission. While waiting for news Rost wrote to
Yancey, on April 7, that there was no hope from Europe until the United States should be ready to treat
with the Confederacy as an independent power, and
he thought it was to the interest of the South to
make concessions to secure an alliance with the
North. Seeing that the Confederacy would have a
big war debt to pay, he suggested that the South
should intimate to the North its willingness to agree
to make its tariff equal to that of the North for a limited time, dispensing with frontier custom houses and
having practically free trade with the United States.
He was willing to give the North commercial advantages in order to avoid frontier troubles, and said that
if other nations complained they could be reminded
of their course in the Confederacy's hour of need.[29]
In bad health, and discouraged, Rost resigned in

[27] Despatches of Slidell, No. 1, Feb. 11, 1862. Rost's interview of Jan. 31 was in regard to the blockade, and the
number of vessels leaving Cuba for Confederate ports.

[28] Despatches of Rost, March 21, 1862.

[29] Rost to Yancey, April 7, 1862.

May and left Madrid with his family.   The following
September his health was still wretched and he had
not changed his views.[30]   He said that France waited
for England, that England would do nothing so long
as she could keep peace at home, and that Spain would
be the last power to act.[31]

[30] Despatches of Rost, Paris, Sept. 13, 1862.

[31] Perry, who represented the United States at Madrid in
1861, before the arrival of Carl Schurz, stated that the sympathies of the Spanish government at the beginning of the
war were favorable to the " faction " which seemed to offer
some hope of dividing the United States and diminishing
her power in the western hemisphere.   He said that Preston,
of Kentucky, during the latter part of his term as United
States minister at Madrid, had endeavored to impress the
governing classes with the belief that the aristocratic and
chivalrous society was in the South, and that the *sans culottes*
democracy was at the North.   Perry stated that the conservative classes were at the North, and the filibusters at the
South.   From speeches of Southern leaders at the outbreak
of the Civil War he showed that they contemplated annexation of Cuba, San Domingo and Mexico, and that the Union
of South and North was the best guarantee to Spain of her
own peace in North America.

CHAPTER V

Mission of Mason and Slidell

On October 12, 1862, Secretary Hunter received from W. H. Trescot, of Charleston, a telegram of which the following is the substance: "Our friends left here last night at one o'clock. Their escape was favored by having a fast steamer with good officers, and by the darkness and rain. The boat will be back in about a week and nothing should be said of it in the meantime."[1]

"Our friends" were James Murray Mason and John Slidell, who on September 23 had received their instructions as commissioners to England and France, respectively.[2] It was felt that the Confederate claims for recognition had been recently strengthened, and the commissioners were sent to obtain aid in every way possible. Both had been prominent men in national affairs.

James Mason was born in Fairfax county, Virginia, in 1798. He was a grandson of George Mason who had been prominent in the Revolution. He graduated from the University of Pennsylvania in 1818, practiced law in Virginia, served in the state legislature, and was a member of the state constitutional convention of 1829. In 1833 he was elected to the United States House of Representatives. In 1847 he entered

[1] With Despatches of Mason.
[2] Confed. "Dip. Cor.," Vol. I.

the United States Senate, of which body he remained a member for fourteen years, and for ten years was chairman of the committee on foreign affairs. He was the author of the fugitive slave law of 1850, and was always a strong opponent to anti-slavery agitation. He had urged secession in Virginia when a majority favored the Union, and took a prominent part in changing the decision of his state. He was a member of the Confederate Congress when appointed commissioner.

John Slidell was born in New York about 1793, graduated at Columbia in 1810, moved to New Orleans in 1819, and began the study of law. After 1828 he became prominent in Louisiana politics and in 1842 he was elected to Congress where he served one term. In 1845 he was sent as commissioner to Mexico, but Mexico refused to receive him. In 1853 he entered the United States Senate and remained until his state seceded in 1861. He represented the extreme views of the South, and was active on committees, though not prominent in debate. In sending these two commissioners to Europe the Confederacy hoped soon to receive such support as would enable it to break the blockade.

The investment of the Southern ports was becoming severe. At the beginning of the war the United States navy undertook to blockade the coast of 1900 miles, capture seaports, acquire control of bays and sounds, assist in opening the Mississippi, destroy Confederate cruisers, and protect United States commerce. Most of the steam vessels were abroad when Sumter fell and there was then no cable to call them home, but the resources of the North soon created a large navy. On April 27, 1861, Lincoln, in order to stop the trade and supplies of the Confederacy, declared a blockade of all the Southern ports, and slowly this became more and more effective. The cotton exports of $202,000,000 in 1860 fell to $42,000,000 in 1861, and to $400,000 in 1862. This was a serious blow to the South, which was dependent on England for supplies. A social and industrial revolution had improved the conditions in the free states, but during the century there had been very little change in the slave states. The flow of European immigrants passed by the South to carry their skill, energy and free labor to the new homes in the Northwest, so that the resources of the slave states remained undeveloped, owing to their peculiar industrial system. The South had no ships, no gun factories and no machine shops. Even medicines had to be bought in a foreign country. But the English manufacturers and merchants, and four million laborers, depended upon American raw cotton, of which the South in 1860 had raised 4,700,000 bales. Smuggling naturally took place in spite of the blockade, but by means of the increase of Federal vessels, and by sinking the hulks of vessels in the channels leading to Charleston, the investment became so effective that cotton fell to eight cents in South Carolina and rose to fifty cents in England—notwithstanding the fact that Nassau had become a centre for blockade-runners which carried it out on moonless nights and during storms. The distress of the South increased, for want of manufactured goods, and the people could not thrive under isolation from Europe.[3]

[3] T. E. Taylor: Running the Blockade, pp. 16-32, 44-54.

Would England and France recognize the Confederacy and oppose the blockade?

Mason, with power to make peace, had been directed to " proceed to London with as little delay as possible," in order to state the Confederate position and urge recognition and opposition to the blockade as a means of shortening an unnecessary war and subserving the interests of England as well as of the Confederacy. He was instructed to say that a dominant majority in the United States had violated the original compact which had been made between sections with diverse social systems, and that the Government no longer protected the Southern system; that the South, seeking self-government, had decided to form a new union of more homogeneous materials and interests, but that the old institutions would be retained, the form of government not being changed, and that secession would furnish no precedent for the overthrow of lawful authority by revolutionary violence; that the United States had rejected the offers of amicable adjustment by peaceful separation; that, notwithstanding the advantage of organization which the United States had at the beginning of the struggle, the Confederacy now had a responsible Government, a united people, 200,000 men in the field and bright prospects, while the North was suffering from failures; that the English people had a deep political and commercial interest in the establishment of the Confederacy because the latter would not be a rival, but a customer, of the manufacturing and commercial nations—that it would favor free trade, prevent the United States from any longer controlling the cotton supply, and end the former Southern desire to seek

protection and balance of power by the annexation
of contiguous territory. The instructions stated that
the South had resolved to seek protection by separation instead of by annexations, and would no longer
threaten to disturb the peace of the world, but would
be a bond of peace between the nations:

It was urged that the recognition of the Confederacy
would be in accord with the previous policy of England. Lord John Russell, in recent despatches to
Lord Cowley on the Italian question, referring to the
consistent principles upon which England had acted
since 1821 (at Troppau, Laybach, Verona, and in
the cases of South America, Greece and Belgium),
said: "She uniformly withheld her consent to acts
of intervention by force to alter the internal government of other nations; she uniformly gave her countenance, and if necessary her aid, to consolidate the
de facto governments which arose in Europe or
America." The Confederate instructions stated that
to withhold recognition would encourage the intervention of the United States, and invited the application of English principles. Hunter desired England
to treat the case of the Confederacy as she had that of
Italy, concerning which Russell had recently said:
"We, at least, are convinced that an authority restored
by force of arms, maintained by force of arms, constantly opposed by the national wishes, would afford
no solid and durable basis for the pacification and welfare of Italy." Hunter's instructions also insisted that
England should enforce the Declaration of Paris upon
the question of blockade; that a war shutting up cotton was directed against manufacturing nations and
humanity as well as against the producing nations;

and that cotton should be made neutral, like transit routes, and protected by most of the chances of war.[4]

The strict blockade made it difficult for Mason and Slidell to leave the Confederacy. Going to Charleston, they awaited a favorable opportunity. They found three United States steamers and a sloop-of-war patrolling the harbor. On October 3 they contemplated taking the route through Texas and Matamoras unless they were otherwise directed.[5] But the next day, before receiving a reply from Hunter, they decided that the route by Mexico would be impracticable and unsafe. They found that the *Gordon*, a good sea boat of 500 tons, could go at any time, and by any route, to Nassau or Havana, and that it could be bought for $62,000, or chartered to either port for $10,000 for the trip, the Government to pay for its value if captured. On October 9, the *Gordon* was chartered and its name changed to *Theodora*, and on the night of October 12, Mason, Slidell, with his wife and four children, J. E. Macfarland, and George Eustis [6] and wife, started on their journey to Europe. As they left the harbor, a shower of rain increased the darkness, and they passed within a mile and a half of the nearest United States ship without being captured. When near Nassau they learned that they could not obtain a steamer from that point to St. Thomas, and instead of landing they determined to go to Cuba.

The *Theodora* reached Havana October 17, but the

[4] Confed. " Dip. Cor.", Vol. I, pp. 146-60, Hunter to Mason, Sept. 23, 1861.

[5] Despatches of Mason. Telegram, Oct. 3, 1861.

[6] Macfarland and Eustis were the secretaries of Mason and Slidell, respectively.

Confederate party disembarked at Cardenas, where they were hospitably treated by a planter until they were ready to go to Havana. At the latter port, the British consul, Mr. Crawford, introduced them to General Serrano, who received them unofficially. Slidell wrote that they found almost universal sympathy in Cuba.[7] After their departure from Charleston had become known in the Confederacy, there had been an expression of much delight. The Richmond *Examiner* of October 29, said that the bold, straightforward manner of Mason at London would wield an influence in England which would enable him to sign a treaty of amity. But Wilkes, stopping at Havana, resolved to prevent both Mason and Slidell from reaching Europe.

On November 7, the steamer *Trent*, with the Confederate party on board, left Havana for St. Thomas, and the next day in Bahama channel a second shot, fired across her bows from the *San Jacinto*, caused her to stop. Lieutenant Fairfax of the *San Jacinto* was sent on board with instructions from Wilkes to capture Mason, Slidell, their secretaries, their baggage and despatches. Captain Moir of the *Trent* was indignant but courteous. The commissioners refused to leave the vessel peaceably, but they arranged their baggage and, under protest, yielded to arrest. The *Trent*, though its seizure had been contemplated, was allowed to proceed with its excited passengers, some of whom indulged in emphatic words of anger. The *San Jacinto* reached Fortress Monroe November 15, and sailed by way of New York to Boston, reaching

[7] Despatches of Slidell, No. 1, Paris, Feb., 1862.

the latter place on November 24. During the voyage
Mason and Slidell were kindly treated, being allowed
to occupy Captain Wilkes' cabin. They were taken to
Fort Warren and given comfortable quarters.[8] In
their baggage were fine liquors and cigars, but their
despatches had been given to Mr. Hanckel of Charleston, who, on his arrival in England on the *La Plata*
from St. Thomas, delivered them to Yancey, Rost and
Mann.[9]

From Fortress Monroe on November 15, the telegraph informed the American people of the *Trent*
affair. The people in the North had known of the
appointment of Mason and Slidell; many also had become anxious at the news of their departure, and
there was a storm of applause at the news of their
capture. Even the Cabinet was elated and Congress
gave a vote of thanks to Wilkes. Lincoln recognized
that, if England protested, the United States ought to
deliver the prisoners, on the ground that their seizure
was a violation of the American principles concerning the rights of neutrals. Jefferson Davis, in a message to the Confederate Congress, said that in the
seizure the United States had assumed a right to
general jurisdiction over the high seas, and that a
claim to seize Confederates in London would have
been as well founded. Many felt that the anxiety of
the Washington Government to prevent the Confederate diplomatists from reaching Europe showed a
weakness, and that the seizure would endanger relations between England and the United States, and

[8] Despatches of Mason (to Hunter), London, Feb. 2, 1862,
No. 1.
[9] U. S. and C. S. A. Naval Records, Series 1, Vol. I, p. 155.

strengthen the hands of not uninfluential persons in England who were urging a policy of interference in the American quarrel. Seward waited to see the course of the English Government, but November 30, he informed Adams that the seizure was not authorized by the Washington Government.

The report of the seizure reached London November 27, and the British press indignantly demanded immediate reparation. The British Government began to arrange for the increase of the British naval force in American waters, and in a few days the transportation of troops to Canada was begun. The London press declared that Seward desired a pretext for a quarrel with England, but Thurlow Weed, who was in London on government business, denied the report through the *Times*. Even the manufacturing classes represented by Bright, Cobden and Forster, who were friendly to the United States and hoped to see the doom of slavery, were silenced for the moment, but they counselled moderation and were confident that the United States had not authorized the capture. The law officers of the crown advised Lord Russell that an American man-of-war would have a right to board a British mail steamer, open her mail bags, examine their contents, and, in case despatches from the enemy were found, carry the vessel to a United States port for adjudication, but that she had no right to seize Mason and Slidell and leave the vessel to continue its voyage.

On November 29, after a Cabinet meeting, Palmerston submitted to the Queen and Prince Albert the draft of a proposed despatch to Lord Lyons urging the duty of Seward to deliver the prisoners and

to offer a suitable apology for the aggression.   After
its form had been rendered less offensive, Russell sent
a copy to Lord Lyons (by Conway Seymour, November 30), together with a private letter, instructing him
to leave Washington if, after a delay of seven days,
there should be no compliance with the demand.   This
ultimatum intimated that a crisis was impending.
A messenger delivered it to Lord Lyons on December 18, and its substance was given to Seward in a
courteous manner the next day.

European opinion generally declared the seizure to
be a violation of neutral rights; on the other hand,
the American press as a rule opposed the surrender
of the prisoners and was ready to risk a war.   The
leaders at Richmond saw the great disadvantage which
such a war would bring to the United States, and they
hoped that, while breaking the blockade in America
and the cotton famine in England, it would result in
permanent disunion by establishing Confederate independence.

The newspapers announced friction between Lord
Lyons and Seward,[10] and this was followed by the
information that Prince Albert, the friend of the
United States, was dead, but the Lincoln Administration was determined to make a friendly adjustment
of the difficulty with England.   At a Cabinet meeting
on Christmas Day, and the day following, it was
finally decided that, notwithstanding public opinion,
the most expedient course was to surrender the prisoners for diplomatic reasons, skillfully stating this
policy to be in accord with the principles for which
America had long contended.[11]

[10] W. H. Russell: Diary.   [11] Nicolay and Hay.

International law forbids a neutral to perform any act which will aid the belligerent in conducting hostilities. Among such acts are the transportation of officers, soldiers, despatches of a military character, arms or military stores, and vessels so engaged are liable to be confiscated. Wilkes had a right to search the *Trent* for such contraband of war. But Mason, Slidell and their secretaries were not contraband goods, and there seems to have been no right to seize them while they were on board the *Trent* on the high seas. Diplomatic ministers of recognized states are entitled to special immunities and the protection of other governments, but the government represented by Mason and Slidell had no recognition except as a belligerent. The United States, however, could not justify the seizure of the Confederate commissioners on the ground that they were political offenders unless there had been some treaty providing for the extradition of such offenders. If there had been some valid reason for seizing the *Trent* and taking her into an American port, the commissioners might have been legally arrested while in American waters, but the *Trent* in carrying Confederate passengers had not violated her duty as a neutral ship.

Though Seward disavowed the act of Captain Wilkes, he carefully added: " If the safety of the Union required the detention of the captured persons it would be the right and duty of this Government to detain them. But the effectual check and waning proportions of the existing insurrection, as well as the comparative unimportance of the captured persons, . . . happily forbid me from resorting to this defense." In the later discussions of the principles involved, Russell informed Seward that Great Britain could not have submitted to Wilkes' act " however flourishing might have been the insurrection in the South, and however important the persons captured might have been." Feeling in the United States was strong against the English attitude at a moment of national embarrassment, but under the lead of Sumner, Congress and the people were influenced to support the surrender.

On December 30, Lord Lyons directed Commander Hewett, of the British war vessel *Rinaldo*, to receive the released prisoners at Provincetown, Massachusetts, and to treat them with the courtesy due to unofficial persons. On January 1, 1862, they were received on board and expected to go to England by way of Halifax, but on account of bad weather they turned to the Bermudas from whence they sailed to Southampton. ·

The concession of Seward was a sore disappointment to the Southern hopes of European complication, and, notwithstanding the hopes of Mason, the prospects at London were by no means encouraging. The London *Times* (January 11), recommending that the Commissioners be treated simply as inoffensive visitors to Europe, said: " They are here for their own interests, and . . . rather disappointed perhaps that their detention has not provoked a new war. . . . They must not suppose, because we have gone to the very verge of a great war that they are precious in our eyes. We should have done just as much to rescue two of their own negroes. . . . Let the Commissioners come up quietly to town and have their say with anybody who may have time to listen to them. For our part, we cannot see how anything they may have to tell can turn the scale of British duty and deliberation."

When Mason and Slidell landed at Southampton, a series of disastrous reverses to the North, followed by sluggish action, caused many abroad to consider that the North and the South would never be united again. England and France were suffering from lack of cotton, and the South was suffering from a congestion of it. Napoleon was planning to realize the dream of his predecessors by founding an American empire to perpetuate his dynasty in Europe. The Civil War was his opportunity, and he was anxious to win glory by playing the rôle of a mediator in favor of the South. He promptly granted an interview to Slidell, who " insisted on the insufficiency of the blockade, and the vandalism of the ' Stone Fleet.' " [12] The current of feeling in France ran strongly against the North. Slidell had interviews with Napoleon and the French Cabinet, who appeared to rejoice at Confederate victories and regret her defeat. He learned that Napoleon had asked England to join with him in recognizing the South; but that England had leaned to the side of the United States, and had declined to act. Russell refused to respond to the Confederate protest against " the paper blockade." He afterwards (May 6) said that though thousands in England, on account of the closing of the Southern ports, were obliged to

[12] Slidell's instructions of Sept. 23, 1861, directed him to seek recognition and commercial intercourse, and to suggest the importance of opening water communication to the great coal fields of western Virginia, which would be valuable and convenient for the French steam marine.

resort to the poor rates, the British Government had sought to take no advantage of the obvious imperfection of the blockade, and had scrupulously observed the duties due to a friendly state.[13] Still, there were many in England who, fearing the tendency towards democracy, and opposing the Liberals in their desire to Americanize English institutions, did not deplore the disruption of the American Union. One of these, James Spence, had just published a book entitled " The American Union," in which he strongly sympathized with the secession movement, and said that slavery was not its real cause. A writer in Blackwood's Magazine for January, 1862, desired to claim no ties of relationship with the performers in the "convulsive dance" which was being executed in America, and urged recognition of the Confederacy.[14]

Mason reached London January 29, and on February 2, he wrote Hunter that the ministry seemed " to hang fire," but that there was a prevalent opinion in well-informed circles that a resolution for recognition would soon be introduced in the Commons as an amendment to the Queen's speech. He did not then anticipate that Earl Russell would refuse to receive him. A few days after his arrival, Parliament met. Mr. Gregory, who had visited the Southern States, in 1860, found him a place in the Commons to hear the Queen's speech, which disappointed him by saying nothing about the blockade.[15] He wrote that

---

[13] Jefferson Davis: Confederate Government, Vol. II, p. 343.

[14] Blackwood's Mag., Jan., 1862, p. 118; April, 1862, pp. 514-36.

[15] Despatches of Mason, No. 2, Feb. 7, 1862.

" our friends in Parliament " thought best not to attempt the amendment for recognition, while the Queen was in mourning, and that they proposed first to try opposition to the blockade. On February 7, by advice of Gregory, who was " steering " him, Mason applied for an interview, and was received unofficially at Russell's home. The despatch reporting that interview never succeeded in getting through the blockade; but subsequent events show that Russell gave no encouragement.[16] Mason said afterward that the minister's personal sympathy had always been against the Confederates. Mason, eagerly watching for mail that never came, was disappointed because he received no words of encouragement from Richmond, and on May 15 wrote Benjamin that the public mind at London " should be kept assured." [17]

[16] On Feb. 17, 1862, Mason submitted to Russell a list of vessels entering and clearing Cuban ports engaged in commerce with Confederate ports. On April 1, he supplemented the list, showing there had been 28 vessels for January and February. On Aug. 4, Russell asknowledged the receipt of his information. [55 Brit. and For. State Papers, p. 723.]

[17] Despatches of Mason, No. 10, May 15, 1862.

CHAPTER VI

Hunter, still hoping that England and France, acting from commercial and political motives, would endeavor by force of arms to break the blockade and end the war, on February 8, instructed Mason that Mr. Davis would not deprecate intervention, but that he desired that the treaty of peace should enlarge the Southern agricultural area, give the Confederacy possession of Chesapeake bay by which to concentrate and control the Western commerce, and make it independent of the North. He urged that the Confederacy should have Maryland, Kentucky and Missouri, and all south of those states, together with New Mexico and Arizona, through which the Southerners could have railroad connection with the Pacific. He stated that the South needed North Carolina, Virginia, Kentucky, Missouri and Maryland to produce food supplies so that the remaining states could devote their entire attention to supplying the demand for cotton and sugar. Besides, it was held that if Maryland, Kentucky and Missouri should go to the North, it would end the hope of a balance of power, and lead to war or to a Southern reunion party to secure peace and trade. It was claimed that, aside from political reasons, it was England's commercial interest "to enlarge the area from which she draws tribute." [1]

[1] Instr. to Mason, No. 4, Feb. 8, 1862. Congress also passed a resolution declaring its opposition to any peace which

It was not until June 23, that Mason replied. In the meantime the Confederate Government had been born in a storm on February 22; on March 8, the Merrimac had made an unsuccessful effort to break the blockade; defeat and reverses had only resulted in sterner stubbornness, and Benjamin, still confident of success, declared the Confederacy only needed arms and ammunition; on March 5, Congress had resolved never to affiliate with the Northern invaders; [2] Count Mercier, the French minister at Washington, visited Richmond on a mysterious errand; [3] missionaries with plenty of money were sent abroad to aid and direct public opinion; [4] Benjamin, claiming despatches were not contraband of war, was contemplating the organization of communication with Europe by French despatch vessels; Slidell was instructed to offer Napoleon seven million dollars in cotton [5] to indemnify him for the expense of a fleet to relieve the Confederacy and establish communication with Europe; [6] Mason

should exclude any of the soil of the Confederacy. C. E. Evans (Ed.): Confederate Military History (Atlanta, 1899), Vol. I, p. 436 et seq.

[2] Instr. to Mason, No. 1, April 5, 1862.

[3] Despatches of Mason, No. 8, April 2, and No. 10, May 15, 1862. J. B. Jones: Diary, May 21, 1862.

[4] Instr. to Mason, No. 3, April 12, 1862.

[5] Ibid.

[6] Benjamin, in a " confidential " letter, on April 12, wrote Slidell that there were certain points on which the interests of England and France were so distinct, if not conflicting, that Napoleon might not be precluded from acting alone on the basis of certain commercial advantages. He stated that, as a rule, Confederate relations should be on the same footing with all nations, leaving commercial relations as free as possible, but that while struggling against vastly superior resources no means to open Southern ports and successfully

was asked to say that England by a few words could encourage the Northern peace party to stop the war; but the occupation of the Confederate ports and the vigorous blockade by Federal forces gave little hope for any interference. On March 10, Earl Russell had said that separation would probably be a result of the war, but in May, when Lord Lyons embarked for England, it was understood in Richmond that he would " report the rebellion on its last legs."

Napoleon asserted that he was ready to cooperate in declaring the blockade ineffective; but said that Russell had dealt unfairly in sending his previous proposals to Lord Lyons, who made them known to Seward.[7] Slidell reported that Napoleon, in an interview with Lindsay (on April 11), agreed that the blockade was inefficient, and said that he had twice addressed the British Government through the French ambassador at London in regard to taking steps to end it, but had received no definite response. The Em-

end the war should be neglected. He said that Mr. Davis, as a means of inducing France to abandon her acquiescence in the United States interdict (blockade) on Confederate commerce, would be willing to concede to the French Emperor the right to introduce French products free of duty for a certain period. It was seen that temporary embarrassment of the French finances might deter Napoleon from initiating a policy likely to necessitate naval expeditions. Slidell was instructed that if, after cautious inquiry, it should appear probable that this obstacle might be removed by the grant of a cotton subsidy to defray the expenses of such expeditions, he might stipulate to deliver 100,000 (or more) five-hundred-pound bales of cotton in the Confederacy. It was estimated that France could sell the cotton for 20 cents per pound and that the vessels which sailed to convey the cotton could take cargoes of merchandise and sell them, in the Confederacy, at four times their cost in Europe.

[7] Despatches of Mason, April 21, 1862.

peror said that he was still ready to act promptly, in cooperation with England, by sending a fleet to the mouth of the Mississippi to demand free ingress and egress for merchant vessels, and he authorized Lindsay to so inform Lord Cowley and to ascertain whether the latter would recommend such a course to England.[8] Lindsay saw Cowley on Sunday, April 13, and immediately reported to Napoleon that Cowley thought that England was not prepared to act, and that the proper moment for action had passed. Napoleon then requested Lindsay to see Lord Palmerston and Russell, to tell them all that had occurred; to manage to communicate his views to Derby and Disraeli of the opposition; to get the views of Russell; and to return. Lindsay returned on the 17th and met the Emperor on the 18th. In reply to his note, Russell had informed him that he could receive no communication from Napoleon except through the regular diplomatic channel. Disraeli had concurred in the Emperor's views. He had no reason to suspect a secret understanding between Russell and Seward as to England respecting the blockade, but he said that any initiative which France might take would probably be supported by a majority in Parliament and that Russell, in order to avoid a change of ministry, would assent.[9] Napoleon was interested in Disraeli's suggestion, and thought that the best course was to make a friendly appeal to the United States to open the ports, at the same time accompanying it with a proper demonstration of force, ready to act in case the United States should fail to take New Orleans, but he de-

[8] Despatches of Slidell, April 14, 1862.
[9] Ibid., April 18, 1862.

cided to wait for more news, and asked Lindsay in the meantime to observe secrecy. Perhaps Napoleon meant what he said, but while he was saying it, the Federal guns opened fire and soon New Orleans fell. Charles Wood of England wrote Slidell denying that the British Government was unwilling to act in American affairs. M. Billault, the minister *sans portfolio* of the French Government, said that the whole Cabinet, except Thouvénel, had been in favor of the South, and that if New Orleans had not fallen recognition could not have been delayed much longer.

In June, Mason wrote Benjamin that he saw little prospect for " the suggested form of mediation unless the cotton famine should urge the Government to act." [10] Seward justified his obstruction of Charleston harbor by saying that the holes of the three thousand miles of coast line could not all be blocked by ships alone. On May 6, Russell said that though the irregularity of the blockade had injured thousands, yet the British Government had never sought to take advantage of obvious imperfections in order to declare it inoperative. Mason had heard nothing further as to the purpose of Mercier's visit to Richmond and was much disappointed as to the results achieved. Napoleon was still waiting. Russell and Palmerston both denied that France had proposed joint mediation, and said that such a policy would be inopportune. Mason complained that even the recent seizure of British ships on the high seas, between England and Nassau, had not caused the British Government to intervene. Though he found much sympathy for the Confederacy, and suggested that the cotton famine

[10] Despatches of Mason, No. 12, June 23, 1862.

might urge the Government to act, he thought it inexpedient even to renew the request for recognition, unless it should be done as a demand of right, to be followed by his retirement to the continent as evidence of Confederate dignity. Caleb Hughes, the Confederate agent for buying foreign supplies, wrote from London (July 3), that there was much Southern sympathy in England, but that no one could see how the Government could interfere—though in case the South should win against McClellan, and at Charleston, he did not see how recognition could be deferred.

The Richmond authorities had expected that England, in the interests of trade, would favor the Confederacy on the question of blockade, and that British vessels would seek Confederate ports for cotton. In October, 1861, they had prohibited two British vessels, the *Bruce* and the *Napier*, from proceeding out to sea from Wilmington with their cargoes of naval stores, but they offered compensation for the cargoes, and denied that it was their policy to prohibit the exportation of cotton except to prevent its use by the United States. On July 7, Mason asked Russell for an interview, and for a statement of his attitude upon the rules of blockade, and whether it would be practicable to require blockaded ports to be designated. On July 10, Under-Secretary Layard simply acknowledged the receipt of his letter and made no allusion to his request. Mason wrote home that it was difficult to hold intercourse under such circumstances, and that the British Government would probably use its own pleasure as to abiding by the rules of 1856.[11]

[11] Despatches of Mason, No. 14, July 30, 1862. In 55 Brit. and Foreign State Papers, p. 724 et seq.

The news of the defeat of the United States army
under McClellan, before Richmond, reached London
and Paris by July 15, and for several days Confederate
efforts were vigorously pushed. Slidell, in an interview with the Emperor at Vichy, on July 16, explained the conditions and resources of the South;
proposed to pay him in cotton for vessels to break
the blockade; informed him that the United States
had negotiated a treaty with Mexico, agreeing to give
$11,000,000 to aid Juarez against France; and sug-
gested that the Emperor now had a chance to secure
the Confederacy as a faithful ally in return for recognition. The Emperor had no objection to Slidell's
presenting his demand to Thouvénel for recognition.
He said that he had seen the nature of the contest
and that separation was a mere matter of time, but
that " the difficulty was to find a way to give effect to
his sympathies; that he had always desired to preserve the most friendly relations with England, and
that in so grave a question he had not been willing to
act without her cooperation; that he had several times
intimated his wish to England, but that he had received
no favorable response; and, besides, that England had
a deeper interest in the question than France, and
was wishing for him ' to draw the chestnuts from the
fire for her benefit.' He regretted that France had
ever respected the blockade, and said that Europe
should have recognized the Confederacy in the summer of 1861, when Washington was menaced and the
Southern ports not yet all closed."

Lindsay's · carefully studied motion for mediation
had been dangling before the House of Commons for
some time, and even Lord Brougham, who, since the

days of Jefferson, had been known as the friend of the
United States, said that America should listen to the
voice of friends and stop the war. Russell and Palmerston, however, feared that an attempt at mediation
would only irritate both of the contestants. On July
17, Mason informed Russell that there was no authority for saying that the Confederacy would be
offended by such an attempt.[12] The next day Lindsay,
in a long speech in the Commons, reviewed the causes
of the war and the " compact " nature of the former
Government. He attributed the cause of the struggle
not to the opposition against slavery, but to taxation
without representation. He stated that emigration
had favored the North, decreasing the proportion of
Southern representation in Congress without decreasing the taxes of the property-holders in the South. He
said that reunion was hopeless; that many people even
in the United States were anxious for England to
mediate to relieve the American Government of an
embarrassing situation, and that France was ready to
join.[13] Others declared that the establishment of the
Confederacy would lead to the manumission of the
slaves. Whiteside favored secession and the recognition of a *de facto* Government, as in the case of
Texas. Taylor and others took the opposite view.
Taylor said that the war had been postponed for many
years by concessions to slavery until that institution
now struck at the interests of freedom in the North.
He gave warning that intervention would lead to a terrible conflict with the United States. In reply to the
statement that the tariff was the cause of the war,

[12] 55 Brit. and Foreign State Papers, p. 728.
[13] 168 Parl. Debates, July 18, 1862.

Forster quoted from A. H. Stephens' speech that "the South went to war to establish slavery as the corner-stone of a new republic," and drew attention to the fact that the South Carolina Declaration of Independence did not mention the tariff.[14] Palmerston said the thirty-years war was a joke compared to the Civil War; but he denied that England would be justified in assuming the independence of the Confederates, and said that recognition would lead to direct intervention. Lindsay's resolution, therefore, was not pressed to a vote—because there was no reasonable assurance of its success. Mason wrote that it was vexatious that the British Government could not be driven to a decided position "in harmony with the public sentiment" of England, and began to hope for a new ministry. He said that Derby could take the helm at any time; but that there were political reasons for not ousting Palmerston while the Queen was in mourning, and while there were fears of her going insane.

Slidell, after an interview with Napoleon, wrote Mason that both should ask recognition at the same time. Slidell presented his letter on July 23. Thouvénel agreed with him that the application to England and France should be simultaneous, though he advised him to wait. On July 24, Mason, coöperating with Slidell, sent a letter to Russell in which he said the Confederate States asked recognition as a European duty. At the same time, desiring to state *orally* that a failure of England to grant recognition would operate as an incentive to the United States to

[14] 168 Parl. Debates, pp. 527-78.

protract the struggle, he sent a private note asking for an interview. Russell declined the interview because he thought no good could come of it. Mason then supplemented his previous letter by stating that a word of recognition would encourage many in the North to speak openly against the continuation of the war.

On August 2, after a Cabinet meeting, Russell replied that the British Government had never presumed to form a judgment on the question of the right of withdrawal of " certain Confederates," nor upon the previous conduct of the United States. He left such cases to be judged by interpretations of the United States, and not by England. He informed Mason that Secretary Seward affirmed that a large portion of the disaffected population was restored to union and loyalty, and that the Confederacy owed its main strength to the hope of assistance from Europe. He said that in the face of fluctuating events and contradictory allegations, and the uncertainty of Confederate stability and permanence, the British Government was " determined to wait," and could only hope for a peaceful termination of a bloody and destructive contest. On August 4, Mason wrote Benjamin " the British Government shuts its eyes to accumulating proof . . . and relies on the open mendacity of Seward." He hoped that division in the Cabinet, together with Napoleon's attitude, might drag the Cabinet into a " disgraceful reversal of its decision." [15]

Lord Campbell in the House of Lords called for Mason's correspondence; but Russell did not think

[15] In Mason's despatch, No. 14, begun July 30, 1862. In 55 Brit. and Foreign State Papers, p. 733.

it then expedient to submit it, stating that it was unofficial. Russell also declared that he had no communication with any foreign power upon the
subject of recognition, but that he would favor communication with the maritime powers if the Government should adopt a new line of policy. Malmsbury
suggested that England should act with the other
powers, whenever the time should come, upon questions of blockade, recognition or mediation, and that
Lord Lyons should not be long absent from Washington. Russell stated that there had been intimate
and unreserved communication, and no difference of
opinion, between England and Napoleon, and that
in case it became the duty of England to make a communication upon American affairs it would be very
deliberately considered, on account of the feeling in
the United States as to the sympathies of Great
Britain.[16]

Davis said that Mason's whole correspondence
showed that the feeling of the British Government was
unfriendly to the Confederacy, and not in harmony
with public opinion, and that there might be a change
of policy later. Benjamin, on October 28, in a letter
which was captured and published before it reached
Mason, contrasted the friendliness of French statesmen with the " rude incivility of Russell." But notwithstanding Mason's difficulty in holding intercourse
with the Government, and his failure to obtain recognition, Benjamin, elated over McClellan's defeat and
the military situation, advised him to remain in Eng-

[16] 168 Parl. Debates, Lords, Aug. 4, 1862. Also, Despatches
of Mason, No. 15, Aug. 5, 1862. [Received by Benjamin on
Oct. 25.]

land, where he could disseminate favorable impressions and where contingencies might arise to make his presence important.[17] Davis, however, agreed that the Confederacy should not be put in the attitude of a supplicant. Mason's house continued to be a resort for Confederate sympathizers. The *Index* and other papers were used to deny that the United States aimed at emancipation, and Confederate aid associations were formed to encourage sympathy with the South.

In the case of the cruiser *Alabama* the English Government apparently had favored the Confederates. The departure of the *Florida* had caused the United States consul at Liverpool, with a wakeful and agitated mind, to watch for new vessels. In May, 1862, " No. 290," which was building in Laird's dock-yard, was under suspicion. The building went on, however, and the vessel was completed. A young lady christened it *Enrica*, and its testing trip was satisfactory.[18] As early as July 4, the British Government had promised Adams that the customs officials should keep a strict watch on the vessel. On July 26, Bullock received information from a private but reliable source that it would not be safe to leave the vessel in Liverpool another forty-eight hours, and, as previously agreed with Laird, he arranged for another trial trip out of the harbor, at the same time informing Captain Butcher that the ship would not return. Though the report of the British law officers was not given until July 29, the signs indicated that it was time to get out,

[17] Instr. to Mason, No. 7, Sept. 26, 1862.
[18] Bullock: Vol. I, Chap. 5.

for inquiries were becoming very frequent and uncomfortable. Bullock claimed that no officer of the British Government ever gave him a hint that would lead him to anticipate the future action of the Government, but Mason kept him informed of all he heard as to naval affairs, and, though gathered merely from the conversations of those who were accustomed to observe the conduct of the ministers and draw their own conclusions, the information often proved correct. Bullock says " it is probable that through private friends Mr. Mason could and did have very favorable opportunities of learning the general, and in some cases, the specific purposes of the Government."

On July 29, " No. 290," which was soon to be known as the *Alabama*, under pretence of taking out a pleasure party, including ladies and gentlemen of the family of John Laird, M. P., left Liverpool in spite of Mr. Adams' warnings. After a sail of fourteen miles, the excursionists were transferred to the *Hercules* for return, and the *Alabama* sailed away to do service for the Confederacy. In reply to Adams' request for explanation, Russell stated that the delay of England was due to the sickness of the Queen's Advocate, Sir John D. Harding, which " made it necessary to call in other parties, whose opinion had been at last given for the detention of the gunboat, but before the order got down to Liverpool the vessel was gone." The *Alabama* was commissioned on the high seas, and Seward never ceased to call her a pirate, nor to press England to seize her, though she was flying the Confederate flag.

After the close of the second campaign in Virginia, both Palmerston and Russell contemplated the right or expediency of mediation or intervention.[19]   On September 14, Palmerston, in a note to Russell, suggested the offer of joint " good offices " by England and France.   Three days later Russell wrote: " The Federal army is driven back to Washington and . . . I agree with you that the time is come for offering mediation to the United States with a view to the recognition of the independence of the Confederates. . . . In case of failure . . . to recognize the Southern States as an independent state."   He proposed a meeting of the Cabinet, and said that if it should determine upon mediation England should propose it first to France, who should cooperate in proposing it to Russia and other nations as a measure decided upon by England, and he suggested that the latter should make herself safe in Canada.   On September 23, Palmerston replied, pronouncing the plan excellent, and said: " Of course the offer would be made to both the contending parties."   He suggested that in case of a defeat of the Federals, which might make them ready for mediation, that " The iron should be struck while it was hot; " but that if the Federals should come out best, England should wait and watch awhile. In October there was an impression in the United States that England would soon grant recognition and follow by mediation or intervention.   The English Chancellor of the Exchequer said the South had an army and would soon have a navy.[20]   Mallory, at that

---

[19] Mason wrote: " I look with renewed confidence to the effect on the Emperor."   Slidell had not yet received a reply to his note of July 23.   [Despatches of Mason, No. 17, Sept. 18, 1862.]

[20] Parl. Debates, March 27, 1863.   Quoted by Forster.

time, had sent Mr. G. N. Sanders to England under contract to construct six iron-clad steamers, to be paid for in cotton.[21]

On October 17, Adams wrote to Secretary Seward that the United States should try to achieve decided success by February to prevent the possibility of recognition of the Confederacy by England. The Cabinet meeting, called for October 23, was recalled as unnecessary, but some English statesmen complimented Davis upon having " made a nation." [22]   Lord Donnoughmore and Fitzgerald, both warm friends of the Confederacy, told Mason that Palmerston would probably not enter into a treaty with the Confederacy[23] unless it should agree not to permit the African slave trade; but bankers were proposing schemes to raise Confederate finances in Europe. Lindsay was planning for direct intercourse between France and the South at the close of the war, and Mason, watching for the slow arrivals from the South of " calm and dignified revelations of truth," was gaining hope, though he had received no epistle from Benjamin of a later date than April 14.[24]

Napoleon was at this time shaking hands with Slidell and listening to proposals to build a Confederate navy in French ports; and, a few days later, when the cotton famine " was looming up," and simultaneous with his expedition of 35,000 reinforcements to " establish stable government in Mexico," he formally invited England and Russia to intervene in the Amer-

[21] Despatches of Mason, No. 16, Sept. 18, 1862.
[22] Ibid., No. 20, Nov. 6, 1862.
[23] Ibid., " Unofficial," Nov. 4, 1862.
[24] Ibid., No. 20, Nov. 6, 1862.

ican war by offering a six months' armistice with the blockade removed. Dayton had heard reports of Napoleon's hostile designs, but he had doubted whether Slidell ever exchanged a word with the Emperor. Lord Cowley at Paris had recently denied that France had made any proposals on the American question, and said that no action was contemplated.[25] Thouvénel expressed surprise, and Mason suggested that the English denial probably referred only to official communications. Slidell had entire confidence in Napoleon, but stated that English statesmen were full of duplicity and hypocrisy. He spoke to Napoleon concerning the British denial, and the latter, smiling, suggested that in diplomacy nothing existed unless it was formally written. Thouvénel, before his resignation, told Slidell that the British denial of official knowledge of Napoleon's views was a "mauvaise plaisanterie," for there had been "des pourparlers très réels" on the subject. Slidell, entertaining little hope from England, on October 27, had an interview with Drouyn de L'Huys, to whom he recapitulated the views which he had expressed to Thouvénel in July. He referred to Russell's statement that the purpose and policy of France on American affairs were the same. He mentioned the conflicting statements as to whether France had communicated Napoleon's views to England, and showed L'Huys a letter from a leading member of the British Parliament, insinuating that France was playing an unfair game. L'Huys said that he had been too recently in office to know what Thouvénel had said or done, and when Slidell

---

[25] Despatches of Slidell, Oct. 20, 1862.

tried to show him how divergent were the interests of France and England on the subject of American affairs he said that there were grave objections to France acting without England.[26]

It appears that the armistice plan originated with Napoleon. On October 22, at St. Cloud, Slidell shook hands with the Emperor and asked him to break the blockade. The Emperor averred that his sympathies were with the Confederacy, but that England might embroil him with the United States if he acted alone, and that he preferred to make a proposition for an armistice of six months with the Southern ports. He stated that the refusal of his plan by the North would give such strong reason for recognition, and perhaps for intervention, that England might be induced to cooperate. Slidell was pleased with the plan, and on November 8, Mason wrote that there was no doubt, but that the proposal had been made officially to Russia and England, and that it was " confidently asserted that Russia would assent to it." The French note, dated October 10, was read to Russell on November 10. No copy was left, but it was published in the *Moniteur*. Russell replied on the thirteenth, declining immediate action.[27] Russia kept the promise made through Gortchakoff to Bayard Taylor earlier in the war, and refused. Napoleon now contemplated mediation through the French minister at Washington, but seeing that the United States would reject such a suggestion, he proceeded with his plan to attack the Monroe Doctrine in Mexico—a policy

[26] Despatches of Slidell, Oct. 28, 1862.
[27] 172 Parl. Debates, July 2, 1863. Layard in the House of Commons.

which could conciliate neither England nor Spain. Some in the North would have favored the French tender of mediation. Mr. Cox in the United States House of Representatives, on December 15, said that the recent elections indicated that " the eagle must use the dove."

The report of the French proposals to England and Russia reached New York on November 25. A few days later, after the news reached Richmond, Benjamin decided that it was a favorable time to further encourage England and France to come to the rescue, by insisting on the restoration of pre-blockade conditions and by taking steps to obtain a monopoly of the trade with the Confederacy. In a letter to Mason [28] on December 11,[29] he said that there were indications that Europe would soon recognize the Confederacy and that trade with the South would be brisk. To encourage Europe to take measures to break the blockade, he said that the Confederacy, in the interests of permanent peace, would expect a treaty of free trade with the United States at the end of the war, and that the rush of the Southern people to get commodities might enable the agents of Northern merchants by their cupidity to monopolize Southern products and become the intermediaries in Southern commerce. To prevent this monopoly, he urged that the European

[28] Instr. to Mason, No. 11, Dec. 11, 1862.

[29] Mason, still looking forward to a cotton famine, on Dec. 11 (No. 23) wrote: "We hear little, but I think events are maturing which must lead to some change in the attitude of Europe." The *Alabama*, in a successful cruise, had taken British property in some instances. When British merchants complained, Russell intimated that they should apply to the Confederate prize courts for redress.

governments, looking toward an early renewal of trade, should encourage their citizens to purchase Southern products *en depôt* before the close of the war; to establish West Indian depots of supplies needed by the Confederacy, ready for immediate introduction; and to prepare merchant steamers for sale in Confederate ports, in order to provide communication with Europe. He urged that the cessation of Southern commerce was not due to the blockade, but to the seizure along the coasts, or on the high seas, of neutral vessels " bound to points where not a blockade vessel was ever stationed," and that, by stopping such seizures, many neutral vessels, which before had not dared to sail for fear of capture, could transport a large supply of Southern staples upon which the North hoped to get the profits. He said that Europe, by encouraging trade with the Confederacy as a belligerent, could prevent the seizure of neutral property by the United States, and thereby make it unnecessary to destroy resources at the approach of the Federal army. On March 2, Mason sent a copy of these instructions to Russell, and the latter merely thanked him for the information.

On October 31, Mr. Davis had complained that England, after asking the Confederacy to concur in the adoption of principles of international law regarding neutrals, had shown herself unfriendly by deviating from her own principles, that no blockade was binding unless enforced, and by refusing to reply to requests for explanation.[30] Mason was instructed to protest against the British modification of the Decla-

[30] Confed. " Dip. Cor., Great Brit.", p. 38. Instr. to Mason, No. 9, Oct. 31, 1862.

ration of Paris, and on January 3, 1863, he brought the complaint to the attention of Lord Russell.[31] On February 10, in replying to his note,[32] Russell stated that England would practically adhere to the rule of 1856, which was aimed against paper blockades, but added that the escape of vessels on dark nights or during adverse winds did not make a blockade ineffectual and that the neutral powers had no excuse for asserting that the United States had not maintained an effectual blockade. In was in vain[33] that Mason urged (February 18) that the departure of vessels was notorious; that Confederate vessels had raised the blockade of Charleston and Galveston and that the duties collected at Confederate ports on foreign goods were twice as much as before the war.[34] In January, Stephens said that there had been a change of tone in the British press since the preceding summer, when Lord Lyons visited London, and that the latter having never become acquainted with Southern men had probably influenced the change.[35]

In December, many in the Confederacy had despaired of the intervention by European powers, and only hoped that the Great Power above would intervene and create an armistice by freezing the Chesapeake. In January the newspapers published the intercepted correspondence of Benjamin, in which Russell was much berated and Napoleon was charged with designs on Mexico and Texas.[36] Lincoln's eman-

[31] Despatches of Mason, No. 24, Jan. 14, 1863.
[32] In 55 Brit. and Foreign State Papers, p. 734.
[33] Despatches of Mason, March 19, 1863.
[34] Ibid., No. 31, March 19, 1863.
[35] Johnston and Browne: Life of A. H. Stephens.
[36] J. B. Jones: Diary, Jan. 23, 1863. Instr. to Mason, No. 15, Feb. 7, 1863.

cipation proclamation was received with favor in England. After two years of the irrepressible conflict many in the North had changed their early feelings against emancipation. On March 6, 1862, Lincoln had proposed that Congress should provide for remunerating persons in the loyal slave states who would free their slaves. This was based on the idea that there was a strong Union sentiment at the South, and was proposed as a war measure. Slaves had been a great aid to the South by supplying food while the whites fought. After the defeat of Lee at Antietam, Lincoln decided to declare the freedom of all slaves belonging to persons at war with the United States, and when his proclamation was issued it gave no strength to the Confederate sympathizers in England. The North now fought not only for the Union, but also for emancipation; and the English workingmen, notwithstanding the prophecies of the South, and the dangers of a cotton famine, prayed for the North and the emancipation of slaves.

On January 17, the French Minister of Marine advised the French admiral off Mexico to protect some vessels belonging to M. Bellot which were returning to Havre laden with cotton, and Bellot suggested to Mason that this seemed to suggest intervention for getting cotton to Matamoras.[37] Mason was elated over the recent democratic victories in the North, and said that the Commons would respond unanimously if Palmerston would recommend recognition;[38] but he was not hopeful as to any favorable action by the British Government. A few days later he wrote that

[37] Despatches of Mason, No. 28, Jan. 31, 1863.
[38] Ibid., No. 27, Jan. 15, 1863.

both the ministry and the opposition agreed that it was not a favorable time for recognition. Derby stated that recognition without intervention would have no fruits. "With those willingly deaf," said Mason, "it was vain to argue." [39] Mason suggested that the United States might provoke a conflict with England in order to avert an internecine war at home. But, by March,[40] he was provoked that the British Government was determined to do nothing objectionable to the United States, and he feared that Napoleon [41] could do nothing owing to his ill-timed Mexican expedition and the complications which resulted from the outbreak of Poland. Benjamin, reading the British debates, also saw little hope from that direction, but he "awaited the onset on the Atlantic and the Mississippi with calm confidence." Layard said that the British Government had given orders to keep a strict watch on vessels suspected to be preparing for the Confederacy in English ports.[42]

When Campbell urged that it was the duty of England to recognize the Confederacy and send an ambassador to Richmond, Russell replied [43] that though Napoleon had actually proposed to the United States to negotiate with the Confederacy, no offer of good offices could now end the contest. Though Russell doubted the ultimate success of the United States, he favored British neutrality, leaving the belligerents

[39] Despatches of Mason, No. 30, Feb. 9, 1863.

[40] Ibid., No. 31, March 19, 1863.

[41] The British Government claimed to have no official document from France as to mediation.

[42] 169 Parl. Debates, Commons, Feb. 24, 1863. Palmerston in reply to Hopwood.

[43] Parl. Debates, March 23, 1863, pp. 1714-34.

to conclude their own quarrel. In his speech of March 23, he said that England had nothing to be ashamed of in her past intervention—that it had always been in behalf of the independence, freedom and welfare of a great portion of mankind, and that he would be sorry if it should ever be for any other purpose, no matter how much English interests were affected. He predicted that if interference should ever be necessary again, it would again be " in the cause of liberty and to promote the freedom of mankind." In concluding his speech, he said: " Depend upon it, my Lords, that if that war is to cease, it is far better it should cease by a conviction on the parts of the North and South that they can never live again happily as one community and one republic, than that the termination of hostilities should be brought about by the advice, the mediation or the interference of any other power." [44]

Mason saw a double meaning to part of Russell's speech, and suggested that he was not disposed to recognize a state with slavery. He was certain the Confederacy could take no action with England beyond the protest at that time.[45] During the spring and summer Russell remained firm, and said the United States blockade of 2500 miles was as legitimate as the English blockade of 2000 miles was in the war against Napoleon. In June Mason wrote that Russell repudiated the rules of 1856 and that the Confederacy

[44] On May 20, Benjamin wrote Mason that even if the defeats of the United States forces had no effect on Europe, and even in the face of the strong blockade, the Confederates were still determined to secure separation from the United States.

[45] Despatches of Mason, No. 31, March 19, 1863.

would have to watch him when the time came to make treaties.[46]   In September he wrote again that Russell, with unchanged opinions, was resorting to evasions of the convention of Paris.[47]

In the spring of 1863, Davis and Benjamin hoped that by disclaiming all designs on Cuba, and by agreeing to guarantee the island to Spain, the Government at Madrid could be induced to take the initiative in recognition.   They appointed Slidell as special commissioner to Spain,[48] but the latter received no intimation from Madrid that his presence there would be acceptable and did not go, though he held long conversations with Isturitz, the Spanish ambassador at Paris, who professed sympathy for the Confederates.[49] In June Slidell contemplated plans by which Spain could be induced to take the initiative in recognition, and cooperate with France in breaking the blockade.[50] Napoleon gave assurance that he concurred in the plan, and it appears that the Spanish Government was sounded upon the subject; but after the news of Gettysburg and Vicksburg, Isturitz informed Slidell that nothing could be effected at Madrid.

[46] Despatches of Mason, No. 40, June 20, 1863.
[47] Ibid., No. 44, Sept. 4, 1863.
[48] Confed. " Dip. Cor., France." Instr. to Slidell, March 22 and May 9 (No. 16), 1863.
[49] Despatches of Slidell, No. 36, May 28, 1863.
[50] Ibid., No. 38, June 21, 1863.

CHAPTER VII

CONTROVERSIES

During the spring of 1863, the fate of the Confederate States hung in the balance. Doubt succeeded expectancy. The Confederate bonds were floated in Europe above par on March 28; but, in a few weeks, Mason was unable to keep them propped up even by " bulling " the market. After the publication of captured Confederate correspondence relating to vessels building in England, Palmerston became very alert in investigating cases brought to his attention. But Confederate friends in Parliament kept up an agitation in American affairs. They protested against the American seizure of British vessels near the Confederate coast; they complained of American prize court proceedings, and brought accusations of American enlistments in Ireland.

In the last week of March, 1863, Forster and others in Parliament, complaining that Confederate vessels were building in Liverpool and referring to the neutrality of the United States in the Crimean War, urged the Government to prevent further departures of vessels like the *Alabama*. Bright gave warning that the United States, which had the sympathy of the English workingmen, and was receiving large numbers of Irish immigrants, might be inclined to remember England's unfriendliness. Baring desired Russell to allay irritation by expressions of anxiety to avoid a recurrence of such incidents. Laird, who built the *Alabama*, replied that the Northern armies were also obtaining war supplies in England, and that he would rather build one hundred *Alabamas* than laud the institutions of the United States, whose " ubiquitous spies made her boasted liberty an absurdity." The Solicitor-General quoted American decisions and the opinions. of Hamilton, Webster and Pierce to show that the United States did not forbid its citizens to sell war supplies, and said that the Government had acted promptly and in good faith to prevent the departure of the *Alabama*. As precedents of the American policy, he alluded to the cases of the *Caroline* at Niagara, and Walker in Honduras. Palmerston, in closing the debate, said that neutrality was difficult to execute, but that English neutrality, whether warm or cold, was honest, and that the Government was ready to act on evidence.[1] Mason, a few days later, in writing Benjamin of the success of the Confederate loan, said that the debate was " damaging to Yankee pretensions as well as to their advocates."

The seizure of the *Alexandra*[2] on April 6, by order of the British Government, caused several to make protest in Parliament that the vessel was not building for the Confederacy, and, at the same time, to offer objections to the Federal stone fleet in Charleston harbor, the large emigration of Irish[3] and shipment of arms to the United States, and even to eulogize the

[1] 170 Parl. Debates, pp. 33-72 and 90-101.
[2] J. B. Moore: International Arbitrations, Vol. I, p. 586.
[3] Benjamin instructed Mason to inform Earl Russell that there were " extensive enlistments in Ireland of recruits for the armies of the United States." Instr. to Mason, No. 21 April 29, 1863.

growing success of the Confederacy. Cobden said that the equipment of ships of war was a different question from that of traffic in fire-arms, and that they should be seized in English ports even after their escape from the place of building. Collier thought that armed vessels left United States ports in 1793, and said that the American Government could not complain of the construction of law in the English courts followed the example of the United States.[4] But he stated that England had no right to refuse to enforce the law against the Confederacy.

Many long, low, greenish-gray blockade-runners were fitted out in the Clyde to engage in the trade between Nassau of the Bahamas and Confederate ports. The United States found it difficult to stop this trade. Nassau merchants complained of the law of the American Congress by which vessels bound from New York to that port were refused a clearance, but the British Government was unable to induce the Federal Government to change its orders.

As the Federal navy increased along the Atlantic, part of the trade retreated to the Rio Grande and especially to Matamoras, which, from 1862, had become a seat of flourishing traffic with both Europe and New York. The United States had captured several neutral vessels engaged in this commerce, but, later, made the claim that these vessels were not really destined to Matamoras, but that they intended to discharge their freights into lighters to be conveyed directly to Confederate territory.

When the news arrived at London that Captain

[4] 70 Parl. Debates, Commons, April 24, 1863.

Wilkes of the United States Navy had captured the *Peterhoof* while she was on her way from London to Matamoras, Mason and his friends cooperated to induce the British Government to take some action. A deputation headed by Mr. Crawford, a London member of Parliament, waited upon Russell and asked him to protest, and it was believed for a while that he would demand her release without reference to a prize court.[5] The *Peterhoof* was one of the vessels which had been recommended to the protection of the French admiral off the coast of Mexico, and Mr. Mason had sent by Mr. Mohl, who sailed on the vessel, triplicates of five despatches which Benjamin had never yet received, and which Mohl subsequently found necessary to destroy in order to prevent their capture.[6] The *Peterhoof* was taken to New York as a prize. Archibald, the British consul, refused to open the packages which had been taken from the sealed mail-bag, and the latter was soon forwarded to its destination, but the vessel was held for the decision of the court. Mr. Spence at once asked the British Government to relieve his vessels from carrying mail.

Although Russell had desired to keep the subject from being discussed in Parliament at that time, Mr. Peacock, in the Commons, precipitated a debate on April 23, by calling for the correspondence. He had understood that Russell had refused to allow certain vessels to carry the mail. He and Mason were both encouraged by the recent publication of a letter of

[5] Despatches of Mason, No. 33, March 30, 1863. [This despatch was carried by Hobson of Richmond, who found it necessary to destroy it.]

[6] Ibid., No. 39, June 12, 1863.

Adams, who, by the advice of W. H. Aspinwall of New York, J. M. Forbes [7] of Boston and R. J. Walker, had offered protection to a vessel sailing to Mata-moras with ammunition for the Mexican Government to use against France, and Mason now wrote that the British Cabinet might grant recognition and adopt a bolder front as a policy to prevent drifting into war with the United States.[8]

Layard, in reply to Peacock, said that the Government could not furnish the correspondence; that it had not refused to allow vessels to carry mail, but that the owners of the vessels, fearing that Confederate correspondence might be found by a visiting Federal vessel, had asked to be relieved.[9]

Hugh Cairns was surprised that the Government seemed to admit that the United States could take correspondence from an English vessel and place its fate before an American prize court. Malins hoped that England would not allow American dictation to make her so timid that she dare not enforce the obli-gation of vessels to carry mail-bags. The Solicitor-General merely referred to Russell's letter of Novem-

[7] Forbes and Aspinwall had been sent to England by the United States Government with instructions to negotiate pri-vately for blocking the progress or changing the destination of the Confederate cruisers then building in English ship-yards. They failed to purchase the cruisers, but their repre-sentations to prominent Englishmen, who were fearful of provoking a war, had some influence in inducing the British Cabinet to stop the sailing of the rams and to purchase them for the Government. [Sarah F. Hughes: Letters and Recol-lections of John Murray Forbes, 2 Vols, Boston, 1899.]

[8] Despatches of Mason, No. 34, April 27, 1863. " The recent debates in Parliament," said Mason, " have this good effect at least—they keep up agitation on American affairs."

[9] 170 Parl. Debates

ber 28, 1862, to Lord Lyons, which stated that the right of search must depend upon circumstances. Lord Robert Cecil said that England waited for Palmerston's decision and expected it at once, but Osborn proposed that it was wise to drop the discussion, and Peacock consented to withdraw his motion.

Lord Russell wrote Lord Lyons on April 24 that the Matamoras trade was perfectly legitimate, even if part of the goods was afterwards carried to Texas. On the same day, in the House of Lords, he seemed to admit that the United States had a right to require an examination of sealed packages taken from seized ships. He decided that if the English Consul, on opening a mail-bag, should find a letter to the Confederate Secretary of State, he could send it to the prize court unopened. The Earl of Hardwick was pained by this decision, stating that it made the British Consul a tool of the United States. He desired to see an " impression made upon the . . . dis-United States " by a fearless stand which he claimed would be the best method of preventing collision.[10] On April 27, Russell stated that it was not then desirable to state the opinion of the law officers of the Crown; but he agreed with Seward that the mail-bags of a neutral, if duly certified and authenticated, should not be opened or detained in case of the seizure of a merchant vessel, but should be forwarded immediately to their destination. At the same time he intimated that the United States was the sole judge of whether a vessel should be captured on suspicion.[11] On April

[10] 170 Parl. Debates, Lords, April 24, 1863.
[11] Ibid., April 27, 1863. For correspondence between Great Brit. and the U. S., see Parlia. Papers, " North America, No. 5."

30 he announced that the *Peterhoof* would not be released, but that her mail-bags had been forwarded. The United States Supreme Court, in the *Peterhoof* case, decided that the blockade could not be extended to the Mexican half of the Rio Grande; that the trade from London to Matamoras, even with intent to supply Texas, was not a violation of the blockade and could not be called unlawful; but that contraband of war on a voyage to a neutral port, with a probable ulterior destination to the Confederacy, were liable to condemnation.[12]

On May 2, Mason wrote Benjamin that the British Government, in its anxiety to prevent collision, seemed determined to yield everything to the United States.[13] He understood that Adams had clandestinely made his peace with Russell, but he still predicted that the public would not be satisfied with this settlement of the question. Marquis Clanricarde recommended that a squadron be sent to the Gulf of Mexico, but he was informed that such an act would mean war. On May 18, in the Lords, while asking for copies of the proceedings in the United States prize court, he intimated that those courts " set aside the whole international law of the world." Russell denied his charges and said that the United States judges had always been quoted with respect. In a calm speech, he referred to Clanricarde's speech as a " desultory lecture on international law," and proceeded to show the error of his charges.[14] He stated that it was nat-

---

[12] A treatment of the Nassau and Matamoras trade, and the *Peterhoff* case, may be found in Montague Bernard's " British Neutrality," Chap. 12.

[13] Despatches of Mason, No. 34, April 27 and May 2.

[14] 171 Parl. Debates, pp. 1818-32.

ural for the United States to suspect vessels bound for Nassau; and that while successful English captains exulted over running the blockade, those who failed and lost their vessels came to the Foreign Office with an air of injured innocence.

Many Irish were emigrating to the United States, some to join the army. Peel said that the Government had knowledge that United States agents were in Ireland, and Mason, stating that Adams had tormented the ministry as to Confederate agents until it would be alert to establish counter-charges against United States agents, employed detectives to obtain evidence of enlistments in Ireland, but no clear discoveries were made.[15]

The Confederate authorities at Richmond, angered by their failure to establish diplomatic relations with England, and, by the evident care which the British Government exercised to prevent giving offense to Seward, refused to recognize the exequaturs of the British consuls in the Southern states. On December 19, 1862, Mr. Bunch, the British Consul, complained of the forcible detention of an unnaturalized Irish deserter, and stated that his letters had not been answered. The Richmond authorities replied in scathing terms. In the early part of 1863, several members of the Confederate Congress favored recalling the diplomatic agents and notifying the foreign consuls to leave the country. Mr. Davis held that the British consuls, having been appointed under the original compact, of which the Southern states had been members, should be allowed to stay so long as they sought

[15] Despatches of Mason, No. 38, Paris, June 4, 1863.

not to evade nor deny Confederate authority. But England, while refusing recognition, had authorized Lord Lyons at Washington to exercise authority over the British consuls in the Confederacy, thus ignoring the existence of the Confederate Government, and, in June, Davis ordered that no further communication should be allowed " between consuls of neutral nations in the Confederate States and the functionaries of those nations in the United States," [16] stating that there was now ample opportunity for correspondence by Confederate fleets and neutral steamers between neutral ports and the South.

Since February 20, Davis had refused to recognize Moore as consul at Richmond. But the latter continued to perform his duties. Two Irishmen, Moloney and Farrell, claimed exemption from enrollment as conscripts on the ground that they were British subjects. Moore, who had been asked by Benjamin, to show his commission and had not done so, in April presented the two cases of the Irishmen to the Secretary of War who, after ordering an investigation, found that both men had exercised the right of suffrage and were thus subject to military duty. Moore, incensed by his treatment, on May 5 wrote to J. B. Caldwell of White Sulphur Springs of Virginia, that from 1826 to 1858, he had lived in despotic countries where he had met with more official courtesy on complaint of grievances than he had received at the hands of his own blood and kin in the Confederacy.

In June, Davis also refused to recognize the consul at Mobile. In the preceding November the Bank of Mobile, as agent for the state of Alabama, informed

[16] Instr. to Mason, No. 24, June 6, 1863.

Magee, the British Consul, that the state, owing English citizens interest-coupons for the sum of forty thousand pounds, payable in London, asked to place coin in the consul's hands for safe transportation at the expense of Alabama. On November 14, Magee replied that he had asked the British Consul at New Orleans whether the British *Rinaldo* could be sent to take the coin from Mobile to Havana, from whence it could go to London. Later, the British *Vesuvius* received thirty-one kegs of specie, amounting to $155,-000. The American commander of the blockading squadron offered no objection, saying "we cannot examine an English man-of-war; we trust all you do will be right and proper." The specie was received in England and paid to the British subjects. Lord Lyons, as soon as he heard of the intention to transmit the specie, sent despatches to Mobile forbidding it, but the *Vesuvius* had already sailed when his despatches arrived. Magee, having been dismissed, Warner, a member of the House of Commons, in the following May, asked whether he had been inconsistent with British neutrality and whether the United States had suggested his removal. Under-Secretary Layard replied that the permission for the *Vesuvius* to do private business was in violation of the pledge given to the United States, and that a dismissal was made before receiving the complaint of the American Government. Though he did not know whether the specie was intended for the payment of interest on the Alabama bonds, or for use for purchasing privateers in Europe, he felt that the British Government had taken the right course."

[17] 170 Parl. Debates, p. 1952, May 19, 1863.

In May, the Richmond *Whig* contained an article complaining that Mr. Cridland, who had sometimes acted in place of Moore in Richmond, was accredited as consul to Mobile under the United States Government. The article, suggesting that the appointment might tend to excite the Southern people to "take the liberty of making a remark" before the close of the war, said: "We know that sundry private citizens of the South, nick-named ministers, are cooling their heels to no earthly purpose in the ante-chambers of St. James and the Tuileries; and this useless refrigeration of the *ossa calcis* of Messrs. Mason and Slidell has been going on for above a year. Intimations of this have reached the 'so-called.'" On May 18, Mr. Cridland sought an interview with Benjamin, called his attention to the article in the *Whig*, and denied that he was going to Mobile except as a private citizen to look after certain interests of the British Government. There was no objection to his going unofficially, but, after his arrival, a telegram from Admiral Buchanan stated that he had papers showing him to be acting consul at Mobile by appointment of Lord Lyons. Cridland was at once informed that he would not be permitted to act as consul and a hint was given him that it would be agreeable if he would leave Mobile.[18] On June 11, Benjamin wrote Mason that he hoped the British Government might be induced to change its whole policy and soon instructed him to bring to its attention all matters relating to consuls. As to the specie sent from Mobile, he said that "according to the principles of the modern public code debts due

[18] Instr. to Mason, No. 25, June 11, 1863.

by a state are not subject to the operations of the law of war, and that, notwithstanding the recent United States confiscation laws (of August 6, 1861), they were beyond confiscation; that England had always abhorred such breaches of faith, and during the Crimean War had paid to the enemy money that she knew would be used against her; that the recent confiscation laws of the United States had caused the Confederacy to pass (August 30, 1861) a law for the sequestration of the enemy's property, but that it exempted public debts; that the United States, in trying to prevent the remittance of specie, either hoped that she herself would be able to get it by the fortunes of war or desired to dishonor Alabama. Benjamin held that if Alabama was still a part of the Union the United States had no right to prevent the payment of her debts; and that if she was a member of the Confederacy, Lord Lyons, by his cooperation with the United States concerning the British consuls in the South, had been unfriendly to the Confederacy.[19]

In July, Russell wrote Mason concerning the cases of both Moore and Cridland, and intimated that the consular agents should have been allowed to remain. Mason informed him that the Confederacy would doubtless be willing to receive agents properly accredited.[20]

The extradition of one Hester, who committed a murder on board the Confederate privateer Sumter, which had landed in a port under British jurisdiction, became a subject of correspondence between Russell

[19] Instr. to Mason, No. 25, June 11, 1863.
[20] Despatches of Mason, No. 44, Sept. 4, 1863.

and Mason in June and July. Hester was impris-
oned by the British authorities, and the London Government offered to deliver him in the West Indies or
in a Confederate port, in case the United States would
allow a British vessel to pass the blockade. Seward,
or Adams, protested against the delivery of the prisoner through the blockade, and on July 25, Russell
informed Mason that the British Government had decided that he could be detained in custody by the
British authorities no longer than might be necessary
to dispose of him on the shore at the Bermudas.
Mason expressed regret that Russell had not adhered
to the original purpose of delivering the prisoner.[21]

[21] Despatches of Mason, No. 41, July 10, 1863; No. 42,
July 21, 1863; No. 43, Aug. 6, 1863.

CHAPTER VIII

THE CRISIS IN ENGLAND

The crisis in England came in the middle of 1863 when Lee was in the heart of the North. Napoleon, shaking hands with Slidell in friendly conferences, consenting to the building of Confederate vessels, denying the English rumors that he was not ready to act, and sitting with the map of the United States unrolled before him, only waited for Lee to take Washington in order that he might grant recognition.[1] Roebuck and Lindsay, by a stroke of amateur diplomacy, in which they said that Napoleon had proposed joint mediation to England, made an attempt through parliament to force the British Government into cooperation with France. But Palmerston opposed double diplomacy, and the government refused " to pull Napoleon's chestnuts from a fire that was too hot for imperial hands." Lindsay, Roebuck, and other friends of the Confederacy, were soon depressed by the news of Lee's retreat, and Mason received instructions to quit London.

Notwithstanding the recent publication of Benjamin's correspondence suspecting Napoleon of occult designs in Texas, the Emperor in the spring and

[1] Dayton wrote Seward (July 10) that news from the U. S. gave him anxiety; that it was already hard enough to prevent recognition, and if Lee should take Washington he could foresee the probable results.

summer of 1863 professed great friendship for the Confederates and showed a disposition to favor them. On April 14, Mocquard, Napoleon's private secretary and confidential friend, stating that he was directed by the Emperor, sent Slidell a copy of a despatch from Adams to Dayton concerning a Confederate cruiser which was expected to enter a French port.[2] It appears that all despatches passed through the French Minister of the Interior, and, if of political interest, were telegraphed to Napoleon—so that Slidell did not doubt that the copy was handed to him as early as the original reached Mr. Dayton at the American legation.

A year before, Napoleon, in a conference with Lindsay and Slidell, said he was ready to act with England, but, as an objection to his initiating official communications with London upon American affairs, he stated that Earl Russell had dealt unfairly in sending his previous proposals (as to the blockade) to Lord Lyons, who made them known to Seward.[3] Since that time England had rejected Napoleon's proposal for mediation upon the basis of a six-months' armistice, and he did not care to take the initiative in any more proposals.

In June, 1863, news from the United States, and the condition of French affairs, again encouraged the Confederacy to ask for recognition. Roebuck and Lindsay were preparing to insure the success of a motion which it was proposed to offer in Parliament on June 30. There were rumors in England that

[2] Despatches of Slidell, April 20, 1863.
[3] Despatches of Mason, July 2, 1863, and No. 8, April 21, 1862.

the Emperor thought recognition would be unwise at that time, and Lindsay was anxious to see him before the motion should be offered, for he saw that Palmerston would probably inform Parliament of the rumors of the reports concerning Napoleon's adverse views. On June 13, Lindsay enclosed to Slidell a letter from Roebuck which referred to Napoleon and the proposed interview as follows: "You know that I am not a great admirer of that great personage, but still I am a politician—so is he, and politicians have no personal likes or dislikes that stand in the way of their political ends. I therefore would act as if I had no feeling either friendly or hostile to him—he could do the same as to myself, and therefore I have no fear but that he would listen to all I have to offer by way of suggestion and advice . . . . and good might come of our interview." [4]

On June 18, Slidell obtained an interview with the Emperor who said that without the cooperation of England with her strong navy, recognition, by creating a rupture with the United States would jeopardize French commerce and the success of the Mexican expedition. He stated that other powers of Europe had no navies, but Slidell suggested that Spain had a fleet, and that a Confederate guaranty of Cuba, and an assurance of French concurrence, might induce her to take the initiative in recognition. Napoleon agreed that France in such a case would act even without England. Speaking of the possibility of forcing the English cabinet to act or to give way to a new ministry, and asking an interview for

[4] Despatches of Slidell, No. 38, June 21, 1863.

Lindsay and Roebuck, Slidell stated that Lord Malmsbury, who was friendly toward the Emperor, would probably be the new English Secretary of Foreign Affairs in case of a change in the government.[5] Napoleon replied that the Tories were very good friends of his when in the minority, but that their tone changed very much when they came into power. He made an appointment, however, to receive Roebuck and Lindsay, and gave his permission for Slidell to give an authorized unqualified denial of the correctness of the rumor in England that he thought it unwise to recognize the Confederacy. Slidell in his report to Benjamin stated that Napoleon added: "I think that I can do something better: make a direct proposition to England for joint recognition. This will effectually prevent Lord Palmerston from misrepresenting my position and wishes on the American question. I shall bring the question before the cabinet meeting to-day, and if it should be decided not to make the proposition now, I will let you know in a day or two through Mr. Mocquard, and what to say to Roebuck."

On June 19, Slidell's friend in the French Foreign Office wrote him that the council had decided to contradict the reports that France was less favorable to the Confederacy, and also to remind the English Government of previous French propositions. On June 22, Mocquard wrote Slidell that the Emperor requested him to say that L'Huys, the Minister of Foreign Affairs, had written Baron Gros, the French ambassador at London, to sound Russell on the sub-

[5] Despatches of Slidell, No. 38, June 21, 1863.

ject of recognition, and to say that the French Cabinet was ready to discuss the subject.[6]

On June 20, Mason having received an account of Slidell's interview with Napoleon sent a note to Lindsay and Roebuck, and they went to Paris that night to urge the Emperor to invite England formally, before June 30, to join France in recognition, and that, in case England should refuse to coöperate, he should act alone, with the assurance that England would follow or have a change of ministry.[7] On June 25, Slidell wrote Benjamin that their interview with the Emperor at Fontainebleau was highly satisfactory, and that they "were authorized to state in the House of Commons that the Emperor was not only willing but anxious to recognize the Confederate States with the coöperation of England. The Emperor, however, did not promise them that he would make any formal proposition to the British Government. But a few days later, the Paris correspondent of the *Times* said that Russell had received a communication from France, through Baron Gros, looking toward the conclusion of the war in America. On June 29, Roebuck asked Gros the substance of his communication to Russell on this subject, and Gros replied that he had made no formal communication. The next day, Lord Campbell, in the House of Lords, asked Russell if he had received such a document or verbal communication.[8] Russell replied that the French ambassador had told him "an hour ago" that he had not even received an order to deliver to him such a communication.

[6] Despatches of Slidell, No. 38, June 21, 1863.
[7] Despatches of Mason, No. 40, June 20, 1863.
[8] 171 Parl. Debates, June 30, 1863.

On June 30 Roebuck presented his petition in the Commons, in favor of entering into negotiations with the great powers of Europe with the object of recognizing the Confederate Government. He reviewed the establishment of the colonies in America; the American Revolution, in which he said that France in aiding the colonies had borne a similar relation to them as that which England now bore to the Confederate States; and the opposition of the South to the tariff since 1827. Announcing that secession was now successful, he stated that if the United States had kept growing she would have been the greatest bully in the world; and though he did not favor slavery he was determined to try to prevent the reconstruction of the Union. He said that England by recognition could avoid the misery of the cotton famine; and that, if recognition was delayed, the people would look to the Government as the cause of their misery and sweep the existing Cabinet from its seat. Roebuck, in telling of his interview with Napoleon, accused the Cabinet of misrepresenting the Emperor's views, of concealing his offers, and of disclosing to Mr. Seward the nature of the Emperor's despatches. He said that Napoleon was stronger than ever in favor of recognition, notwithstanding reports to the contrary; that on account of the leakage of previous overtures he could not make a formal application to England; but that he had authorized Lindsay and himself to say to Parliament that he was ready to act with England.

Roebuck's motion evidently had little chance of success. Robert Montague in discussing the legal aspect of recognition, and historical precedents, favored strict neutrality, feeling that England might as well declare war against the United States at once as to adopt the policy of recognition which would certainly lead to war. He stated that the Confederacy should not be aided to fight its own battles, and that Napoleon should be left to pull his own chestnuts from the fire. Clifford denied that the Confederate States were in rebellion, and prophesied military despotism and failure in the United States, but he also favored neutrality. The Chancellor of the Exchequer[*] did not believe that the restoration of the United States, by force, was obtainable, however much those who favored American institutions might dislike to see great visions destroyed; but he did not fear American expansion, nor think that the United States should be divided in order to prevent it from becoming a menace to England. He said that England should suppress passion and treat the matter as one of facts. Though he thought that nineteen-twentieths of the House favored an end of the war, he considered that Roebuck's motion was untimely and inconvenient. Forster, whose father had been killed in a slave state, favored neutrality not only because it was a duty, but because a war with the United States would endanger Canada and commerce, and because he was opposed to any more division and strife in the Anglo-Saxon race. Lord Robert Cecil defended the course of Napoleon and suggested that the fear for Canada would not influence England. But Bright had no faith in the

[*] 171 Parl. Debates, p. 1807.

scheming and land-hungry Emperor of France who, he said, ran the chance of being " far too much represented in this House." He considered that Lincoln represented a moral and peaceful party, and warned England not to lift her hand " to aid the most stupendous act of guilt in history." " The more I study this war," said he, " the more I conclude that it is improbable that in the future the United States will be broken into separate republics. Even if separation occur, sympathies will later bring the whole continent under one central government." George Grey could not understand the extraordinary statement of Roebuck as to what Napoleon said about the danger of making proposals to the English Government, and he referred to the apparent contradiction between the statements of Roebuck and Baron Gros.

On July 2, Layard, the Under Secretary of State, answered Roebuck's accusation against the British Foreign Office.[10] He stated that the Emperor's despatch of November 10, 1862, which was the only one to which Napoleon could have made reference, had been published at once in France, and then in other newspapers; and that it had been communicated to Seward by Mercier, the French minister, and not by Lord Lyons. He further said that, since the French communication of the previous November, France, notwithstanding the statements of Roebuck, had not made any overtures to the British Government upon the subject of proposed intervention, mediation or recognition; that Gros of his own accord had stated

[10] 172 Parl. Debates, July 2, 1863.

that he had received no such communication from Paris; and that Earl Cowley at Paris knew of no such communication. Roebuck asked if France had not made a proposal in the spring of 1862. Layard had looked over every despatch and could find none upon that subject.

Mason, July 2, said that the debates and the language of Gros reduced to a mere shadow the professions of Napoleon to Slidell, Lindsay and Roebuck.[11] At the same time he saw an article in the *Times*, from the Paris correspondent, stating that a private letter from Madrid gave the information that the Spanish Government had been sounded upon the question of recognition, with an intimation that if Spain were ready she would have the support of France. He remarked that France seemed to be playing a complicated diplomatic game. Slidell believed that the Emperor had kept his promise, and that the fault rested either with the French Foreign Office, Palmerston, or with Russell and Layard. Mason wrote that the Commons were agitated by the entanglements, and that four-fifths of the members were with the Confederacy, but that as parties stood Roebuck's motion would probably be lost; and he anxiously awaited news from General Lee.[12]

The debate on Roebuck's motion was resumed on July 10, when the latest report from Lee's movement in the North was favorable to the Confederacy, indicating to Mason that Washington and Baltimore might fall, and make it impossible for the ministry to hold out against recognition.[13] Sir James Fergu-

---

[11] Despatches of Mason, No. 41, July 2, 1863.
[12] Ibid., No. 42, July 10, 1863.   [13] Ibid.

son stated that the Confederacy seemed to be no longer on the defensive, but that the debate should be postponed until the result of the campaign was learned. Though the debate was postponed until July 13, there was a long discussion on July 10. Palmerston said that all knew the wishes of Napoleon now; and, while stating that England was ready to interchange views with France on American affairs, he suggested that Napoleon should know that conversation between himself and two members of Parliament was not a question for discussion in the Commons. He hoped that Roebuck would let the debate drop, claiming that it could not go on without a revival of personal discussions as to what Napoleon had said in private. Lindsay explained that in the previous four years he had held several conversations with Napoleon upon the subject of navigation—some of which had occurred since the Civil War—and that he had told nothing except when Napoleon gave him permission. He vouched for the truth of what Robeuck had said, but he desired to avoid such discussions in the House. He said that he felt for the Southern people, but others replied that the Confederacy need look for no sympathy from the workingmen of England. O'Donoghue declared that disunion would be one of the greatest calamities to the world and protested against the feeling of hostility to American prosperity in which Roebuck's motion had been conceived.

After a long discussion, much of which related to Napoleon's statements, Layard still declared that he himself had gone through all the papers and that no despatch sent by France to the British Government had ever been sent to the American Government. He also mentioned a previous case where Lindsay had come from Paris as an amateur diplomatist to make communications which he had no authority to do. Lindsay in reply spoke of his conversation with Napoleon on April 11, 1862, stating that Napoleon had asked him to report it to Russell. As to the recent conference, he said that Napoleon was anxious to recognize the Confederacy, had wished to see him, and had authorized the use of any means to notify the Commons of his readiness to act. He took no offense at what Lord Palmerston had said, but he did not like to be called an "amateur diplomatist" by the Under Secretary. He said that if he was an amateur diplomatist the British Government had made him so by authorizing his talks with Napoleon on the subject of navigation. Palmerston made another speech on July 13, regretting the attack on the Under Secretary, and stating that it was necessary to receive communications through responsible ministers—even if the correspondence should be between Napoleon and Victoria. He said that it was not the habit of the British Government to carry on double diplomacy or irregular negotiations by private individuals. He explained that Lindsay had offered to talk with Napoleon on navigation; and that the Government, considering him informed upon that subject, had accepted his offer with the best intentions. At the request of Palmerston, Roebuck moved to discharge the order for resuming the debate. In doing so he said that there were two great dangers to England which the Government would have to meet: (1) The possibility of reconstructing the Union on a Confederate basis, or, (2) recognition of the Confederacy by France alone.

The statement of Lindsay and Roebuck as to Napoleon became a subject of conversation between Dayton and L'Huys at Paris, and Dayton wrote Seward: "Take it all in all, it was the most futile and abortive attempt to help on the recognition of the South that men in prominent positions ever made." Both English and French officials declared that there were no such official despatches as those to which Napoleon had referred. L'Huys informed Dayton that after the most diligent search he could find no despatch to which Lindsay's statement could possibly apply—except the November proposal for an armistice.[14] Perhaps, in his interview with Lindsay in 1862, Napoleon may have referred to unofficial representations made through the French minister at London, but Secretary Seward positively stated that Russell had never furnished him any communication of the Emperor. Seward distrusted Napoleon, but his distrust probably arose from the rumors and reports which found their way into the newspapers. L'Huys stated to Dayton that the Emperor had at no time made a proposal to England to acknowledge the South, though Roebuck and Lindsay had pressed him hard to do so and had told him that England was ready and would offer recognition if it were not believed that France would refuse to follow—that if he would but say *the word* their proposals in the House of Commons would pass at once; that Napoleon had replied that he had

[14] Dayton to Seward, No. 333, Aug. 5, 1863.

given England no cause to believe that he would not act with her, but that he would not initiate the movement; that when Roebuck and Lindsay asked him if they might communicate his views, the Emperor had replied that his views were no secret, little dreaming that they would use his words in the Commons. An article in the *Moniteur* admitted the readiness of the Emperor to follow England in case the latter believed that acknowledgment of the Confederacy would end the war.[15]

Notwithstanding the assurances of L'Huys, it seems that Napoleon may have sent some kind of a despatch through L'Huys, asking Gros to sound Palmerston and Russell and to notify them that he was ready to join in recognition if England would make the official proposal. Mocquard in explaining the subject to Slidell said: "On the next day after the interview of Messrs. Roebuck and Lindsay with the Emperor, the Minister of Foreign Affairs telegraphed Baron Gros to inform Lord Palmerston 'officiously' that, should Great Britain be willing to recognize the South, the Emperor would be ready to follow her in that way." Either Gros did not get the telegram, or, seeing the feeble support which Roebuck's motion met, he denied receiving any official communication on the subject of recognition—as he had a right to do if his despatch was purely confidential.

It is possible that if Lee had won, and the draft riots had not failed in the North, and if Vicksburg had not fallen, that England and France might have

[15] Dayton to Seward, No. 329, July 30, 1863.

intervened and sent iron-clads to America. Some still hoped for foreign aid and complications, and said that if France and England feared reconstruction of the Union, they would manifest their purpose when they heard of the recent Confederate calamities. Still others, seeing that the United States would continue the war, would have been willing to be included in the new Mexican empire, whose notables were now asking France for an emperor.[16] A few favored the abolition of slavery as a means of obtaining recognition. By August, it became evident that what nature and man's genius had bound together could not be separated by the storms of a single generation. Peoples might come and pass away but the Mississippi would roll on through a united country.

Parliament was prorogued July 28, and the expectations of the Confederate sympathizers were much depressed by the news from America.[17] The Confederate engagements in Europe for an army and navy required large sums, and Confederate affairs in the stock market became more and more doubtful. The loan fell to 70; and Mason, seeing that another could not be expected, advised that the Confederate authorities at Richmond should take control of the shipment of cotton by fast steamers, and avoid the exorbitant rates of the blockade runners. On August 10, in reply to Mason's note of July 16, Russell stated that he saw no reason to change his opinion on the subject of the blockade.[18] Mason reported that

[16] J. B. Jones: Diary, July 31, 1863.
[17] Despatches of Mason, No. 43, Aug. 6, 1863.
[18] Ibid., No. 44, Sept. 4, 1863.

England would still resort to evasions of the Declaration of Paris. Confederate agents had been sent to Ireland to stop Irish emigration to the United States, by assurances of Southern friendship, but Mason doubted whether they could make much impression. Mason saw, in fact, very few crumbs of comfort; but he wrote Benjamin that if Russia should modify her policy toward Poland so as to remove apprehension of European war, France, compelled by her interests in Mexico, might take a position of value to the Confederacy. He suggested that the authorities at Richmond should define their policy with the view of endeavoring to obtain France and Mexico as allies against the supposed future designs of the United States.

After the failure of Mason to obtain recognition, in the summer of 1862, the Southerners had become irritated, and many desired the recall of the diplomatic agents.[19] The withdrawal of Mason was contemplated by the Government, but it was decided that his recall would interfere with Slidell's arrangements for the purchase of war materials. The press complained that, while the Confederacy should have agents abroad, the dignity of the country was compromised by having them sit or kneel at the gate of kings to petition for admission to the family of nations. It was stated that, since European ministers had spoken so plainly, no one now believed in the delusion of European recognition and that self-respect demanded the withdrawal of the diplomatic agents; that Europe wished to see the war pro-

[19] Instr. to Slidell, Jan. 15, 1863.

tracted till both sides should become exhausted, and would interfere only when it was clear that the South could not succeed alone.[20]

In the spring of 1863 England published the correspondence between Mason and Russell on the legality of the blockade, and when it reached the Confederacy the immediate withdrawal of Mason was strongly urged. Editorials suggested that he had no position from which to retire, save that of a waiter on the pleasure of the English Government. Others, adopting the policy of Davis, saw no humiliation in allowing him to remain in London "to be ready for any event which might turn up." They remembered that they had received valuable assistance from some of the English people who were "not so cold as Russell." But a strong party in the Confederacy continued to speak of Mason "cooling his heels in the ante-chamber of St. James to no earthly advantage."[21]

On August 4, Benjamin, seeing by the parliamentary debates that England would decline overtures for a treaty, wrote Mason that his residence in London was "no longer conducive to the interests nor consistent with the dignity of the Confederacy," and advised his withdrawal.[22] In a private note, however, he asked him to use his discretion if the British Government showed any sign of a change of policy. On September 21, Mason, after consulting Slidell, notified Russell and the newspapers of his reasons for withdrawal.

[20] Richmond Dispatch, March 31, 1863.
[21] Ibid., April 8, 1863.
[22] Instr. to Mason, No. 30, Aug. 4, 1863.

The London papers for which the Confederate press agent (Hotze) wrote editorials to "affect the public mind," commented upon Russell's very marked and impolitic partisanship in favor of the United States, stating that he licked the feet of Adams and bit every one else who ventured within the length of his chain—while rifles and Irishmen were sent to New York in shiploads with impunity. The *Morning Herald* (September 23) spoke of the inconvenience which would result from England having no means of communication with the South, and said that Davis had reluctantly reached his determination after enduring much provocation and lack of courtesy from Russell, who, in order to please the indignant American minister, had not even been disposed unofficially to converse with Mason as a private citizen, concerning interests of British citizens in the vast territories over which Davis affirmed himself the ruling executive. Alluding to the continental idea that Russell was "a very bear of diplomacy," the *Herald* suggested that the bear had found his keeper, and inquired: "How much dirt is this nation to eat in order to escape the bugbear of an American war?" It was urged that the Confederacy, with its seat at Richmond unshaken by the hosts from the North, had a right to expect more sympathy than it had received in Europe; and that it was unwise for Russell to grow colder with the waning fortunes of the Confederacy, while Napoleon was growing so friendly that rumor spoke of a possible alliance of France, Mexico and the Confederacy to cut the Gordian knot of the American difficulty. But Russell, remaining unmoved in his policy, replied (September 25) that the reasons for declining Confederate overtures were still in force, and that he regretted that circumstances had prevented the cultivation of Mason's personal acquaintance.

Mason still complaining of Russell's evasions in favor of the North on the question of the blockade, withdrew from London to Paris to await orders from Richmond.[23] He decided that it would be best for him to remain in England—or at least in Europe. Accustomed to dealing in futures, he was not yet disheartened. Who could say when there might cease to be a Palmerston and a Russell in the Cabinet. To Jefferson Davis on October 2, he presented his views in substance as follows: "I await orders. We think best for me to stay in Europe. Notwithstanding the reluctance of those really our friends in the Commons to vote for Roebuck's motion, . . . it resulted from no disaffection to our cause, but was due to the peculiar structure of parties in England just now. Palmerston's personal popularity is the mainstay of his administration, and if his party were overthrown it might be returned. The opposition members think that if he were out of the way they could come in with their strength greatly increased —and he is now far advanced in years, and subject to sharp attacks of the gout or its incidents. Were there a new administration, or one reconstructed on the loss of its chief, or any event which would displace Lord Russell, it is thought that the policy of

[23] Despatches of Mason, No. 46, Sept. 25, 1863 (received at Richmond on Oct. 23). On Sept. 25, Russell wrote Mason that the reasons for declining Confederate overtures were still in force. [Despatches of Mason, Oct. 19, 1863.]

England in regard to our country would undergo great modification."

Mr. Davis in his message to Congress strongly criticised the Governments of Europe for refusing to admit the Confederacy into the family of nations.[24] Nevertheless, in view of the very disturbed condition of European affairs, the wars which might arise therefrom, the probable relations of France and Austria in Mexico, and contingencies and unexpected relations in which the Confederate interests could not wait for the delays of uncertain communication, Mason was appointed commissioner to the continent with duplicate full power addressed in blank so they could be used for any capital in Europe.[25]   He never had any occasion to use them.   Yet he continued to draw his salary of $12,000 per year until the end of the war, conferring alternately with Slidell at Paris, and with Southern sympathizers in the British Parliament who were seeking to embarrass the Palmerston ministry.   He watched the ebbing tide of the Confederacy's fortunes and hoped against fate until the last.[26]

[24] The Richmond Examiner (J. M. Daniels), Dec. 10, 1863. Davis was criticised at Richmond for "bad taste" in complaining too much of the foreign powers. [J. B. Jones: Diary, Dec. 9, 1863.]

[24] Instr. to Mason, No. 34, Jan. 25, 1864.   The Confederate Senate, on Jan. 18, had confirmed the appointment of both Mason and his secretary.   Macfarland's salary was $3600.

[26] The tenacity with which some clung to the hope of foreign recognition and support is surprising.   It appears that their ideas as to English sympathy with the cause of the secessionists were very much exaggerated.   In April, 1864, L. Q. C. Lamar, who had recently returned from his fruitless mission to Russia, in a speech at Macon, Georgia,

said England was almost unanimously Southern in its sympathies, and that the majority in Parliament were sympathizers with the Confederacy, but that the Cobden-Bright element held the balance of power. He declared that Napoleon, the artful politician, was friendly, but was opposed by his Chamber of Deputies and could do nothing. He considered that the Confederacy was favored by Austria and Spain, and by Italy through the Pope, and might be able to secure as an ally Mexico, under the rule of Maximilian. [The Weekly Register (Lynchburg), April 23, 1864.]

CHAPTER IX

NAPOLEON, AND THE PROJECTED CONFEDERATE NAVY

While Napoleon was contemplating an American empire around the Gulf, Slidell was planning in France for a Confederate navy, and Mason was commissioned to await contingencies.[1] Some who favored rushing headlong into political combinations for " gigantic increase " urged entangling alliances with France. Henry St. Paul, in a pamphlet published at Mobile (November, 1863) on " Our Home and Foreign Policy," stating that France had contemplated and panted for it, proposed making the gulf a Franco-Confederate lake, of which Cuba and the French islands would be the central key, by which the isthmus could also be brought under control.

Louis Napoleon desired to perpetuate his dynasty by a military revival and a strong foreign policy. Even before the civil war he dreamed of restoring to France her long-lost colonial empire. A professor in the University of Virginia told Benjamin of an hour's conversation which he had with the Emperor in 1859 or 1860. He said that the latter drained him by questions, and was especially eager to talk of Mexican affairs. The professor had just returned from Cuba, but he found Napoleon apparently better informed than himself concerning the condition of affairs in the gulf. He knew the exact number of guns on Morro

[1] Instr. to Mason, No. 32, Nov. 13, 1863.

Castle and how much the United States spent on the Florida fortifications. He seemed to seek in Mexico a compensation for the lost colonies in the West Indies, which he said could not be peaceably recovered. He stated that France must soon have a *pied-à-terre* on the Florida coast to protect her gulf commerce. " Nous ne voulons pas d'un autre Gibraltar de ce cote-là." He seemed also to revolve in his mind the possibility of getting a foothold in Louisiana. In asking as to the disposition of the French in Texas, the tendency of the German colonists, and the feeling on the Mexican border, he twice said " La Louisiane n'est ce pas qu'elle est Française au fond? . . . Eh bien, il faut reconstruire l'empire là bas." [2]

At the opening of the civil war Napoleon saw his opportunity, and he was favored by the conditions around the gulf. Spain was ready to introduce her authority in San Domingo; and England and Spain were cooperating with France in contemplated intervention in Mexico in order to collect claims resulting from the revolutions there. The United States, however, would not join the European powers, but soon expressed a readiness to help Mexico in the settlement of her claims. In the early part of 1862 England, Spain, and France landed troops at Vera Cruz. Mexico soon arranged with England and Spain by negotiations, and they withdrew their forces. Napoleon refused the terms offered, and by invitation of the clerical party declared war against Juarez. He expected the Confederacy to be successful, and hoped that thereby the United States would be prevented

[2] Confed " Dip. Cor.", France, Benjamin to Slidell, Feb. 7, 1863.

from interfering with his designs. French journalists stated that intervention was rendered necessary by the ambitious views of the United States as to expansion. The American Government was apprehensive that Spain might renew her cooperation with France. Perry at Madrid suggested to the Spanish Government that it was time for her to end her participation in the Mexican affair. Referring to the possible large merchant navy which might traverse the waters between Mexico and France, he suggested that the strategical position of the Spanish colonies should make Spain careful. For a while the influence of the United States at Madrid was lessened by the report that Mexico was to pledge territory for a loan from the American Government, but Spain held aloof from Mexican affairs.

The Confederate officials expressed no disapproval of the policy of either France or Spain in Mexico and San Domingo. They informed Spain that they desired to see her power grow. Slidell in 1862 told Napoleon that the Confederacy would have no objection to his taking the west end of San Domingo.

The Confederates were much encouraged by Napoleon's attitude. In May, 1861, the Duc de Morny, the greatest person in France after the Emperor, informed Rost that the recognition of the South was only a matter of time. France only waited for England. In April, 1862, Napoleon freely stated to Slidell that he was ready to send an Anglo-French fleet to the mouth of the Mississippi to break the blockade, but New Orleans soon fell and postponed the chances of Confederate recognition. In the fall of 1862 Napoleon had been ready to mediate for a six months' armistice but England and France had refused to join him. Apparently his friendship grew in the spring and summer of 1863, but Lee was driven from the North and England firmly declared against coöperation in recognizing the South, and Napoleon soon found it inconvenient to facilitate plans for building a Confederate navy in his ports. Gradually the signs of the times rudely destroyed his vision of a great Latin empire beyond the seas.

While Napoleon, declaring the necessity of a stable government in Mexico to prevent the United States from controlling the entire gulf, was preparing, in the summer of 1862, an expedition for Vera Cruz, his consuls at Galveston and Richmond were acting in such a manner as to make Benjamin suspicious that the Emperor, in accordance with the traditions of the French policy, had secret and occult designs on some of the Southern states, as well as on Mexico. Under date of August 18, Theron, the French consul in Texas, in a letter to Governor Lubbock, confidentially asked his views as to whether the annexation of Texas to the United States, and its subsequent secession and incorporation with the Confederacy were good political movements, and whether the reëstablishment of the republic of Texas would be beneficial. He stated that he was seeking information to guide him in his political correspondence with his government. Lubbock forwarded this letter to Davis; and shortly afterwards Benjamin, in a communication which was captured and published in the newspapers [3] of the following January, informed Slidell as to the discovery of

[3] Richmond Examiner, Jan. 23, 1863.

a political intrigue believed to have been set on foot by the French consul for the purpose of detaching Texas from the Confederacy. Benjamin suggested that it was the intention of Napoleon to hold Mexico as a colony, and to establish Texas as a weaker power between Mexico and the Confederacy so that he might feel secure—or that it was his purpose to take Texas under his protection as an independent republic, so that he could get cotton to offset the India supply of England, thus making Texas as subservient to French interests as if it were a French colony. Benjamin asked Slidell to investigate.

The Richmond *Examiner*, whose editor was not an admirer of Benjamin, feeling that the publication of this captured despatch would give the Yankees more news than could possibly have been given by any Confederate newspaper, and tend to disgust Napoleon with the Confederate cabinet—and, at the same time, ironically feigning to believe that the despatch was a fabrication—said that two idle French consuls might have conceived the "silly idea" of sandwiching Texas between two *strong* governments, but that so stupid a conception could not possibly have attracted the serious attention of even the feeblest secretary of state.[4] L'Huys voluntarily spoke to Dayton concerning the alleged intrigue, and said that he would severely censure ("pound them"), the French consuls, for assuming to interfere. Seward seems to have attached no importance to Mr. Benjamin's fears, nor to have apprehended any danger from the various rumors as to French designs. He considered that

[4] Richmond Examiner, Jan. 26, 1863.

the French element around New Orleans had become entirely Americanized. At the close of 1862, in writing to Dayton that the relations between France and Louisiana did not have any political significance in the relations of the two countries, he said that there was no hook in Louisiana upon which French intervention could grapple.[5]

Notwithstanding the suspicions of Benjamin, Napoleon did not appear to take offense. He still professed to be ready to coöperate with England in any policy affecting the Confederacy, and a few months later he even appeared willing to act with Spain alone if the latter would take the first step. In March, 1862, Spain had not been ready to take the initiative in recognizing the Confederacy. At the close of 1862, when by the mutations of Spanish affairs General Serrano was called to the portfolio of foreign affairs in the O'Donnel cabinet, Slidell saw a possibility that Spain might review her decision, and he recommended that the Confederacy should be represented at Madrid. On March 22, 1863, Benjamin appointed Slidell to act as special commissioner to that court; and, on May 9, sent him instructions to assure Spain that the South, since secession, no longer desired Cuba, nor sought to extend its boundaries, but that it foresaw future aggression of the United States for acquisitions, and was willing to form an alliance with Spain, and to guarantee her possession of Cuba. When Slidell received his instructions Serrano had gone out with the other members of the O'Donnel cabinet.

[5] U. S. Dip. Cor., 1863, parts 1 and 2, pp. 640, 642, 646 and 702. Dayton to Seward, Feb. 13, 1863. Seward to Dayton, Dec. 29, 1862, March 2, Sept. 26, 1863.

Slidell did not go to Madrid, but he held long conversations with Isturitz, the Spanish ambassador at Paris, who stated that the sympathy of himself and his government was with the Confederacy, and that Spain was prepared to act with France and England, but that she could not take the initiative in recognition and risk the results of a war with the United States.[6] Slidell suggested that Spain and other powers might unite with France without the coöperation of England, and with apprehension of consequences no more serious than " Seward's ebullitions." Isturitz seemed to admit that Spain would be favorably disposed to his suggestion, but he did not commit himself. He wrote Miraflores, the Spanish minister of foreign affairs, that Slidell would promptly go to Madrid in case he should receive an intimation that his presence would be acceptable.[7] Napoleon, on June 18, was more favorably disposed than ever to a general European recognition of the Confederacy; but he feared the large navy of the United States, unless he could receive English coöperation. Slidell suggested that Spain had a navy, and that, by a guaranty of Cuba and with assurance that France would concur, she might be induced to act. Napoleon gave the assurance, Slidell informed Isturitz, the Paris correspondent informed the London *Times*, and Benjamin expected a treaty; but after the defeat of the Confederacy at Gettysburg and Vicksburg, Isturitz stated that nothing could be effected at Madrid.

The Confederates at this time were calculating upon success in obtaining a navy in French ports. In an

---

[6] Despatches of Slidell, May 28, 1863.
[7] Ibid., June 21, 1863.

interview of October, 1862, Napoleon had intimated to Slidell that if the Confederacy would arrange to build ships in France, the builders would not be interrupted, and that by making some plausible plea the vessels would be allowed to leave. The two had just been speaking of a plan of joint mediation for a six months' armistice, when Napoleon changed the subject by asking why the Confederacy had not created a navy. Slidell said: " If the Emperor would give only some kind of verbal assurance that the police should not watch too closely when we put on the guns and men, we would gladly avail ourselves of it." The Emperor replied: " Why could you not have them built as if for the Italian Government? I do not think it would be difficult, but I will consult my ministers." Slidell was further encouraged, in December, by an interview with Mocquard, though in the early part of January the latter said that Napoleon found greater difficulties as to building the ships than he had anticipated.[8]

On January 7, M. Arman, a deputy of the French legislative body, came to Slidell with a proposition to build steamers, and the latter, feeling that he came at the Emperor's instance, asked him to wait until he learned the action of the Confederacy upon the proposition of European bankers to float a loan. L'Huys, who was consulted as to building the vessels, said that he preferred to close his eyes to the affair until some direct appeal should be made to him, and that Slidell had better communicate with him through his " friend," except when there was something special.

[8] Despatches of Slidell, Jan. 11, 1863.

The Minister of Marine officially assured Slidell and Deputy Voruz that the builders of the corvettes "for commercial purposes in the Indian ocean" would be permitted to arm and equip them, and that the vessels would be allowed to go to sea.[9] The Emperor also informed Arman that there would be no difficulty in arming the steamers.

By the last of March the success of the Confederate loan seemed to be assured and Mason and Slidell advised that the building of vessels should begin. On April 15, Captain Bullock made a contract with J. L. Arman for four clipper corvettes of the *Alabama* type, to run between Shanghai, Yedo and San Francisco, and built with the contemplation of a sale to the Emperor of China or of Japan. Arman arranged with M. J. Voruz of Nantes for two of the vessels. Bullock, soon after, received Mallory's note, of May 16, stating that the Confederate Congress by a secret act had appropriated £2,000,000 for building iron-clad ships of war abroad. Expectations at Richmond had become much aroused by the hopes held out by France. In an interview with Napoleon on June 18, Slidell, in thanking him for his sanction of the contract for building the four corvettes, stated that the Confederacy was also prepared to build several iron-clads if he would only give verbal assurance that they would be allowed to proceed to sea. To this request Napoleon replied that if the ships were built it would be necessary to conceal their destination. Slidell urged that it would be no violation of neutrality for the Emperor to give his permission to the Confeder-

[9] Despatches of Slidell, March 4, 1863; Feb. 16 and 18, 1864.

acy, and mentioned the precedent of a ship built for the Chilean Government, but the Emperor said there was a distinction.[10] On July 16, Bullock closed another contract with Arman for two iron-clad vessels. There was no official assurance, as in the case of the corvettes, that the vessels would be allowed to go to sea; and afterwards, when Slidell found that they could not leave except under the apparent ownership of some recognized government, he stated that he did not know of the contract until it was made.[11]

It will be seen from the foregoing statements, as reported by Slidell, that Napoleon only promised that the vessels should be built, and allowed to sail if their real destination could be kept concealed. But the secret of their destination becoming known through no fault of his, in the face of American protest he finally found it inexpedient to favor the Confederacy in its plans to secure a navy.

On September 10, 1863, a mysterious stranger walked into the office of John Bigelow, the United States consul at Paris, and informed him of Bullock's contract to secure Confederate vessels by having them built for China. The stranger was Peterman, a clerk of M. Voruz, who had abstracted his employer's correspondence. Bigelow at once informed Seward and Dayton, who brought the matter to the attention of the French Government.[12] Arman claimed that he was no longer dealing with the Confederacy; but, on October 22, L'Huys informed Dayton that the Min-

---

[10] Despatches of Slidell, No. 38, June 21, 1863 (in cipher). Despatches of Mason, No. 40, June 20, 1863.
[11] South. Hist. Ass'n Papers, Vol. XIV, p. 454.
[12] Bigelow: France and the Confederate Navy.

ister of Marine had notified both Voruz and Arman of the withdrawal of the authority which had been obtained for the armament of the four vessels.[13] Sometime later, when Dayton placed into the hands of the French authorities full proofs as to the Confederate vessels, L'Huys expressed amazement.

Slidell became uneasy, and on November 6, wrote to Napoleon that the confident assertions of the agents of the United States Government, and certain remarks made at the office of foreign affairs, and of marine, caused him to apprehend that orders might be given to interfere with the completion of the vessels, and he stated his confidence that Napoleon would take necessary steps to prevent such interference. Three days later L'Huys asked Slidell to call November 9. He then told him that what passed with the Emperor was confidential, and that France being bound by a declaration of neutrality would not risk a war with the United States. Slidell replied that the vessels were building by an invitation of Napoleon, who had originated the idea, and he invoked an adherence to the promises confidentially given.

The Minister of Marine (November 19) drew a broad line of distinction between corvettes and ironclads, stating that if the latter be allowed to sail in spite of the remonstrances from Washington and in violation of the declaration of neutrality it would be an overt act of hostility. He informed Arman that the iron-clads would not be allowed to go to sea except as the property of some non-belligerent government, and Bullock, after consulting Mason and Slidell,

[13] U. S. Dip. Cor., 1863, Vol. II.

determined to sell them. Bullock also desired to dispose of the corvettes, which he said were built only to act in conjunction with the iron-clads in raising the blockade. Slidell, however, suggesting that a few months might change affairs, was in favor of using the corvettes as cruisers like the *Alabama*. " I know the Emperor's feelings are as friendly. as ever," said he, " and the new ministry in England may enable him to indulge them. The chapter of accidents is always in the long run fruitful of great and unexpected results. Perhaps it may be better to go on and complete the ships." Davis and Mallory agreed that it was best to complete the vessels and take chances.

A short time later, Slidell's hopes received a fresh shock. The steam sloop *Rappahannock*, pierced for four guns and purchased by Confederate agents in Great Britain, left November 25, without armament or war equipments, and by permission entered the French port of Calais for repair, to adjust her engines, and to complete preparations for her voyage to the Confederacy. Napoleon wrote Persigny that he had given orders that she might leave the French port, but that the American minister must not know it. A few days later, however, by an order which Benjamin called unfriendly, the French Government prevented the vessel from proceeding to sea with more than thirty-five officers and men. This being insufficient to manage the vessel she was detained at Calais.[14]

Slidell soon had fresh evidence that the turn of events in America and Europe, and the policy of England, were forcing Napoleon to endeavor to conciliate

[14] Rp. of Mallory, Sec'y of the Confed. Navy, Richmond, Nov. 5, 1864.

the United States. James Williams, a confidential agent, had spent two weeks at Miramar in frequent communication with Maximilian, and wrote Davis that the latter was disposed to enter into an alliance with the Confederacy. Slidell was told by his friend in the foreign office that Maximilian would recognize the South, but when the latter, while at Paris, did not receive him, he wrote that the whole policy of the Emperor had changed. Mercier was on a visit to Paris, and Mason suggested that perhaps Lincoln had sent a message to the Emperor offering to recognize the Mexican Government if France would not recognize the Confederacy.[15]

Arrangements for extricating vessels in England also met with serious interference. The British Government had detained several steam rams upon complaints that they were building for the Confederacy, and Earl Russell soon found occasion to warn Mr. Davis that British neutrality must be respected. In December, 1863, Seward sent Russell a copy of what purported to be an annual report of Mallory of the Confederate navy.[16] It alluded to Confederate vessels building in England, and to contemplated Confederate operations in Canada. Seward stated that "The recognition of the insurgents without navy, ports, courts, or coasts, as a belligerent, was deemed by

[15] Despatches of Mason, March 16, 1864. Despatches of Slidell, Dec. 3, 1863, Mar. 16, 1864, and May 2, 1864.

[16] U. S. Dip. Cor. Instr. No. 789, Seward to Adams, Dec. 20, 1863. As to the spurious character of the Mallory report, see Adams to Seward, Nos. 574 and 579; Seward to Adams, Nos. 824 and 883; Adams to Seward, Nos. 596 and 640; and Seward to Dayton, Feb. 25, 1864. Also, Despatches of Mason.

them . . . as an invitation to use the British ports," and he urged that for the British Government to tolerate the Confederate agents while they were carrying on their avowedly hostile purposes against the United States could not be called neutrality.

In March, 1864, Lord Russell asked Lord Lyons to convey to Davis in a spirit of neutrality and impartiality a protest against the efforts of the agents of the "so-called" Confederate States to build or purchase war vessels in British dominions for use against the United States—stating that they gave the United States just cause for serious complaint, even if the vessels were armed out of port.[17] He further stated that even if it should be difficult to prove in a court of law that the parties procuring the building of these vessels were Confederate agents, nevertheless it was so undersood everywhere, and the British were satisfied that Davis would not deny it.[18] There were no regular diplomatic or consular agents near Richmond, and Lord Lyons (April 1) by permission of the United States Government sent Russell's protest to Richmond by special messenger. Davis replied (April 6) through Burton N. Harrison, his private secretary, protesting against the term "so-called," stating that the British plea of neutrality was clearly contradicted by British action in favor of the United States, and refusing to notice Russell's argument upon a question which was still before the highest courts of England.[19]

[17] Despatches of Mason, March 16, 1864.
[18] Despatches of Adams to Seward, No. 596, Feb. 12, 1864. Enclosure.
[19] Frank Moore: The Rebellion Record (N. Y., 1861-65, 8 Vols), Vol. VIII, p. 513, et seq. Mrs. Davis: Jefferson Davis, Vol. II, Chap. 48.

A few days later Benjamin instructed Mason that he could use his own discretion about going to London, in case he thought his presence would be useful there.[20] Mason had already been going to London to help " keep the public mind awake," to combat the anti-slavery sentiments of his friends, to organize Southern societies, and to communicate to Lord Robert Cecil information which he might use in combating the Government.[21] He was feeling the pulse of the opposition and of public opinion, but he could expect nothing from the British Government unless Grant should be driven from before the gates of Richmond.[22]

At the beginning of 1864 the vigilance and protests of the United States officials in France had caused the French Government to notify the builders that vessels for the Confederacy must not leave, and Arman saw that his only opportunity was to make a fictitious sale and have the vessels delivered to the Confederacy on the ocean. Bullock, feeling that he had been deceived, refused to agree to Arman's plan. Maury returned to the Confederacy (February) to report the failure to get out vessels from either France or England. It was a painful disappointment.[23] Mason wrote that there was no excuse for the defeat in France where the Confederate agents had a right

[20] Instr. to Mason, April 18, 1864.

[21] Despatches of Mason, No. 1, Paris, Jan. 25; No. 2, Paris, Feb. 8; No. 3, London, Feb. 18; No. 4, London, Feb. 18; No. 5, March 11, 1863.

[22] On June 22, 1864 (Instr. to Mason, No. 36), Benjamin wrote that the British action regarding the *Tuscaloosa* was an " outrage."

[23] Despatches of Mason, No. 3, London, Feb. 18, 1864.

to expect better results.[24] A month later he said that there was no more hope from France than from Austria, notwithstanding Napoleon's mysterious policy and his "fairest professions sedulously made." Again in July he wrote: "We have been duped by that power and worse." Bullock stated that in future it would be necessary to be very cautious in dealing with France. Perhaps Napoleon had expected Confederate victory, or contemplated an alliance which would give him an opportunity to allow the vessels to go, but he finally found it necessary to discountenance any arrangement which would offend the United States. Bullock had finally agreed to the fictitious sale of the corvette to a Denmark banker, to be delivered to the Confederacy on the sea, but Arman sold them outright, claiming that he did so by the order of Napoleon. The two Bordeaux corvettes and the ram were sold to Prussia. The builder at Nantes declared that he would deliver the other two corvettes at sea but Slidell was not confident. On June 2, in a letter stating that ex-Senator Gwin with a recommendation from Napoleon was on his way to colonize Sonora with persons of Southern birth and proclivities, Slidell advised that no further attempt be made at that time to fit out a navy in Europe—but he said that the *Confederacy would need a navy at the close of the war*.[25] Napoleon still studied the United States map, but he ceased to see Slidell, except occasionally at the races.

Of the prospective navy only one vessel was ever

[24] Despatches of Mason, No. 5, March 16, 1864. Ibid., No. 7, Paris, April 12, 1864. Ibid., No. 11 July 8, 1864.
[25] Despatches of Slidell, June 2, 1864.

delivered to the Confederates. About the last of January, 1865, the ram *Stoerkodder*, which Arman pretended to have sold to Denmark, sailed from Bordeaux. She changed her name to *Olinde* on the French coast, discharged her Danish crew, and taking on arms, sailed to Spain as the *Stonewall*. France declined to meddle with the vessel after it reached Spain. Commodore Craven, of the United States navy, arrived to prevent its escape but he mysteriously failed. The *Stonewall* escaped to Nassau and finally reached Havana, where it was sold for $16,000, though the captain-general was willing to make the contract read $100,000. The war had then ended and it was too late to attempt to break the blockade. Bigelow afterwards instituted suit against Arman for money received from Confederate agents, but the claim was rejected.

The failure to get out vessels in France was a blow from an unexpected quarter.[26] It disappointed both Davis and Benjamin who seem already to have had grave doubts of the good faith of Napoleon. Davis while walking through the capitol square with some Richmond ladies said: " We have no friends abroad."[27] Benjamin ceasing to put his faith in foreign powers and expressing expectation of an early victory without them said (April 18): " It has been, perhaps, fortunate for us, notwithstanding the awful price paid in blood . . . that European powers have remained so inconceivably blind to their own interests in this trouble. The end is seen to be approaching and we . . . shall have no favor to reciprocate, but many

[26] Instr. to Mason, April 16, 1864.
[27] J. B. Jones: Diary, March 21, 1864.

wrongs to forget—some, perhaps, for which to ask
for redress." In September, 1864, Benjamin furnished Slidell with a long catalogue of acts of the
French Government—in France, in the Confederacy
and on the Mexican border—which he said had been
injurious to the Confederate States.[28] He stated that
England had scarcely disguised her hostility, but that
the Emperor had obscured his under profuse professions of friendship. He decided, however, to defer
complaints against the French Government until a
more favorable season. There were rumors of prospective French aid until the visions of both the Confederacy and Napoleon vanished in the fall of Richmond. But there was no longer a cordial feeling
toward the Emperor, and Davis, while travelling
through Europe after the war, refused to call upon
him.[29]

[28] Instr. to Slidell, Sept. 20, 1864.
[29] J. W. Daniel: Jefferson Davis, p. 45.

CHAPTER X

CONFEDERATE OPERATIONS FROM CANADA

The plans in the British Parliament had failed; the British war vessels kept a close watch at the mouth of the Mersey to prevent the escape of Confederate vessels; Spain would not act; and France, owing to the vigilance of the United States officials, had become more careful than had been anticipated, leaving doubt as to whether a Confederate navy would be allowed to sail even if it were secretly built in European ports. The decrease of Confederate opportunities in Europe, together with the desire to embarrass the United States Government, and to create national complications, caused the Confederates to turn to Canada as a base of operations.

The Richmond authorities in making their plans placed much reliance upon the disaffection (against the Lincoln administration) which existed in portions of the North, and which found expression in the organization of the Knights of the Golden Circle and the Sons of Liberty. Some even expected a counter-revolution. The West, at the beginning of the war, had been much excited as to the Confederate policy on the waters of the Mississippi. On February 25, 1861, the Confederate Congress had passed an act for free navigation of that river. In January, 1863, Foote, in the Confederate Congress, offered a resolution tempting the Northwest to make peace. A few days later he stated that if Indiana and Illinois should recede from the war and aid the Confederacy he would be willing to furnish them an army for protection against Lincoln. A month later it was stated in Richmond that a gentleman from the Northwest declared that Ohio, Kentucky and Illinois would secede and form a new confederacy, or join the South. Though this was not reliable, the people began to discuss whether Virginia would be willing to take back her " erring children of the Northwest," and whether the cotton states would oppose such an accession.[1] In March, it was suggested that conscription in the North might cause a new civil war that would result in giving aid and comfort to the Confederacy. In the following June, Mr. Vallandigham of Ohio, whom Lincoln had banished to the Confederacy for an intemperate speech in Mount Vernon, Ohio, was in Richmond, and told Ould that, if the Confederacy could only hold out for the year, the peace party of the North would sweep the Lincoln dynasty out of existence. In September, J. C. Jones asked Davis for permission to run the blockade to confer with Secretary Bates of Lincoln's Cabinet on terms of peace by assuring the United States that none of the Northwestern states would be admitted to the Southern Confederacy.[2] In February, 1864, one of Morgan's secret agents, who had spent several months in the North, doubted whether Lincoln would be able to recruit the army by a draft, and stated that there was a perfect organization all over the North for a revolu-

[1] J. B. Jones: Diary, Jan. 24 and 27, Feb. 14, March 3, June 22, 1863.
[2] Ibid., Sept. 10, 1863.

tion, and for the expulsion or death of the aboli-
tionists.[3]

As early as February, 1863, Mr. Mallory had favored
an expedition against Johnson's Island for the purpose of releasing Confederate prisoners. Davis and
other members of the Cabinet, fearing complications
with England, opposed the expedition, but it was
finally arranged. The plans, however, miscarried.
In November, 1863, Lord Monck, Governor-General
of Canada, telegraphed Lord Lyons at Washington
that there was a rumor of a Confederate plot to capture
steamers on Lake Erie, release Confederate prisoners,
and then to invade the United States by an attack
upon Buffalo. On the night of November 11, Lyons
notified Seward, and a close watch being kept along
the frontier by both Canada and the United States, the
Confederates made no attempt to execute the plot.
Lieutenant Minor soon returned from Canada and
stated that his contemplated expedition had failed on
account of the gratuitous action of Lord Lyons.[4]

Notwithstanding the close watch kept by Lord
Monck, the United States Government in 1864 expressed much anxiety concerning the large number
of Confederates in Canada and the suspicious-looking
vessels in Canadian waters. Seward had been protesting vigorously against the British policy, and there
was a widespread belief in the United States that the
Confederates received assistance which the British

[3] J. B. Jones: Diary, Feb. 22, 1864.
[4] Lieut. Minor's letter of Feb. 2, 1864. In Naval War
Records, Series 1, Vol. II, No. 36, House Docs., Vol. XLI,
54-1, 1895-96.
J. M. Callahan: The Neutrality of the American Lakes
and Anglo-American Relations, pp. 145-46.

Government could have prevented. With the rise of controversies, the Confederates contemplated the contingency of an Anglo-American war which would embarrass the United States and aid the cause of secession. In April, 1864, Seward said: " We must finish the Civil War soon or we shall get into a war with England." Two months later he declared that British sympathy was clearly with the South.

In February, 1864, the Confederates expected to gain some advantage from the *Chesapeake* affair. On December 5, 1863, J. C. Braine and H. A. Parr, with twelve equipped men, boarded the United States steamer *Chesapeake*, leaving New York for Portland. They pretended that they were passengers for Portland. On December 8, while on the high seas, they captured the vessel, after a brief struggle, made prisoners of those on board, and sailed to the bay of Fundy. Near St. Johns, New Brunswick, the passengers, and most of the crew, were released, and Captain Parker took command. While the *Chesapeake* was receiving coal from a British vessel in Sambro harbor, Nova Scotia, the United States gunboat, *Ella and Annie*, entered the harbor and seized her; but, after reaching the sea, orders were received from a Federal officer to deliver her to the British authorities at Halifax. The United States Government requested that the men engaged in capturing the *Chesapeake* on the high seas should be delivered to the United States. Davis and Benjamin decided to assume responsibility for the seizure of the *Chesapeake*, stating that the original conception of the plan was probably by Captain John Parker, alias Locke, a British subject, who had enlisted as a Confederate privateer, and whose vessel had become unseaworthy. They stated that Braine and Parr were Confederate citizens and that they had intended to take the *Chesapeake* through the blockade at Wilmington.[5]

On February 15, Benjamin instructed Hon. J. P. Holcombe to go to Nova Scotia to defend the men and to claim the vessel. In case the authorities refused to give him an official interview, he was to remonstrate firmly and inform them that the Confederacy would hold England responsible. He received $3000 salary, and $5000 for expenses in carrying out his instructions. He was also given $25,000 to secure passage to Bermuda for Confederate prisoners who had escaped to Canada.[6] Holcombe's instructions asked him to insist upon the following points: (1) That citizens of the Confederacy had a right, during the war, to make captures even without a commission, and that while engaged in such enterprises they were neither pirates nor murderers. (2) That the *Chesapeake*, while in a neutral harbor, was beyond the reach of legal recapture, and that voluntary rendition of the vessel gave the United States no right to retain it. (3) That the Richmond admiralty court, and not those of a neutral power, had jurisdiction in determining whether the *Chesapeake* was a good prize of war. (4) That this particular case was not affected by the English prohibition against privateers carrying prizes to English ports, as the vessel went to the English port only to get fuel. (5) That England had recognized the Confederates as belligerents. (6) That if the British authorities had delivered the vessel to the North, they must reimburse the Confederates

[5] Instr. of Benjamin to Holcombe, No. 1, Feb. 15, 1864.
[6] Instr. to Holcombe, No. 2, Feb. 24, 1864.

Holcombe found Confederate sympathizers in Canada; but, in April, the Confederate Government, acknowledging that it had been led into error, disclaimed the seizure of the *Chesapeake*.[7]

In April, 1864, just before Grant began his advance to Richmond, the Confederacy had recognized its perilous condition. Many, both North and South, were weary of war. The Confederate Congress, believing that an organization in the North and West would aid the South, secretly appropriated a million dollars to be used by Confederate agents.[8] In March, Mrs. ———, of Maryland, whose son was in a Federal prison, had already received secret service money, and had gone to Canada on some enterprise in which she expected aid from Catholic priests and nuns.[9] On April 27, Jefferson Davis sent Jacob Thompson and C. C. Clay as special agents to Canada to carry out instructions [10] received orally, by which that country was to be made the base for striking the United States in the back.[11] Thompson, on April 28, received bills of exchange for $900,000.

A subsequent report of Thompson to Benjamin (from

[7] Instr. to Holcombe, April 20, 1864.
[8] See N. Y. Herald, July 28, 1872.
[9] J. B. Jones: Diary, March 22, 1864.
[10] Their credentials are in Confed. " Diplomatic and Consular Commissions." On April 30, Benjamin wrote Slidell: " We have sent Jacob Thompson of Mississippi, and Clement C. Clay of Alabama, to Canada on secret service in the hope of aiding the disruption between the Eastern and Western States in the approaching election at the North. It is supposed that much good can be done by the purchase of some of the principal presses, especially in the Northwest." [Confed. " Dip. Cor., France."]
[11] Benjamin to Thompson, April 28, 1864.

Toronto, December 3, 1864) indicates the nature of his mission. By conferences with disaffected men, some of whom hoped that without war the South would soon consent to reconstruction, Thompson encouraged the organization of an insurrection in the North; he advised with Colonel Martin in regard to burning New York City, and with Captain C. H. Cole, who made a tour of the lakes, studying forts, channels and people preparatory to plans for the release of Confederate prisoners and the inauguration of operations in which the prisoners were expected to assist; he aided a plot undertaken by J. Y. Beall for the capture of lake steamers. By Benjamin's instructions, he urged the people of the North to convert their paper into gold and withdraw it from the market. John Porterfield of Nashville was sent to New York with $100,000 to use in purchasing and exporting gold.[12]

On July 9, Thompson wrote Benjamin from Windsor: " We have sixty escaped prisoners who are ready for any enterprise." He said that nothing could be done in the Eastern States, but suggested that the Confederate movements to Kentucky and Missouri would facilitate a movement in the West, where there was much discontent against the Lincoln Government. In a letter sent by Captain Hines, he stated that " the work " would probably not begin before the middle of August and that much caution would be necessary. About the same time there were rumors from Canada that the Confederate agents had machines in Canada which were to be mounted on lake vessels and shipped to destroy Northern cities.

[12] Report of Thompson to Benjamin, Toronto, Dec. 3, 1864.

The coming presidential election in the United States was at this time an absorbing question and the Confederates were reckoning upon some chapter of possible accidents to defeat Lincoln. Some in the North, like Wendell Phillips, the stormy petrel of political troubles, thought Lincoln was going too slowly in his policy. Others who opposed military arrests and the suspension of the habeas corpus, said that he was going too fast and that recent reverses justified efforts to obtain peace. Some had opposed the war policy from the beginning. But the nearly universal desire of the Union party was to renominate Lincoln and to support the campaigns of Grant before Richmond and Sherman before Atlanta. The Baltimore Convention which met June 7, declared in favor of maintaining the integrity of the Union, of ratifying an amendment for emancipation, of constructing a railway to the Pacific, of paying the public debt and of re-electing Lincoln. It opposed any compromise with secession.

Many of the opposition had charged Lincoln with refusing to negotiate for peace on reasonable terms. A. H. Stephens, who desired peace, had been stopped before he reached Fortress Monroe on his way to Washington, and had not been permitted to come within the Union lines because he had refused to state the object of his visit.[13] In July, 1863, Colonel Jacques, a Methodist clergyman, serving in Rosencranz's army, returned from an unofficial visit to Rich-

[13] President Davis to Gov. Vance, Jan. 8, 1864. On Dec. 30, 1863, Vance had urged efforts to secure peace. [Weekly Register (Lynchburg), June 4, 1864.] See also Stephens' "War Between the States," Vol. II, pp. 557-80; and Nicolay and Hay's "Abraham Lincoln," Vol. VII, pp. 369-74.

mond and reported that he had proposals for peace. He said that prominent men in the South were willing to give up slavery, but that they would not take the initiative in a movement for peace. On June 14, 1864, Davis issued a manifesto stating that the Confederacy was willing to negotiate on points which required adjustment and that it desired the United States to cease the war against secession. He stated that if the United States would withdraw its armies, the war would be at an end. On July 8, Col. J. T. Jacques, in company with J. R. Gilmore, a novelist (Edmund Kirke), made an " unofficial visit " to Richmond, where Davis listened (July 17) to their plans of adjustment—to decide, by majority vote, whether there should be union without slavery or disunion with it. Davis pronounced their plan impracticable, said that the Confederate States seceded to get rid of the rule of the majority, and would not consider proposals for peace except on the basis of independence.[14]

About the same time another peace comedy [15] was being enacted on the Canadian boundary. After a recent conference at Niagara Falls between Thompson, Clay and several prominent citizens of the United States, the Confederate agents decided to open a correspondence looking toward negotiations for peace. Holcombe in the following November wrote Benjamin that it was intended that the correspondence should have effect in rendering probable the defeat of Lincoln at the polls.[16] Clay and Holcombe opened

[14] Nicolay and Hay, Vol. IX, p. 212. Benjamin to Mason, Aug. 25, 1864. Register (Lynchburg), Aug. 27, Sept. 24, 1864. Gilmore, Recollections of Lincoln; Atlantic Mo., Vol. 59.

[15] The Index (London), Aug. 4 and 6, 1864.

[16] Despatches of Holcombe (Richmond), Nov. 16, 1864. Also, N. Y. Herald, July 31, 1872.

communication with Greeley, and G. N. Sanders expressed his willingness to go to Washington on a peace mission.[17]   In the early part of July, Greeley wrote Lincoln that Colonel Jewett was at Niagara in communication with Confederates who had power to make negotiations for peace.   Lincoln had no faith in Jewett's story, but replied July 9: " If you can find any person, anywhere, professing to have any proposition of Jefferson Davis in writing, for peace, embracing the restoration of the Union and the abandonment of slavery . . . say to him he may come to me with you."   A few days later he again wrote: " I am disappointed you have not reached here with those commissioners . . . I not only intend a sincere effort for peace, but I intend you shall be a personal witness that it is made."   On July 20, Major John Hay, Lincoln's private secretary, arrived at Niagara with the following note:

" Executive Mansion, Washington, July 18, 1864.

To Whom it may concern:

Any proposition which embraces the restoration of peace, the integrity of the Union, and the abandonment of slavery, and which comes by and with an authority that can control the armies now at war against the United States will be received and be considered by the Executive Government of the United States, and will be met with liberal terms on other substantial and collateral points, and the bearer or bearers thereof shall have safe conduct both ways.

ABRAHAM LINCOLN."

[17] The Weekly Register (Lynchburg), Aug. 6, 1864, p. 214.

It was discovered that the Confederates at Niagara with whom Greeley opened peace negotiations had no authority from the Confederate Government.[18] They were endeavoring to have Lincoln take the initiative in the peace negotiations and to recognize the official status of the Confederate Government. Lincoln considered that the Niagara Confederates were coöperating to aid the anti-administration movement by creating an impression that he was opposed to peace except on the basis of immediate emancipation. On August 24, Lincoln wrote a letter with the intention of sending Henry J. Raymond to propose peace without mention of slavery, but events soon occurred to weaken the extreme peace men and the letter was never used.[19]

Thompson and Clay, by confidential conferences with men from the Northwest, had declared the readiness of the Confederacy to seize Illinois, Indiana and Ohio. Peace meetings were inaugurated at Peoria and other places, but the fire soon diminished and the nerves of the leaders began to relax.[20] The return of Vallandigham in June encouraged the opposition to attempt to defeat Lincoln by the ballot-box. The half-formed project of an insurrection was given up with the hope of success at the polls. The leaders of the anti-administration party had called a national convention on July 4; but after the Baltimore Convention, hoping to receive advantage from some new chapter of accidents, they agreed to postpone the meeting to a more inconspicuous date. Thompson, in his

[18] Instr. to Mason, Aug. 25, 1864.

[19] Nicolay and Hay.

[20] Thompson to Benjamin, Toronto, Dec. 3, 1864.

report to Benjamin, said this postponement interrupted the calculations for a general uprising in the North. The Democratic convention finally met at Chicago, August 29, the day which had been set for a counter-revolution, and nominated McClellan for president. It was a time of depression and gloom. The terrible fighting in the Wilderness, the horrible slaughter at Cold Harbor, the Confederate raid into Maryland had shocked and depressed the country. Early, defiant, stormed up the Shenandoah; Sherman was delayed at Kenesaw; Chase, tired of providing the funds while others controlled the expenditures, had resigned from the Cabinet, and seemed to see the mirage of the presidency; the Wade-Davis manifesto had been issued in August and the Democrats, attacking the administration and hoping to change the Government, pronounced the war a failure. Mason, also from London, wrote: " I do not see how the war can be carried on when . . . people have no stomachs for the fight." [21]

The Confederates had recently received fresh proof that Europe would not take any action, and Mason saw nothing to do but await events, hoping that the presidential election and the anti-war feeling in the United States, together with the distress in England, would favor the South. In the last week in May, Lindsay had had a conversation with Palmerston to endeavor to conciliate the British Government's support on a resolution for joint mediation in the American war. He wrote Mason that Palmerston favored his resolution, but thought it best to wait. At the

[21] Despatches of Mason, No. 13, Paris, Sept. 29, 1864.

suggestion of Lindsay, Palmerston said he would be willing to see Mason and hear his views if he were in London.[22] Mason did not feel at liberty to approach the British Government without some intimation of its disposition to enter into official relation; but, urged by Lindsay, he went to London, expecting to see Palmerston in case he should be invited. He found that only the news of a great victory against Grant before Richmond would give any hope that the ministry would support Lindsay's resolution.[23] Russell remarked that Adams still spoke confidently. On July 8, however, Mason, in a note to Benjamin, stating that new Confederate successes might cause English public opinion to compel the Government to act, said: " Palmerston has sent me a note that he desires to see me." [24] Benjamin had already (July 12), in a note advising occasional conferences with Lindsay, favored the proposed interview and instructed Lindsay to meet Palmerston's advances with courteous but lofty bearing." [25]

On July 14, Palmerston received Mason and Lindsay in a friendly manner at his home. He asked Mason his opinion of the nature and probable length of the war; the probable results of the presidential election upon it; whether the United States would be as much opposed to intervention as formerly, and what prospects the South had. Mason, in his reply, stated that the North was strongly against a continuation of the war and indicated that the United States

[22] Despatches from Mason, No. 8, Paris, June 1, 1864.
[23] Ibid., No. 9, London, June 9, 1864.
[24] Ibid., No. 11, July 8, 1864.
[25] Instr. to Mason, No. 37, July 12, 1864.

would be forced to cease hostilities and make peace. He did not doubt the final success of the Confederacy. Though he did not urge recognition, he suggested that recognition alone by any European power would stop the war. Palmerston, though friendly, did not define his policy for the future.[26] Lindsay, unable to conciliate the ministry, abandoned his resolution.[27] On July 25, Palmerston, in reply to Lindsay in the House of Commons, said that the Government lamented the sacrifice of life and property in America and the distress in England, but in the existing state of affairs there would be no advantage in entering into concert with European powers to propose mediation.[28] Mason soon returned to Paris, from whence he wrote,[29] a few weeks later, that he might be able to do some good at Frankfort by efforts to prevent emigration to the United States and aid a catastrophe to United States securities. Palmerston had stated that recognition would be of no value unless England should intervene by raising the blockade, but Benjamin said that recognition from whatever quarter would end the war and that nothing else would. He insisted the Confederacy did not seek intervention, but he expected nothing from England except a "policy dictated by the United States." As Benjamin was writing, Davis was on a tour through Mississippi, Alabama and Georgia endeavoring to dispel increasing disaffection

[26] Despatches of Mason, July, 1864. Duplicate copy in Mason's MS. Record Book. Ibid., No. 14, Nov. 10.

[27] Ibid., No. 12, Aug. 4, 1864.

[28] 176 Parl. Debates. Also, Despatches of Mason, No. 12, London, Aug. 4, 1864.

[29] Despatches of Mason, No. 14, Nov. 10, 1864.

for the Confederacy. But Benjamin wrote: " There is no reason for despondency." [30]

From the moment of the Chicago convention, the stars in their courses seemed to fight against both the Confederacy and the Chicago platform. During a flow of rhetoric and the march of torchlight processions, following the nominations, Hood was preparing to evacuate Atlanta. The Union success at Mobile knocked the second plank out of the platform. McClellan seemed to see the poison of death in the platform and his letter of acceptance he practically repudiated part of it and disappointed the Confederates in their expectation of an early end of the attempts to preserve the Union. In September, Napoleon shook hands with Slidell at the races, and agreed with him that McClellan's letter was disappointing. Slidell said the war would probably continue till a revolution broke out in the North. As the campaign proceeded, the thunder of great guns announced new Union victories. Peace did not appear so far distant, but it was the peace of reunion.

The crisis on the lakes came September 19, 1864, when the steamer *Philo Parsons*, running between Detroit and Sandusky, was captured by Confederates who had boarded her as passengers. The Confederate flag was unfurled and the vessel started on her way to Sandusky to capture the armed steamer *Michigan*, but the design failed and the *Parsons* was taken back to

[30] Instr. to Mason, Sept. 2, 1864. The Confederate Congress prepared a manifesto (July) which Mason, Slidell and Mann, in November, decided to engross and present to the principal European powers. [Despatches of Mason, No. 14, Nov. 10, 1864.]

the Detroit river and left at Sandwich in a sinking condition.[31] Mr. Seward had just prepared a statement of the *Parsons* affair for the British Government when the news arrived at Washington that twenty-five desperate men had plundered St. Albans, Vermont, and escaped on stolen horses into Canada.[32] Excitement in the United States followed. It was felt that Canada was responsible for her Confederate guests, and that their bad conduct might endanger the peace with Canada. This feeling was not mollified by the declaration of Lieutenant Bennett H. Young, commander of the St. Albans raiders, that he went to Canada as a commissioned officer in the provisional army of the Confederate States [33] and that he had violated no law of Canada. False reports continued to alarm the people and to add to the excitement which naturally existed upon the eve of a great presidential election. On Sunday, October 30, church

[31] Thompson to Benjamin, Dec. 3, 1864.

[32] Seward to Adams (19 Instr., Great Brit.), No. 1136, Oct. 24, 1864.

[33] The St. Albans raiders were afterwards tried in the Canadian courts. Mason, learning that Lieutenant Young had acted under orders of war, took steps to appeal his case to the courts of England in case it should be necessary. [Despatches of Mason, No. 15, Dec. 16, 1864.] In December Sanders wrote from Montreal to Richmond asking for copies of orders showing that the Vermont raid was authorized by the Confederate Secretary of War. [J. B. Jones: Diary, Dec. 15, 1864.] It appears that Thompson had no knowledge that the raid was contemplated, but Sanders in his testimony before the court at Montreal stated that Young acted under the instructions of Clay. Davis issued a proclamation assuming Confederate responsibility for Young's raid [N. Y. Times, Jan. 1, 1865], and Seddon, the Confederate Secretary of War, said that the raid was authorized by instructions of June 16, 1864. [N. Y. Times, Feb. 19, 1865.]

services at Detroit were disturbed over the report from Toronto that one hundred Confederates had left that place for the purpose of raiding Detroit. The State Department at Washington received information that there was a conspiracy to fire all the principal cities in the North on election day, and, on that day, General Butler and General J. R. Hawley, as a precautionary measure, were placed upon lake steamers ready for service at any point in case Confederate sympathizers should attempt to execute any of the reported plots. But no Confederate attempts were made.

After the people had so strongly supported Lincoln at the polls, the Confederacy saw its approaching doom—unless the United States should become involved in foreign difficulties. The Sons of Liberty had been demoralized by the election. Thompson, holding letters from prominent Northern men, and with much money still unused, was not anxious to continue his operations from Canada. " The bane and curse of carrying out anything in this country," said he, " is the surveillance under which we act. Detectives stand at every corner." [84] Holcombe, however, advised further encouragement of disaffection in the North. In a letter to Benjamin dated at Richmond, November 16, he said: " The Northwest is not . . . ready for a revolution. But it is fermenting with the passions out of which revolutions have been

[84] Report of Thompson to Benjamin, Toronto, Dec. 3, 1864. [Received by Benjamin on Feb. 13, 1865.] Published in the N. Y. Herald of July 25, 1872, and in Naval War Records, 1°, Vol. III, No. 379, p. 714. [House Doc., Vol. LXXIII, 54-1.]

created. In Illinois, Indiana . . . a majority are hostile to the present administration . . . it would be a fatal mistake, in my opinion, to abandon all effort to separate this section from the United States because no results have as yet been achieved commensurate with our expectations. . . . We should employ money and talent without stint to give this brooding resentment the proportions of anarchy and civil strife. Let us preserve our communication with our friends in the North, . . . introduce arms . . . gradually and cautiously . . . subsidize leading presses. . . . With arms, leaders and an opportunity, we could strike a deadly blow." [35] Benjamin did not recall Thompson until March 2, 1865. [36]

Confederate operations from Canada caused excited debates in the United States Congress in December, and for a while affairs seemed to be drifting toward an Anglo-American war. The English Parliament became alarmed at the proceedings in the American Congress, but Palmerston, seeking to avoid angry debate (February 11), said: " We cannot deny that things did take place of which the United States were justly entitled to complain." The London *Times* became friendlier in its tone toward the United States, and said that the Confederacy was seeking to involve England in the war. The Richmond *Dispatch*, in reply, said that England, seeking her own prosperity, was responsible for the anti-slavery feeling in the North, for secession, and " for the present calamities of this continent," but that her precarious hold on Canada was indicative of the coming day of retribution when

[35] Holcombe to Benjamin, Richmond, Nov. 16, 1864.
[36] See N. Y. Herald, July 24, 1872.

that province would be " tied like a tinpail to the tail of New England." [87]

On February 13, Russell informed Mason, Slidell and Mann by a note, that the Confederates, by not respecting the British neutrality, were attempting to involve England in a war in which she had declared her intentions to take no part. Referring to the seizure of the *Philo Parsons*, the plan to capture the *Michigan*, and the raid into Vermont, he stated that the " so-called Confederate States," by assuming responsibility for such acts and claiming them to be belligerent operations, showed " a gross disregard of her Majesty's character as a neutral power, and the desire to involve her Majesty in hostilities with a coterminous power with which Great Britain is at peace." In conclusion, he said: " I trust you will feel yourselves authorized to promise that such practice shall cease, and shall be entirely abandoned for the future." [88]

[87] Richmond Dispatch, Jan. 14 and 18, and Feb. 24, 1865.

[88] MS. at U. S. Dept. of State: Vol. 88 Despatches, Great Brit. Enclosure in Russell to Adams, Feb. 15, and in Adams to Seward, Feb. 16, 1865.

CHAPTER XI

Near the close of 1864 two Confederate officials at Richmond apprehensive of an approaching crisis were closeted in deep deliberation. One of them had been suffering for days with neuralgia, and once there had been rumors over the city that he was dead; but, still bearing evidences of recent illness, he had returned to his laborious work of reading letters of complaint, examining monotonous detail, and deciding on applications for positions. The other was the picture of robust health—though in his face, over which there usually played a pleasant smile, could now be seen the worry of those troubled times. Both had been hearing the old dull sullen sounds of bombs down the river for weeks and months, and now they were informed that Lee's army was becoming depleted by desertions; that the nitre and mining companies were ceasing operations; that Hood was defeated; that Sherman had seized Savannah; and that persons in high places were aiding Federals to obtain information. They saw the people feeding upon poor supplies and condemning the speculators. The croakers were made gloomier by dismal rain and fogs. Some of the states refused to obey the Richmond authorities and were threatening to make peace with the United States, or to establish a counter revolution.[1] The soldiers and clerks were complaining that rich property holders were exempt from military service. Military officers and disaffected congressmen were quarrelling with the administration. Lee's shelterless men were shivering over feeble fires before Richmond, and pulling the trigger with frozen fingers; and Lee himself was despondent.

In all attempts to secure European recognition or aid by offer of commercial advantages or alliance, or by international complications, the Confederacy had failed; and, in its plans to raise a navy in French ports, it had been duped by Napoleon.[2] Notwith-

[1] Governor Brown of Georgia refused to obey the Confederate authorities. The conditions in North Carolina were such that Governor Z. B. Vance urged Davis (Dec. 30, 1863) to send envoys to Washington to endeavor to bring the war to an end. Davis in his reply expressed the fear that some of the people of North Carolina would inaugurate a movement to give aid and comfort to the Union, and that there would be a civil war in that State. He hoped that Vance, by not too long delaying action for conciliating men suspected of disloyalty to the Confederacy, would make it unnecessary to use "physical force to suppress treason." [South. Hist. Society Papers, Vol. XIV, p. 412. Jefferson Davis to Z. B. Vance, Jan. 8, 1864.]

[2] Davis in his message of November said that the policy of European nations in refusing recognition discriminated unfairly in favor of the United States, and that it was charitable to say that they were indifferent. Referring to the impossibility of peace without independence he said: "The common judgment of history will be unable to absolve the neutral nations of Europe from a share in the moral responsibility for the myriads of human lives unnecessarily sacrificed." On November 25, Earl Russell—in a communication acknowledging a joint note of Slidell, Mason and Mann, which had as an inclosure the manifesto of the Confederate Congress—lamented the "protracted nature of the struggle

standing the immense war debt which had been piling
up, the United States had the confidence of foreign powers, and they feared to oppose her while the
Confederacy was being crushed, and while the
clauses of Lincoln's message contained the Monroe
doctrine coiled up for a spring. Very few now asserted the political power of cotton stored in Con-

between the Northern and Southern States of the formerly
United States of North America," and said that Great
Britain since 1783 had remained connected by friendly relations with both the Northern and Southern States, and that
her policy was strict neutrality. [Despatches of Mason, No.
15, Dec. 16, 1864.] Some thought that there was a relaxa-
tion in Russell's tone, but Mason attached no importance
to the reply. In December some hoped that complications
might arise over the seizure of the Confederate cruiser
Florida in Brazilian waters [Mason to Benjamin, Nov. 10,
1864], and some still looked across the Atlantic to see aid
brought from the East in ships, but Europe spoke not.
The editor of the Richmond Examiner said that a Confederate commission to Brazil might do more service than the
Erlanger loan would ever be able to do. He stated that if
Brazil should demand redress and the United States should
laugh at her that nothing would be more natural than a
Confederate-Brazilian alliance which might also include Mexico and "erect a barrier against the encroachments of the
Hoosier." [Richmond Examiner, Dec. 8, 1864.] Some proposed to enter into colonial or other subordinate relations
with European nations. The Sentinel counselled the Confederate States to resume their places as the colonies of
England, France and Spain—like prodigal sons, or like
young birds that had broken their shells too soon. This
would have been a recantation of the Declaration of Independence in order to escape defeat in a nearly lost cause.
[J. B. Jones: Diary, Dec. 15, 1864.] The same paper shortly
afterwards advised that in order to secure recognition or
intervention—and the good opinion of mankind—that the
Confederacy should inform Europe of its readiness to abolish
slavery. The Examiner (Dec. 30, 1864) preferred to put
military affairs in a really responsible hand, give him *carte
blanche* and *carte noire* and let Europe alone.

federate warehouses, or doubted that the crisis in the English "cotton famine" was over.[3] It was the darkest period in the Confederacy, and President Davis and Secretary Benjamin, seeing a coming cataclysm in which the Confederacy might be swept to its doom, began to feel convinced that intervention by European powers was the only hope —and they resolved to play their last card by sacrificing slavery, as a war exigency, for success against the United States.

It had often been suggested that Europe was prejudiced against the Confederacy chiefly on account of the question of slavery. Mason so interpreted one of Earl Russell's speeches in the House of

---

[3] George McHenry, in a paper on "The Approaching Cotton Crisis" (Dec. 31) endeavored to prove that, notwithstanding the general belief on both sides of the Atlantic, the cotton famine was not over, and the calamity was still in store. On January 5, 1865, the Committee of Ways and Means (F. S. Lyon, Chairman) passed a resolution asking McHenry to furnish such information as he had in his possession relating to "cotton products, cotton trade, and its importance to the commerce of the world." McHenry replied January 8. His belief in 1861 had been that cotton was not then king, and now, although he found himself almost alone, he asserted its political power—if the Confederate authorities would take the proper steps. He stated that a supply of good cotton would, after the lapse of a few months, be of vital importance to England, and endeavored to show that 90 per cent of all the cotton yarns and goods manufactured in England were from southern cotton, the China and Indian cotton being of a damaged or inferior quality. He said that the time was at hand when the British cotton manufacturers would not remain quiet if they were deprived of the raw material to make the fabrics for which there was a demand—that unless the mills obtained a full supply of American cotton there would be a revolution in the British isles. He considered it a mistake to attribute

Lords (March 23, 1863), in which, while urging the present duty of England to stand still, he had stated that if interference should be necessary in the future it would be " in the cause of liberty and to promote the freedom of mankind." Mason saw a double meaning in these words and intimated that Russell was not disposed to recognize a state with slavery. Even the most ardent friends of the Confederacy were opposed to its system of labor. In November, 1862, while Mason was taking dinner with Lord Donnoughmore, a warm Confederate sympathizer, the latter informed him that Palmerston would doubtless not enter into any treaty with the Confederacy unless it should agree not to permit the African slave trade. Mason was surprised, and still

the previous distress in the English manufacturing districts to a cotton famine. He stated that there were large stocks of cotton and cotton goods in England when the war began— enough for three years—and that these goods had been sold at from two to five times the regular prices, and that the supply from the Confederacy had never been fully shut off. He believed that the cotton crisis had been staved off only by the steady arrivals of 4000 bales of American cotton per week, together with that which had been received in the United States. It was to this that he attributed the fact that the neutral powers had been passive viewers of the American conflict. He declared that the American slavery question had not in any degree influenced the course of the rulers of England—that they knew that cotton could not be cultivated by free negro labor and that they would not oppose the South in obtaining necessary help even from Africa. According to his view, England would already have been prepared to offer recognition if the export of cotton from the Confederacy had been prohibited a year before. He expected the famine sometime during 1865, and said, " If recognition or mediation could only be brought about in time to permit of a good cotton planting in 1865, the finances of the South would soon be righted.

more so when Fitzgerald, another member of Parliament, coincided. The Confederate constitution forbade the opening of the slave trade, but Benjamin stated that the Confederacy could not make a treaty on the subject.[4] He informed Mason that after all it was not wise to impose restraints on men for the future, and requested him, in case England should insist on this subject, to refer the matter back to Richmond.[5] In June, 1863, De Leon wrote Benjamin that the prejudice against slavery was so great that the Confederate reasons and arguments were powerless.[6] M. de Lesseps said that France could not acknowledge the Confederacy without some promise of emancipation. De Leon recommended that the Richmond Government should withdraw the commissioners from Europe, stand on its dignity and enlighten public opinion. In January, 1864, Mann informed Benjamin that the Southern Independence association was against "our cherished institution" and had desired kindly to show him that recognition must lead to the gradual abolition of slavery.[7] Mason at the same time wrote that he found it "but vain to combat their sentiment"—though, still expecting to convert them, he told them that the film would fall from their eyes in time.[8] Mr. Spence, who wrote a book and many articles in favor of the South, lost a prominent position under the Confederate Government because his published opinions

[4] Instr. to Mason, No. 14, Feb. 6, 1863.
[5] Ibid., No. 13 (and circular), Jan. 15, 1863.
[6] De Leon to Benjamin, June 19, 1863.
[7] Mann to Benjamin, London, Jan. 24, 1864.
[8] Despatches of Mason, No. 1, Paris, Jan. 25, 1864. [Received at Richmond on April 19.]

were unfavorable to the Confederate institution of slavery.

Many prominent men in the Confederacy had favored the abolition of slavery. Others had proposed drafting slaves into the army. In 1862 John T. Pickett favored emancipation. After the defeat at Gettysburg and Vicksburg in 1863, E. S. Dargon, a member of Congress said that he would agree to abolish slavery in order to obtain intervention.[9] In August of the same year B. H. Micon of Florida proposed that slaves be drafted into the army to fight for their masters. Benjamin in his reply stated the following difficulties: (1) Slaves as property would cost the Confederacy $2000 each. (2) If the Government should hire them they would cost $30 per month, and only $11 per month were paid for white men. (3) The banding together of negro men might be an unsafe experiment, giving facilities for desertion. (4) The males were needed in the mines, on fortifications, and in other fields of labor.[10] The subject was frequently discussed at that time. Lee, in the fall of 1864, recommended the employment of negroes as soldiers, and a few months later he stated to the Senate committee that slaves should have their liberty if put in the field to fight.[11] In the early part of the war Davis refused to respond to the intimations that England or France might recognize the Confederacy without slavery. The constitution gave him no power to treat with foreign nations on the

[9] J. B. Jones: Diary, July 31, 1863.
[10] Confed. " Domestic Letters," Aug. 18, 1863.
[11] H. A. White: R. E. Lee and the Southern Confederacy, N. Y., 1897.

subject of slavery. At last, however, he was persuaded to favor gradual emancipation, and reluctantly he recommended the arming of the slaves.[12] In November, 1864, after Davis's recommendation, the Confederate Congress began a several months' debate upon the proposition for arming and emancipating a part of the slaves.[13] Some declared it was Benjamin's idea for foreign effect, and the press at first strongly opposed it.[14] Howell Cobb thought it would be better to " concede the demands of England and France for the emancipation of the slaves and to enlist them afterwards." In December and January some of the newspapers counselled the Government to propose to Europe that the Confederacy should abolish slavery in order to obtain recognition and ships to break the blockade, but the majority of the leaders did not favor such a course.

In the fall of 1864 Benjamin realized even more fully than Davis that desperate measures and new forces were necessary to secure Confederate success. He informed Davis that future negotiations with Europe must be on the basis of emancipation and the Government seizure of cotton to purchase ships by which to break the blockade. Davis hesitated to act in a matter so clearly extra-constitutional, stating that the Confederate constitution was his supreme court of law. But Benjamin justified his proposition as a war measure; he believed that by emancipa-

[12] J. W. Daniels: Jefferson Davis, p. 59.
[13] Seward's Diary, Nov. 21 and Dec. 17, 1864. Richmond Observer, Dec., 1864. Seward to Adams, No. 1193, Dec. 17, 1864, and No. 1298, March 13, 1865. [Instr. Great Brit., Vols. XIX and XX.]
[14] J. B. Jones: Diary, Nov. 8, 1864.

tion, and a promise to ship cotton, the recognition of France and perhaps of England might be obtained; he urged that the only way to get ships and money was by cotton, the only unexhausted resource of the Confederate Government and the people. Mr. Davis was influenced or controlled by few men, but he had entire confidence in Mr. Benjamin. After careful deliberation, without appealing to Congress, and independent of that body, he finally agreed to accept the last and only hope of an almost expiring Confederacy, trusting that if successful the plan would gradually receive the support of Congress and the states.

In determining what agencies to use in order to carry out this new policy, Benjamin proposed the selection of some one man of sound judgment who would be ready and able to meet contingencies as they might arise. For several reasons it was not considered expedient to work through Mason and Slidell alone. It was seen that they might not be enthusiastic with the new policy, and that it would be better to send some one from Richmond pledged to the new scheme, and with power to act independently of diplomatic agents, or even to dismiss them if necessary. The blockade was very stringent and communication was very hazardous. Speedy action was necessary. There was no time to refer questions back to Richmond. Benjamin opposed sending more than one prominent man on account of the danger of publicity, and of jars and quarrels.

The new plans were domestic dynamite, and it was considered necessary to guard against exposure until after a diplomatic triumph had secured a navy. This was expected to reconcile the people to the means used to achieve the end. At the same time it was desired to send an agent who had a commanding influence in Congress—one who would prove a link between that body and the executive authorities. Such a man was Duncan F. Kenner of Louisiana, the intimate friend of Benjamin. He was an able man of conservative views, a wealthy sugar planter, representing personally and by his family connections one of the largest slaveholdings in the South, and he was chairman of the committee of ways and means in the House of Representatives. He had been educated in Europe and spoke French. He was asked by Mr. Benjamin to go to Europe with general instructions giving him not only full powers as a commissioner to make treaties and bind the Confederate States to the emancipation of slaves, but also with separate instructions to negotiate for the sale of cotton. These instructions were based upon the principle that the Confederacy was a *de facto* Government, and could take extra-constitutional power if necessary to its preservation. Mr. Kenner had before proposed to offer a motion in Congress authorizing a commission to be sent to Europe to promise emancipation for recognition, but had surrendered his determination at the advice of Davis, who did not yet approve his proposal, and begged him not to make the move at that juncture. He now hesitated to accept powers given neither by Congress nor by the constitution.

But Kenner finally yielded to Mr. Benjamin's representation that it was necessary to ignore the constitution in order to save the Confederacy. He still objected to the form of his credentials, stating that his instructions should be more specific as to the plans of emancipation, but Benjamin prevailed. The power given to Mr. Kenner to *sell cotton* was not diplomatic, nor was it necessarily intended to be a matter of discussion with the European Governments, but only with capitalists. The instructions relating to *this* power were entirely separate and distinct from his credentials as a high commissioner, and were much fuller. They gave him power to sell all the cotton in the Confederacy if necessary, to receive the price thereof, and to invest in vessels and war material. It was not expected that any contract to sell cotton to the capitalists would be completed until after the success of diplomatic negotiations with either England or France, when it was expected that France at any rate would wink at the fitting out of a navy in her ports.[15]

In a letter addressed to Slidell on December 29, Benjamin stated that the Confederacy in a four years' courageous struggle for self-government had really been fighting the battles of England and France; that if the war had been against the United States alone it would have long since ceased, but that in calculating the length of the war the Confederacy had not expected Europe to aid the United States by the abandonment of the rights of neutrals, by closing ports to Confederate prizes, by the seizure of vessels intended for the Confederacy, and by indifference to an unequal fight; that, notwithstanding miscalculations and the afflictions caused by the

[15] From notes of an interview with Gen. J. L. Brent in 1898, and from correspondence with him in 1899.

blockade and devastation, the Confederates were determined never to reunite with the North. At the same time Benjamin mentioned Seward's "One war at a time" policy, and warned Europe against future Northern aggression. Then he approached the main question—were there no terms upon which recognition could be obtained? "Will Europe never recognize us till the United States consent?" If so, he said that it might be necessary to deliberate upon the terms that could be secured from the Federals. But he urged if Europe had objections to recognition not already made known that she should give the Confederacy a chance to meet them—or if it were her purpose to exact terms or conditions before recognition, a frank exposition of that purpose was due to humanity—"for," said Benjamin, "it may enable us to save many lives by consenting to such terms in advance of another year's campaign." On December 30 a copy of this despatch was addressed to Mason with a statement that it would be handed to him by Hon. Duncan F. Kenner, whose verbal communication upon the subject embraced in the despatch should be accepted as reliable, and "as emanating from the department under the instructions of the President."

Kenner was delayed, probably by the increased blockade at Wilmington, and Mason was told that he need not wait his arrival before taking steps toward sounding the European Governments. "Confer with Slidell" continued the instructions, "as to measures best adapted to elicit some decisive response from France and England as to their intentions concerning the war after having freely conversed with Kenner and obtained the information he will convey." [16]

It was intended that Kenner's mission should for the time be kept secret. In such a crisis it is not likely that Benjamin gave out any information except so far as it could not be avoided. On December 29, the Senate, in secret session, among other things asked the President for information as to the finances, the condition of foreign relations and as to whether any aid from abroad was expected or had been sought or proposed. No reply was ever sent to the Senate. The Richmond newspapers, at the beginning of 1865 however, indicate that public opinion was being prepared for the new policy. The *Enquirer* said that the absence of a Confederate declaration of the causes of secession, and of the war, had enabled the United States to say that slavery was the corner-stone; that the thirty years' violent anti-slavery discussion in the United States had led anti-slavery Europe " to think our war is to perpetuate slavery; and that an avowal that slavery would not be permitted to prejudice the question of recognition might not be too late, and might induce recognition or intervention." The *Enquirer* followed the *Sentinel* in agreeing to urge upon its readers a policy of emancipation, if it should be necessary as a means of securing recognition and a guarantee of independence by England and France.[17] The *Sentinel*,

[16] Instr. to Mason, No. 39, Dec. 30, 1864.

[17] An editorial from the Richmond Sentinel concluded with this paragraph: " If France and England will enter into a treaty with these Confederate States, recognizing our nationality and guaranteeing our independence upon the abolition of slavery in all these states, rather than continue the war

which was often quoted as an "official" organ, stated that such a proposition ought to be made to England and France. It despondently spoke of the recent reverses [18] as having done much to prepare the minds of the people for the most extreme sacrifices. It said: "Any sacrifice of opinion and sacrifice of property, any surrender of prejudice, if necessary to the defeat of our enemy, is now the watchword." It favored exhausting every resource, and throwing overboard all the cargo if necessary, to keep afloat the storm-tossed ship of the Confederacy. "Let the Government determine what it needs and what it can use," said the editor, "and if it be our land . . . our negroes . . . it shall have them . . . . Our constitution . . . may not provide for all the exigencies of war; questions may arise . . . . when our best welfare will require of our rulers the exercise of a bold responsibility (as in the purchase of Louisiana) . . . . Statesmen have sometimes to throw themselves upon the intelligence of their countrymen and seek their advantage by irregular means." [19]

On January 25, after having had General Lee at his house for tea the day before, Mr. ——— Lyons, informed Mr. J. B. Jones that as a last resort he was in

we should be prepared to urge the measure upon our readers. We believe such a proposition would be favorably received and acted upon by those nations and it ought to be made to them." Some in the North declared this to be from the pen of Davis, and Seward ordered copies of it to be sent to foreign leaders. [Richmond Dispatch, Jan. 7, 1865.]

[18] This despondent tone is also seen in the Whig of Jan 2, 1865.

[19] Richmond Sentinel, Jan. 2, 1865.

favor of sending out a commission to Europe for aid, on the basis of emancipation, etc. He stated that to use negroes as soldiers in the war would mean emancipation, and he thought that Lee always had been an emancipationist. George D. Prentiss, of the Louisville *Journal*, in the early part of January returned from a month's visit to Richmond and informed the Kentuckians in the United States Congress that the Confederate Congress had conclusively resolved to free and arm the slaves—that 200,000 of them would soon be equipped to fight under promise of liberty and a proprietary interest in the soil.[20]

In January before Kenner sailed for Europe there was much discussion in favor of peace negotiations, and several preliminary unofficial interviews finally resulted in the Hampton Roads conference. Governor Vance of North Carolina, in December, 1863, had urged Davis to communicate with Washington with a view of ending the war. Davis replied that he had already made three such attempts, and that it was Lincoln's policy to grant pardons to the Confederates only after they had emancipated their slaves and sworn allegiance to the United States. Mr. Blair, without any official authority, went from Washington to Richmond, in January, 1865, and urged Davis to take steps looking toward a cessation of hostilities. He stated that Lincoln would receive Confederate commissioners, and that he did not sympathize with the radicals in Congress. He expressed a hope that the pride of the South would

[20] Richmond Dispatch, Jan. 13, 1865. Quotes from Northern papers of Jan. 10.

suffer no shock and the Southern [21] territory would
be extended even to the isthmus of Darien. He proposed: (1) The gradual abolition of slavery by the
State legislatures, (2) The Confederate States to return to the Union with their old rights; (3) The incorporation of the Confederate army with the United
States army in case of a foreign war; (4) The past to
be forgotten.[22] He suggested to Davis that slavery
was doomed even if reunion should be prevented
by foreign intervention, and said that rather than
continue the war to make themselves dependencies
of European potentates, after having abandoned

[21] Jefferson Davis: Confederate Government, Vol. II, pp.
612-15.

[22] The Richmond Enquirer about this time stated that the
Confederacy if it yielded would join the North in applying
the Monroe doctrine from Behring's Straits to the Isthmus
of Darien. There was much talk of the Monroe doctrine in
both Confederate and United States papers. [The Index,
Feb. 9, 1865.] Later the Confederacy desired to remove the
impression that it was the first to propose a peace based
upon foreign aggression as a means of sustaining the Monroe
doctrine. The Index of March 16 quotes from the Owl a
paragraph which doubtless relates to Mr. Kenner's official
instructions on the subject of Blair's mission. The paragraph is as follows: " A gentleman of the highest position
and character, and a member of the Confederate Congress
has just arrived in England, having left the South as late
as the end of January. Enjoying as he does the entire confidence of President Davis, he received prior to his departure
the account of Mr. Blair's mission from Mr. Benjamin, the
Secretary of State at Richmond, who used these words:
' The object of the mission was to assure President Davis
that commissioners would be received at Washington to
open negotiations on the following basis: (1) All questions
in dispute to be left undecided, and considered as open
questions. (2) An armistice to be granted, and a league
offensive and defensive to be made to drive the French out
of Mexico.' "

slavery to escape the embrace of the United States, it would be better for the Confederates to send a Southern army to restore the rights of Mexico. He even suggested that Davis might realize previous Southern dreams, and complete the work of Jefferson, by modelling the Mexican states so as to adapt them to the Union, and by extending the United States to the Isthmus.[23] Blair left Richmond on January 16, on a flag-of-truce boat, and Singleton, a peace democrat from Illinois returned to Richmond on the same boat on some unauthorized mission.

Mr. McMullin in a recent resolution[24] in the Confederate Congress had proposed a selection of peace commissioners, and about the time that Blair reached Richmond there were rumors that the resolution had been passed, and that Orr, Gilmore, Stephens, and twelve others had been selected to meet at Grant's headquarters.[25] On January 14 the *Sentinel*, alluding to a rumor that Mr. Atkins of Tennessee had introduced a resolution before Congress in secret session to open irregular intercourse through commissioners with Lincoln, pronounced it treachery and disloyalty.[26] The article was evidently intended as a criticism of the committee on foreign affairs. The editor of the *Sentinel* was public and private printer of the House, and many considered that his paper was the organ of the administration. Several members of Congress were offended by the evident intention

[23] Rhodes, Vol. III.
[24] On Dec. 16, 1864. Several other peace resolutions were offered on the same day. Printed copies may be seen at the Library of Congress at Washington.
[25] Richmond Dispatch, Jan. 16, 1865.
[26] Ibid., Jan. 18, 1865.

of the article in regard to appointing peace commissioners. On January 17, Lester of Georgia moved to suspend the rules in order to allow him to introduce a resolution stating that the imputations of the article were false. The vote stood 32 to 26, but a two-thirds vote was required, and thus the motion failed. Atkins was willing to have his resolution considered in public, instead of in secret session, and intimated that he was willing to assault the administration if necessary. He considered that the *Sentinel* spoke for the administration. W. R. Smith of Alabama, a member of the committee of foreign affairs was offended because the House refused to allow Lester's resolution. He ceased to attend sessions and prepared to return home, stating that he favored honest efforts to end the carnival of blood; that he believed that this policy was sustained by a volume of Southern sentiment, and that it could not be intimidated by the *Sentinel* nor "the power behind the throne of the *Sentinel*." [27]

Lincoln (January 18) informed Blair on the return of the latter from Richmond, that he was ready to receive any agent informally sent with a view of securing peace to "our one common country." But he said nothing of a joint invasion of Mexico. Blair returned to Richmond a second time (January 21) to inform Davis of his interview with Lincoln. Many in the South were urging peace negotiations, and a few days later Davis decided to appoint Stephens, Hunter and Campbell as peace commissioners. Benjamin, with Lincoln's note to Blair before him, in his instructions to the commissioners proposed

[27] Richmond Dispatch, Jan. 21, 1865.

to say simply that they were empowered to confer "upon the subject to which it relates," but Davis (January 28) changed the instructions so that they authorized a conference "upon the issues of the war and for the purpose of securing peace to the two countries." The commissioners expected to go to Washington, but Seward decided to meet them at Fortress Monroe. Lincoln arrived later, and the Hampton Roads informal conference was held on the *River Queen*, on February 3, between Seward and Lincoln and the Confederate Commissioners.[28] Stephens thought that an arrangement for the invasion of Mexico would be a rational and proper enterprise,[29] but Lincoln informed him that whatever Blair said as to occupying themselves with continental questions until the anger of the contestants should cool "was of his own accord and not by authority" from Lincoln; that the restoration of the Union was a *sine qua non*, and that there could be no armistice until this question was settled. The Confederate commissioners could not agree to accept the terms of peace, and after a long informal talk— which ended by shaking hands—Stephens, Hunter and Campbell returned to Richmond and reported the failure of negotiations.[30]

[28] South. Hist. Papers, Vol. IV, pp. 212-14. Benjamin to Davis, May 17, 1877.

[29] John A. Campbell: Reminiscences and documents relating to the Civil War during the year 1865. Baltimore, 1887. Stephens had no hope of European intervention. While going down the river to Hampton Roads he told Campbell that European intervention was only a dream of Benjamin's.

[30] Perhaps Mr. Davis expected different terms than those offered at Hampton Roads. H. S. Foote, who had recently

It was an opportune time to hold an indignation
meeting to reanimate the people, and cautiously prepare them for the contemplated new policy.   Such
a meeting was held on February 9, on Capitol Square
at Richmond.   Hunter presided and made a speech
picturing the future expansion of the Confederacy

resigned his place in the Confederate Congress, said that
the mission of Stephens, Hunter and Campbell was only a
ruse of Davis and a forced concession to the peace men of
the South. [N. Y. Times, Feb. 14, 1865.] Seward, in a
very confidential note to Adams on March 1, enclosed the
contents of a cipher of February 13, from a Confederate
emissary in Canada to Jefferson Davis, concerning the
attempt of Thompson and Clay to get terms of assistance
and recognition from England and France.   Seward believed
that it would throw some light upon the " late rebel proposals to the United States for a conference." [20 Instr.,
Great Brit., p. 75.]   The Richmond Dispatch of March 31,
quoted a Washington letter of March 23d to the New York
Tribune, stating that Clay had recently returned from an
unsuccessful mission to England.   The records do not appear
to indicate any such mission of Clay.   A Confederate correspondent of the London Times had written from New
York in January that there was an unexpected theatrical
change in favor of the South which would make it possible
for Davis to secure independence.   The Times suggested
that the clue to this startling mystery was to be found in
the report that the Emperor of Mexico had conveyed in
trust to Napoleon the province of Sonora to be held and
administered by a French viceroy in liquidation of the claims
of France upon the Mexican government; that it was assumed in the North that this could not occur without the
recognition of the Confederacy by France, and that such
recognition would be followed by England and other powers.
The Times further stated that these presumptions were
strengthened by the anticipations entertained of a Confederate emancipation policy. [N. Y. Times, March 1, 1865.]
By February 9, there was a report at London that ex-
Senator Gwin, of California, who was a good adventurous
leader of the Southern men in California, had been appointed

into the countries bordering on the South.[31]   But he was evidently not in harmony with the recent abolition movement, and probably knew nothing of Kenner's mission to Europe. He said that it was no comfort to contemplate the terms offered by the United States Government—that 3,000,000 negroes would be let loose to wander about as the *lazzaroni* of the land, and that Congress would be constantly interfering between the whites and the blacks. He considered that under the existing system the slaves were provided for and were happy, but that under a system of emancipation they must perish. " In the fierce competition for food between white and negro," said he, " the latter will be blasted like human life before the burning Sirocco and vanish like mist before the sun."

The other speeches were in harmony with Benjamin's recent instructions for negotiations in Europe. Senator Henry of Tennessee said that he would not hesitate to give the negro his freedom and to employ him in the army, and he urged the people to deposit with the Government their gold, cotton and tobacco. Benjamin, after having " worked night after night under infamous Richmond gas-light " studying data and problems, announced that it was

viceroy of Sonora. It appears that before Maximilian went to Mexico, Gwin had laid before him plans for rendering the mineral riches of Sonora available for the Mexican Empire. [The Index, Feb. 9, 1865.] In France it was stated that his views were ultra French and that he would carefully look after French interests. Gwin returned to France on March 2. Many Southerners like Foote had contemplated emigration to Sonora.

[31] Richmond Dispatch, Feb. 10, 1865.

necessary for all the means (cotton, tobacco, bacon, etc.), and men to be given to the Government and the army. He favored emancipating the negroes and placing them in the army, though he admitted it could only be done by the states. He said: "We want means. Are they in the country? If so, they belong to the country and not to the man who chances to hold them now. . . . I would take every cotton bale in the land . . . and make it the basis of means without which we cannot go on. . . . I am going to open my whole heart to you. . . . Let us say to every negro who wishes to go into the ranks on the condition of being made free: 'Go and fight. you are free.'" This speech from the Secretary of State of the Confederacy caused considerable excitement among slaveholders who had no desire to lose their slaves.[32] Ould, in January, had stated that rather than adopt the administration policy of freeing and arming the slaves many in Virginia would seek reconstruction. Wigfall of Texas, Graham of North Carolina, Orr and Miles of South Carolina, were among those who strongly opposed the policy in Congress.

About January 12, Kenner with full powers and letters of credit had gone to Wilmington which he found strongly invested.[33] After the fall of Fort Fisher on January 17, General Bragg suggested that he should sail from Charleston but he decided that he could reach Europe at least a month earlier by way of New York. Returning to Richmond he stated

[32] J. B. Jones: Diary, Feb. 9, 1865.
[33] War Records, Series 1, Part 2, Vol. XLVI, p. 1089.

his plan to Benjamin and Davis who at first opposed
it on the ground that it was excessively perilous to
a man whose prominence, and especially whose inter-
terests in horse-racing before the war had made him
well known in the North, and that his capture would
be almost certain.   The Confederacy had secret service communication across the Potomac, and two of
its officers were detailed to assist Kenner, one to
carry his papers and deliver them to him in New
York, the other to accompany him as far as Baltimore.
The companion was not acquainted with Mr. Kenner,
and was only informed that he was a Confederate
agent who was trying to get to Canada in order to
assist the Confederates who had been arrested for
operations on the lakes.   Reaching the Potomac they
found it full of·ice and dangerous to cross.   The
boatmen hesitated to try the river.   They remained
a few days at the home of a woman to whom they
promised to bring some needles and cloth as they returned.   They finally crossed in the night and proceeded on horseback to a place where they could
safely take a train.   They passed the house of Mrs.
Surratt who had recently moved to Washington;
they spent a night in the woods, and another at the
house of a Confederate sympathizer; and after having passed near Washington they boarded the Baltimore and Ohio train, occupying seats far apart, and
were soon in Baltimore.   Mr. Kenner, after obtaining a suit of clothes which gave him the appearance
of a Pennsylvania farmer, took leave of his companion and boarded the train for New York.   Arriving at his destination early the next morning, he
drove to a New York hotel whose proprietor he

had frequently entertained at his Louisiana home. Taking a room on the upper floor he sent for the proprietor and informed him that he was going to London with a commercial enterprise in view. Through his friend he obtained a ticket to Europe, and also a trunk that had just come off a European voyage and was covered with foreign advertisements of hotels. His presence in New York was kept quiet until his departure.[34] On the steamer he escaped the attention of Government officials and was soon *en route* for England.[35]

Coming events cast their shadows before. By the time Kenner reached Europe the new policy of the Confederacy was already anticipated at London and Paris. Perhaps a copy of Benjamin's instructions of

[34] Memoranda by the late Wm. Wirt Henry of Richmond, March 24, 1899, regarding a narrative which he and the Hon. J. L. M. Curry heard Mr. Kenner give at the White Sulphur Springs, W. Va., several years after the close of the Civil War.

[35] One finds in the Richmond papers no reference to Kenner's departure, but J. B. Jones says in his diary, under date of January 23d, that there were rumors that a commissioner (Louisianian) sailed that day to England to make overtures to that government. In the Richmond Examiner, February 3d, we find the following: " On the whole, we believe the Confederacy has given up the idea of making a present of itself to England, France and Spain, and that however willing we might be to give up slavery as the price of independence, there is no more talk of offering that as a bribe to some foreign power in order to induce it to do for us what we should confess we are unable to do for ourselves." [Also, in London Times of Feb. 20.] Another Richmond paper of February 6th stated that neither the United States nor Europe desired the abolition of slavery and that no rational being in the Confederacy had seriously entertained the suggestion of emancipation for recognition. It seems evident that the editors of these papers knew nothing of the pending negotiations. Did they?

December 29-30 to Slidell and Mason had preceded Kenner. A letter from Paris, dated January 31, stated that there was little doubt that a proposition had been communicated to England and France within the preceding month (and in a manner to leave no doubt of its official character), which suggested that in return for recognition the Confederates were prepared to abolish slavery, or for practical assistance they were ready to offer "physical concrete advantages." The letter suspected from appearances that the proposition would not be accepted. In the *Indépendance Belge,* a few days before February 1, a Paris correspondent stated that he had seen a letter from a member of the Confederate Congress, stating that President Davis intended at an early day to invite Congress to abolish slavery, and that Mason and Slidell had since informed him that if England and France had decided to acknowledge the Confederacy it could only be after the abolition of slavery. He also said that immediately on the adoption of the emancipation measure instructions and probably deputies would be sent to Europe, in order to facilitate the mission of Mason and Slidell. Another correspondent at Paris wrote to the *Index* in February, stating that he knew "from a good source" that neither Slidell nor Mason had communicated to Richmond any views as to slavery hindering the recognition of the Confederacy; nevertheless, he was convinced that the abolition of slavery would gain the favorable opinion of the liberal party, especially in France, and that, as a result, Confederate "political rights would be speedily acknowledged." [36]

[36] The Index., Feb. 2, 1865. About the middle of January, the London Times stated that a Confederate offer to abandon

The *Index* and other periodicals published a statement that after March 4, Lincoln could only be recognized as the President of the states which took part in the election of the preceding November.[37]   The *Index* of February 16 said that England and France both admitted that after March 4, the government of the United States could not be regarded as the *de facto* or *de jure* of the South.   " We are not prepared to say," it continued, "whether England and France will therefore recognize the South on that day. . . . There are, however, some indications that recognition is contemplated, at least by one of these governments . . . Whether or not recognition shall be postponed, under all circumstances a re-union or conquest of the South is to be prevented by recognition, and if necessary by intervention."   This proved to be only a contribution to a volume of unfulfilled prophecies.

Kenner,[38] arriving at London in the latter part of February, found that Mason was in Paris.   He thereupon hastened thither to present his instructions and hold a conference with Mason and Slidell.   When they

slavery could not secure the recognition of Europe, because recognition was withheld for many other reasons.   It was also seen that the abolition of slavery could not propitiate Spain.   [Richmond Sentinel, Feb. 3.]   The Times of February 13 said: " The assumption that the failure of England to recognize the Confederacy is due to the abhorrence of slavery is based on ignorance of the real opinions of Englishmen as to the abstract principles of public policy." [The Richmond Dispatch, March 4.]

[37] N. Y. Times, Feb. 12, 1865.   London Times, Jan. 23.

[38] Kenner may possibly have arrived by the middle of February, for the eccentric *Owl*, whose articles attracted attention from its alleged special sources of information, had resumed publication on February 15, and stated that it was " enabled from special sources " to give the Blair proposals.

came together, Mr. Kenner, seeing that Mr. W. W. Corcoran was in the room, said: " I was directed to show my instructions to Mr. Mason and Mr. Slidell and to no one else." But the latter gentlemen informed him that he could safely proceed in the presence of Corcoran as he was their confidential adviser. The instructions, which were in cipher, were then translated by a clerk of Slidell. Both Mason and Slidell were greatly astonished. Mason at first was disinclined to coöperate in obeying the instructions, but he yielded upon finding that he must assist or be suspended.[39]

Kenner afterwards said that through Slidell he obtained an interview with the French Minister of Foreign Affairs, who asked to defer his reply for two weeks. Mr. Slidell learned, however, that the Emperor was still ready to offer recognition if England would do so. A Confederate " diplomatic council," which had been in session for several days at the Grand Hotel at Paris, adjourned on March 2. Mann and Buchanan had gone over from Brussels to join Mason, Slidell and their secretaries. Members of the council boasted that there would be a peace between the United States and the Confederacy before May 1.[40] The *Index* stated that negotiations which were going on between European governments would " give quite a turn to affairs in America." A Paris letter of March 2, in the London *Telegraph*, said: " Mr. Kenner, a distinguished Confederate, has just arrived and brings

[39] From memoranda of Kenner's narrative, by Wm. Wirt Henry.

[40] N. Y. Times, March 20. Richmond Dispatch, March 25, 1865.

what the Southerners evidently consider good news." [41]
Mr. Mason and Mr. Kenner returned to London on
March 3, to sound the Prime Minister. Mr. Kenner
obtained no interview with Palmerston, though he
afterwards stated that Mason asked for one. While
waiting two weeks for a definite answer from France,
he opened negotiations with the bankers for the sale
of cotton. A syndicate of capitalists offered to invest
$15,000,000, and Kenner was encouraged to expect
$30,000,000, but his plans in this direction depended
upon recognition.

On March 14, Mason had an interview with Palmerston, in which he mentioned the substance of
Benjamin's instructions of December 30. He also
gave the substance of later instructions which Kenner
had received after leaving Richmond. He denied that
an aggressive alliance had been first proposed by the
Confederate commissioners at Hampton Roads. He
stated that Blair had proposed that an armistice be
granted, and that the Union and Confederate armies
be united to drive the French out of Mexico, leaving
internal questions in dispute to be decided later.
While endeavoring to leave the impression that the
United States was planning aggression against neigh-
boring possessions, Mason informed Palmerston that
the Confederacy had made an offer to France to
guarantee the French West Indies in return for alliance. He frequently and studiously reverted to the
suggestion of emancipation in a way that Palmerston
could not have misunderstood, but he " made no distinct proposal in terms of the private note borne by

[41] Richmond Dispatch, March 24, 1865.

Mr. Kenner." He said that the Confederacy might be induced to agree to terms which it would not have accepted under more favorable circumstances. He did not use the word "slavery," but Palmerston could not have had any doubt as to his meaning upon the subject of emancipation of the slaves. Desiring that Palmerston should at the close of the interview have an impression that the Confederate chances were not as hopeless as they seemed, Mason informed him that the change in the Confederate military policy, by which the coast-line was abandoned, encouraged the people by making it possible to concentrate forces in the interior.

Palmerston in reply to Mason stated that England had no reason back of those already given against recognition, and that those reasons still held. He said that while England might have taken exception to the blockade during the first year of the war, it would not have been a good policy—in view of possible wars which England might have in the future in which she might be placed in a position similar to the United States upon the question of the blockade.[42] On Sunday, March 26, Mason had a conversation with Lord Donnoughmore also, in which Mr. Kenner's mission, so far as it related to emancipation, was plainly discussed. Lord Donnoughmore said that it was too late to secure recognition by the abolition of slavery.

Across the Atlantic, at Richmond, on Sunday, two days before Mason's interview with Palmerston, the two leaders of the Confederacy again sat closeted in an all-day interview. The bill for arming and eman-

[42] Despatches of Mason, March 14, 1865. [From a duplicate, in the possession of Miss Virginia Mason.]

cipating 200,000 negroes had at last, after months of consideration, passed the Senate, Mr. Hunter having finally decided to vote for it, and in order to be a law it lacked only the President's signature. But both Davis and Benjamin saw that more than the negro bill would be required to save the Confederacy. Congress had intended to adjourn on March 10, but Davis had asked it to remain a few days. Many supposed that a treaty of alliance with France was expected. There were rumors that France had offered to intervene if the Confederacy would cede Louisiana and oppose the Monroe doctrine.[43] But Mr. Davis had evidently received no dispatches from France. On March 13, the day following the Sunday interview, Mr. Davis sent to Congress a secret message, making no reference to foreign relations, but stating that Congress had so long debated and delayed his November recommendation as to the negro bill, etc., that much of the value was now lost.[44] He asked for additional legislation increasing the power of the executive. It was observed that day that Benjamin's old smile had returned, and it was interpreted to mean a new triumph over Congress, but it was only temporary. Congress on March 16, in a dissentient and defensive reply, said that the executive had not urged the immediate necessity of the negro bill, that he had even seemed to dissent from the policy of arming the negroes, that

[43] Richmond Dispatch, March 13, 1865.

[44] Lee wrote to the War Department March 10, "The situation is full of peril and difficulty and requires prompt action. If my situation is not greatly improved I can neither hold my lines before Richmond, neither can I remove with my army from there." This was sent to Congress with Davis' secret message. [Campbell's Reminiscences.]

he had failed to reply to requests for information as to the condition of affairs, and had left Congress to determine its policy of necessity by consulting the opinion of General Lee.[45]

When the committee waited upon Davis the latter in a vigorous broadside declared that the causes of defeat could not be laid at the door of the executive; but Congress, still refusing to pass his recommendation, adjourned on March 18, *sine die*, after issuing a five-column address advising the Confederacy not to pause or commit suicide. " The shades of our departed heroes hover over us and beckon us on," it said, " . . . The enemy is far spent. . . . Let us stand firm." [46]

When Congress issued its advice, and dispersed, there was little chance of holding out much longer against Grant's campaign of shot and shell. For nearly two weeks the packing and boxing of government archives had been going on quietly. Even farther South there was little chance to prolong the struggle. When Columbia, South Carolina, fell, in February, and the lady employees of the " paper money bureau " returned to Richmond, many wept in real despair. News was scarce, but it was almost all news of defeat. The Richmond newspapers thought that the Northern Menelaus was too persistent in running after the wayward Southern Helen to induce her to return to political wedlock after she had so long trifled with marital relations.[47] But there were now many who were not opposed to returning to the

[45] Richmond Dispatch, March 20.
[46] Ibid., March 31, 1865.
[47] Ibid., March 10, 1865.

old " political wedlock."   " Street-corner generals "
were merely dissatisfied with the plans of the West
Pointers in the field, but many others contemplated
reconstruction or a counter revolution.[48]   Hon. H. S.
Foote of Tennessee, who, from the banks of the
majestic Potomac, on December 24, had proposed to
resign his place in the Richmond Congress,[49] wrote to
Seward on January 30, concerning the " strong Union
feeling of the majority in the South," [50] and on February 6, before sailing for Europe, he suggested as a
political measure that Lincoln should issue a proclamation of amnesty to the *people* of the South.   Foote
said that he had never favored secession.   In March, he
published a pamphlet in London advising his friends
to return to the Union, and he proceeded to do the
same himself.[51]   In estimating Foote's statements, it
is necessary to bear in mind that he was one of the
boldest members of the Confederate Congress in his
opposition to the Davis administration.   But Mr.
Foote's declaration was based upon what he had seen
and heard, and the voice for peace and reunion asserted itself more and more.   In the Virginia House
of Delegates, on March 9, when it was proposed to
reconsider a bill to confer conventional powers on the
General Assembly, Speaker Sheffey made strong op-

[48] On March 5, Campbell, in a note to Breckinridge, referring to the large number of desertions and advising an
investigation of the Confederate resources, said: " Georgia
is in a state of what may be properly called insurrection
against the Confederate authorities."

[49] N. Y. Times, Feb. 3, 1865.

[50] N. Y. Tribune, March 17.

[51] Richmond Dispatch, March 24, 1865.   N. Y. Tribune,
March 17, 1865.   H. S. Foote: War of the Rebellion (N. Y.,
1866).

position, saying that a convention contemplated severance from the Confederacy and consideration of reconstruction.[52] He said: "If other states fly madly from their sphere to blaze awhile, then die out in eternal night forever, let them fly; but let Virginia be one of the calm fixed stars, veiled sometimes in cloud and tempests, but indestructible as the firmament from which it shines. . . . The ship of state is upon the rapids, and . . . if we are to sink, let us sink where we stand." Of the members of the Confederate Congress who were reported to be Unionists, there were nine from Virginia, ten from North Carolina, two from South Carolina, nine from Georgia, six from Alabama, and four from Mississippi.

After the closing of navigation at Wilmington the The London *Times* had altered its tone. Lord Russell's conferences with Mr. Adams were friendlier.[53] On February 13, Russell had notified Mason, Slidell and Mann of complaints that Confederate agents did not respect British neutrality—that they sought to involve Great Britain in foreign complications by attempting to procure war armaments in British waters. He stated that to buy vessels in one place and prepare

---

[52] Richmond Dispatch, March 10, 1865.

[53] A London correspondent said that the Emperor of France might urge the recognition of the Southern Confederacy, but that England would not be shaken by the daily letters of the Paris correspondent to the London papers—that England had turned Quaker, Palmerston was too gouty, and Earl Russell and the Queen desired peace with the United States. "You may cover the lakes with gun-boats," said he to the New York Times, "and England will give the St. Lawrence for a summer outlet for the western products. If you take Canada she will throw in New Brunswick." [N. Y. Times, Feb. 13, 1865.]

them for war in another was manifestly offensive to the British Crown; and that the Confederate instructions for cruisers set aside some of the most settled principles of international law, and broke the English laws of neutrality.[54] This communication, besides being delivered to the three commissioners, was sent through Seward by way of General Grant's lines; and General Lee, receiving it under a flag of truce, forwarded it to Benjamin at Richmond.[55]

When Russell's note came to Benjamin (March 14), his career as a diplomatist had about run its course. For several weeks he had seen very little diplomatic correspondence except what he read in Northern

[54] Inclosure in Russell to Adams, Feb. 15, 1865. The *Sea King*, built in the river Clyde, Scotland, left London October 7, 1864, ostensibly for Bombay, but she was quietly purchased by Confederate agents and a few days later at Madeira was transformed into the *Shenandoah*, the crew and armament going from Liverpool on the *Laurel* which ostensibly sailed for Nassau. During the next year the *Shenandoah* circumnavigated the globe, cruising much of the time until the end of the war against the American whalers in the Arctic and Okhotsk seas, and finally returned to the Mersey, where on November 5, 1865, Commander Waddell asked Earl Russell that his men be released and that his vessel revert to the United States. [C. E. Hunt: Cruise of the *Shenandoah*; J. T. Mason: The Last of the Confederate Cruisers (Century, Aug., 1898).]

[55] When the note was first issued in London the Index bitterly referred to Seward's indecency and stated that though he danced a " can-can, he would not allow England to lift her petticoat one inch to escape the dust, and that England, while hiding her own ankles, shut her eyes to the scantiness of the Federal petticoat." The Richmond Dispatch announced that England had been " brought to play second fiddle in the concert of nations," and philosophically stated that the " greatest bullies are always first to succumb when real danger presents itself." [London Index, Feb. 16, 1865.]

newspapers, and his principal work had been to grant passports. He returned Russell's letter to General Lee (March 21), diplomatically declining to receive through the Federals a communication from a neutral, and expressing doubt as to its authenticity. General Lee suggested that the expression of doubt be omitted.[56] On March 25, Benjamin forwarded to Mason the correspondence relating to the transmission of Russell's note through Grant and Lee, and stated that he only had time to say that it was returned to Grant's lines.[57]

All hope of recognition by England was now gone, but rumors of French alliance or assistance floated in Richmond until the end. The officials took no pains to put the press in possession of authentic information, or to correct false reports.[58] On April 1, the people were " fooled " by a report that a treaty had been signed with Maximilian. The next day the Union army broke the lines, and eight trains started south with the archives and executive baggage of a now hopeless Confederacy,[59] which had for four long years stubbornly but unsuccessfully fought and, to the last, struggled for recognition as a nation. A few still expected to continue the war. On May 1, Mason

[56] J. B. Jones: Diary, March 14 and 21, 1865.

[57] Instr. to Mason, No. 40. No copy appears on the records kept at Richmond, but the original, written on very thin paper, is among the papers left by Mr. Mason.

[58] Richmond Dispatch, Jan. 30, 1865.

[59] Stephen R. Mallory, of Mr. Davis' cabinet, wrote an interesting account of the removal from Richmond which has just been published by his daughter under the caption: " The Last Days of the Confederacy." [McClure's Mag., Dec., 1900, and January, 1901.]

wrote Benjamin: "It is the almost universal opinion in Europe that the war is at an end, but I apprehend no such event." He expected the Confederacy to take a new stand farther South, and to prolong the fight until the North should be forced to come to terms on account of internal dissension.[60] But, fortunately for both North and South, the war had ended.

Notwithstanding the prediction of statesmen that the Union was dead, the Mississippi still flowed unvexed to the sea, with its springs and its mouth both in the control of one people. Not one Confederate was executed for participating in the long political disturbance. Aside from Benjamin and a few other leaders who preferred to live in foreign lands, the brave sons of the South took the oath of allegiance and faced the problems of reconstruction. Kenner, going to the United States Legation at Paris, accepted the provisions of the President's amnesty proclamation, and returned to his native state to recover possession of his estates.[61] Soldiers returned to fields of productive labor to build up what had been destroyed by the cruel fate of war. Emancipation, though not contemplated as a purpose at the beginning of the war, came as a result of it. But the prophecies that territorial aggrandizement would follow reunion remained unfulfilled. The lapse of years, and mutual interests and sympathies, have tended to heal the wounds of war and the irritations of reconstruction, and to-day an undivided nation looks upon England not with the jealousies and suspicions of former days, but as a

[60] Despatches of Mason, No. 21, May 1, 1865.
[61] Mr. Kenner died in July, 1887.

friendly power, and even as a possible ally in case of national danger. Friendly association, the study of industrial conditions, better railway connections, stronger economic interests and higher education have been clearing away misunderstandings. The Confederate armies fought gallantly, but now the veterans of the South are as much a part of the nation as are the veterans of the North or of the West.

NOTE.—There may have been other official " missions " of which there is no official record owing to their secret nature. There were also " missions " of self-appointed agents who had errands abroad, and saw fit to surround themselves with mystery. In some cases, persons who visited Europe to publish books, or pamphlets, to influence public opinion, probably went with the aid and encouragement of the Confederate authorities at Richmond.

Near the close of the war there were rumors regarding various "missions" and of possible or expected alliances. There were those who, in order to win in the war of secession, would have made great sacrifices which would not have been offered at the beginning of the struggle. Their policy was dictated by the feeling that dreads the chagrin of defeat. Though they probably could not have induced Mr. Davis to accept their policy, some of them, in order to obtain foreign aid, would have made promises which they never expected to fulfill. They would have promised France and England to set the negroes free; but at the same time they hoped for international conditions that would have enabled the Confederacy to ignore its agreements without fear of being forced to keep them.   The policy of Mr. Davis was based on higher grounds.   A prominent Confederate has recently said: " If he had been less honest, we might have succeeded in our efforts."

An editorial in the *Washington Post* of March 14, 1901, states the belief that Prince Polignac, who commanded a brigade under General Kirby E. Smith, was sent to Europe [early in 1865] on a very delicate mission, accompanied by Major John C. Moncure. " Gossip had it [at Shreveport, La.] that Polignac went authorized from Richmond to offer Louis Napoleon all that part of the original Louisiana Purchase then included in or claimed by the Southern Confederacy, the consideration being that France would send an army to aid Jefferson Davis and otherwise cooperate in the establishment of his Government in the rest of the Southern States."   The editor says he heard of the mission from Moncure himself, when the latter returned from Europe.

That such a mission was authorized by Mr. Davis, is emphatically denied by Burton N. Harrison, Esq., who was the private secretary of the Confederate President;—and also by General John H. Reagan, the only surviving member of the Confederate cabinet.[62] Polignac himself has cabled a denial (on April 2, 1901).

---

[62] See also letters from Col. James Morris Morgan and others in the *Washington Post* of March 18 and 25, 1901.   The diplomatic archives contain no record of this mission.   The records for the early part of 1865 were destroyed or lost.

APPENDIX

CAUSES OF SECESSION.

The statements of the real causes of secession, and of the beginning of the Civil War, are to be found, not in the archives of Confederate diplomacy, but by following the course of events immediately preceding the war, and by examining the contemporary speeches and writings of the secession leaders.

The assertion that the tariff was a cause of the secession movement was evidently a *ruse diplomatique*, intended for effect upon foreign powers that favored free trade. The subject of the tariff was scarcely mentioned in the discussions of Southern statesmen. Toombs, it is true, on November 13, 1861, while excitedly demanding hasty action, without the formality of State conventions to ascertain the will of the people, characterized the Union as a curse which by tariffs, navigation laws, and otherwise, had legislated against the South. But Stephens, in a reply, on the following day, opposing secession and advising calmness and deliberation in meeting the crisis, said he could not agree with Toombs. He declared that the South had prospered under the American system of government and had been protected and aided in many ways by its provisions. Among other things, he said: the Southern presidents had not opposed the early fishing bounties of New England; the tariff had ceased to distract public councils; the navigation laws had been begun under a Southern president, and no subsequent president had ever recommended their repeal; South Carolina, and also Toombs, had voted for the existing tariff, which was just as low as the South had asked.

The declaration adopted by the South Carolina Convention, in December, 1861, said nothing of the tariff as a cause of secession. Maxey Gregg suggested that it should be mentioned; but Keitt replied that all of the South Carolinian senators and congressmen had voted for the recent tariff, and that no tariff since that of 1832 had caused any desire for secession. The address of the convention to the slaveholding states (prepared by R. B. Rhett), however, had mentioned the tariff, and unequal distribution of appropriations, among other causes of grievance, and had made vague charges about the consolidation of the North and the reduction of the South. Stephens, who was not favorably impressed by the address, said these charges were not well-founded and arose from peevishness rather than from reason. Concerning the tariff, he suggested that "perhaps the less said about it the better," stating that the South though in a minority had controlled the administration for sixty out of seventy-two years, and had made the tariff and the government what they were.

The principal sources of contention were connected with the institution of slavery, which was seeking extension into new territory—even into territory which had not yet been acquired.

Questions relating to slavery had been most prominent after Polk's nomination to the presidency. Stephens, during the Mexican war, fearing the rock which Jefferson had predicted would endanger the Ship of State, favored a policy which would tend to avoid slavery discussions. The natural tendency of slavery interests to seek expansion led to attempts to annex Cuba, and a desire to obtain control of other countries southward—Mexico and Central America; but the chance to acquire new slave territory faded away after the passage of the Kansas-Nebraska bill and the decision in the Dred Scott case. Notwithstanding the efforts of the Buchanan Administration, the Kansas struggle terminated in favor of free soil,[1] and plans to acquire Cuba and part of Mexico failed.

---

[1] Stephens did not attribute the result entirely to the eternal vigilance of the Northern leaders and to the developing sentiment

In April, 1860, the Democratic party split at the Charleston convention. Both factions agreed that personal liberty laws were unconstitutional, that Cuba should be acquired, and that the Pacific railway should be built. The Southern leaders, however, feeling the moral reproach under which they were living, complained that the admission by men from the North that slavery was a wrong, but a wrong for which they were not to blame, had been the cause of the discord, and intimated that the Northern Democrats must pronounce the institution a necessary good.[2] Senator Pugh of Ohio replied: " Gentlemen of the South, we will not do it." Other sources of disagreement arose. Gaulden of Georgia asked that the ruthless restrictions which cut off the supply of slaves from foreign lands should be taken off. Some said that slavery by the intention of the constitution should be encouraged and protected by the Federal government, thus deserting the argument of non-intervention as held by previous statesmen. The Dred Scott decision has been characterized as the rock upon which the party went to pieces. The Southern minority desired the platform to declare in favor of the doctrine of the Dred Scott decision permitting the Supreme Court to settle the question of the rights of property in states or territories. The Western and Northern majority rejected this plan, though they were willing to deny

against slavery. On March 11, 1858, he wrote that the Lecompton constitution would be defeated on account of several Southern members being too drunk to get to the House. " If we are to separate," said he, sadly, " what is to become of us in the hands of such representatives." In the early part of 1860 Stephens expected to retire from politics, and to a friend who asked him why, he said: " When I am on one of the two trains coming in opposite directions on a single track, both engines at high speed, and both engineers drunk, I get off at the first station."

[2] George Fitzhugh, five or six years before, had written a book, " Sociology for the South," which justified slavery not only from expediency but from right—stating that it was the happiest form of socialism, the true relief for pauperism, and better than the *laissez faire* labor policy for the protection of the poor laborer in his struggle for existence. [Also, see De Bow, July, 1855.]

the power of Congress or the territorial legislatures to abolish slavery in the territories. Thereupon, the minority seceded from the convention, leaving the majority to adjourn. In June, the majority nominated Stephen A. Douglas and Herschel V. Johnson. The minority named John C. Breckenridge and Joseph Lane. On May 9th, the Constitutional Union party had nominated John Bell and Edward Everett. On May 16, the Republicans had met at Chicago and nominated Abraham Lincoln and Hannibal Hamlin upon the platform repudiating the Dred Scott decision, opposing the extension of slavery into the territories, but denying any sympathy with interference with slavery in the states, and declaring in favor of the Pacific railway and the homestead law.

The Democratic tangle at Charleston gave the rapidly growing Republican party such an advantage that a majority of the Lincoln electors were chosen on November 6. The South Carolina legislature chose electors on that day and remained in session to learn the result of the election, and then, being encouraged by the governor to expect aid from other states, provided for the purchase of arms and called a state convention to determine upon secession. A shower of expressions on the subject of secession followed.[3]

Some urged a declaration of dissolution by state legislatures instead of by conventions. Cobb of Georgia advised the legislature of that state to declare for secession without waiting "to hear from the crossroads and groceries." Toombs, fearing that a convention, if called by the state authorities, "would vote for abolition rule," said to the

[3] Col. R. B. Rhett of Charleston received a letter from Thomas J. Butler of Mobile, Alabama, dated November 14, saying: " I break down every barrier in order to effect the great object I have had for over thirty years—the disunion of the states and the security of slavery. If I betray unusual feeling and zeal you must attribute it in a degree to a somewhat impulsive temperament, but more to the severe schooling I have had in the lessons of Mr. Calhoun and your illustrious father."

Georgia legislature: " Give me the sword, for, if you do not give it to me, as God lives, I will take it myself." It was in vain that Stephens urged the Southern leaders not to yield to temptation as did their first parents who " reopened their eyes only to discover their own nakedness." [4]

No advice from a conservative could stay the action of the South Carolina convention. In December it seceded, issued a declaration of independence, and adopted an address to the people of the slaveholding states. The declaration, pre-

---

[4] Stephens urged that the South should not break the constitution because she failed in the election, but that she should wait until the North broke it. He called attention to the fact that the House of Representatives and the Senate were largely Democratic, thus tying Lincoln's hands and leaving him no opportunity to do any thing unconstitutional. He saw no reason why the South should take the last step, so long as there was a chance that the Northern and Western legislatures would recede from their hostility towards the fugitive slave laws.

On November 24, Stephens wrote his brother that he had no doubt that redress might be obtained if it was sought in the proper spirit and with an honest purpose, but he feared that such was not the object of the agitators. " We are, I fear," said he, " in the hands of those who are bent upon dissolution at all hazards. Nothing will satisfy them but to get out of the Union. . . . The evil genius of civil discord seems to be rampant." Again, on November 30, while insisting that the popular will should be as fairly represented as possible, he said, " The truth is our leaders do not wish any redress . . . are disunionists per se . . and . . they will carry the state." [Johnston and Browne: Life of A. H. Stephens.]

There were others who threw their weight on the brakes to stop the accelerating movement of the car of secession. One of these was J. A. Campbell, who, although he had emancipated his slaves while a member of the United States Supreme Court, exerted great influence in the government at Richmond during the entire period of the war. On November 26, he protested against secession on the ground that all classes tend towards the same standard of intelligence and submit eventually to the same rule of opinion— stating that the South could gain nothing and that the election of Lincoln was not a sufficient cause for revolt. [Du Bose: Life and Times of William Lowndes Yancey, p. 689.]

pared by Memminger and adopted December 24, declared the right of a state to govern itself or to abolish governments, advocated the compact theory of government, said the Northern states had disobeyed the compact, complained that the ends of 1787 had been defeated and that a sectional party was now in power, endangering the institution of slavery. The address recited that, notwithstanding the prosperity of the United States, discontent had been caused by taxation without representation, by unequal distribution of appropriations, by Northern evasion of the compromises, by abrogation of the limitations of the constitution, and by the attitude of the majority toward the minority. It spoke of the constitution as only an experiment begun when there was no tariff and no negro fanaticism; it did not seek reform but desired only to be let alone. It preferred a system of slavery "where capital and labor are identified in interests" to a system of industry where capital and labor are in conflict.[5]

Stephens was not favorably impressed by the address of the convention. He said that it hardly deigned to specify grievances and that it almost entirely ignored the slavery question—barely glancing at the personal liberty acts which were the real cause of complaint.[6]

Events were now hurrying rapidly to a catastrophe. "The times are fearfully distempered," said Stephens, "We are on the high road to ruin." But when his state seceded a few days later, he resolved to "go down with a fragment of the wreck."

American public opinion had not yet decided in favor of coercion, but expected compromise. Horace Greeley, in the

---

[5] McPherson: Political History of the Rebellion.

[6] In a letter to Lincoln, Stephens said that previous presidents, Washington and Jefferson, had had antislavery opinions, and that in his judgment "the people of the South did not fear that the Republican administration would attempt to interfere directly or immediately with slavery in the states, but that their discontent and apprehension was created by the fear of results of fanaticism like that of John Brown."

Tribune of November 9, favored letting the seceding states go rather than holding them by bayonets. Many in the North and in the border states desired compromise, and various plans were proposed. Thurlow Weed, in his Albany *Evening Journal*, proposed a law for the payment of rescued slaves by counties and the extension of the Missouri compromise to the Pacific. George P. Curtis believed that Massachusetts would repeal her personal liberty law, and the House of Representatives, on December 17, by a vote of 153 to 14 recommended a repeal of these laws as far as they were in conflict with the constitution, but Senator Iverson said that the immediate repeal of all these laws could not stop the progress of the "revolution." Davis and Toombs complained that the North refused to recognize slaves as property in the territories. Southerners were sensitive to the Northern sentiment that slavery was out of harmony with the moral progress of the age. Crittenden of Kentucky, December 18, introduced into the Senate a plan of compromise favoring an amendment to the constitution, extending the Missouri compromise line of division to all territory of the United States so long as it should remain as territory, and providing that when states should be organized in such territory, either north or south of the line of 36° 30′, they should be admitted free or slave as their constitution might provide. Congress was to have no power to shut slavery from the territories; slaves were to be protected as property by all the departments of the territorial government; Congress was never to have the power to interfere with slavery in the states where the laws permitted that institution—not even in places within those states where Congress had exclusive jurisdiction; and payment for rescued slaves was to be made by the United States government. Such was the Crittenden plan to which the Republicans could not agree, and no agreement could be reached on other plans before the issue came.

On December 18, 1860, Senator Powell of Kentucky offered

a resolution for the selection of a committee of thirteen to consider the grievances of the slaveholding states. The Senate adopted it and the Vice-President appointed Powell, Crittenden, Hunter, Toombs and Davis with the Northern Democrats, Douglas, Bigelow and Rice, and the Republicans Seward, Collamer, Doolittle and Grimes. Before they met, South Carolina had seceded. On December 22, Crittenden presented his plan to the committee. Article 1 relating to territories was the most important. It was opposed by all the Republicans and by Toombs and Davis. The Republicans also opposed the other articles. They probably feared Southern fillibustering to get Mexico, Cuba and Central America. Nevertheless there was considerable opinion in the North in favor of the Crittenden amendment. The Northern Democrats and Hunter, Powell and Crittenden would have accepted the compromise but Seward, on December 26, wrote Lincoln that, even with the restoration of the 36° 30′ line, Georgia, Alabama, Mississippi and Louisiana would secede. As a congressional law, instead of a constitutional amendment, Lincoln would have accepted all the compromise except article 1. He believed that the agitation could be stopped for a time by the provision to extend the 36° 30′ line, but would probably be renewed by Southern attempts to seize and annex Mexico. He believed that compromise could only postpone, but thought that the fugitive slave law ought not to be resisted in the North.

The Republicans offered a plan of compromise. On December 24 Seward proposed to the committee of thirteen: (1) That there should be a constitutional amendment that the constitution should never be amended so as to authorize Congress to interfere with slavery in the state. (2) That the fugitive slave law should be amended so as to grant jury trial to the fugitive. (3) That Congress should recommend the repeal of the personal liberty acts that were unconstitutional. Two days later he also proposed that Congress should pass no law for the punishment of persons engaged in the armed invasion of any state from another. Grimes of Iowa was willing to admit Kansas under the Wyandotte constitution, and to admit the rest of the western territories as two states divided by the line of 36° 30′ with provisions for their future sub-division when the population should be sufficient. This would have made New Mexico a pro-slavery pocket borough—though physical laws, even in the face of congressional laws to the contrary, would, perhaps, have prevented slavery from thriving there. Of the above Republican proposals only the first one was carried.

After considering other propositions, the committee of thirteen reported to Congress that they could not agree on a plan of adjustment. Crittenden then proposed (January 3, 1861) in the Senate, that his compromise plan should be submitted to the people. Douglas favored it, but the question never came to a vote in the Senate.

Clingman of North Carolina said that he was astonished that the North hesitated to accept the Crittenden plan; that it gave that section the larger amount of present territory and left undisturbed the right to a vote as to the acquisition of further territory toward the South. Lincoln, however, was opposed to surrendering his principles in order to please those beaten at the elections, whom he feared would next ask for Cuba as a condition for remaining in the Union. He stated that the constitution was the same as before the election, and that there never was a more shallow pretext for extorting a compromise. "There is in my judgment," said he, "but one compromise which would really settle the slavery question, and that would be a prohibition against acquiring any more territory." In a letter to Seward on February 1, 1861, he said, "I am for no compromise which permits extension of slavery to soil now owned by the nation, or allows any trick by which the nation is to acquire territory and allow some local authority to spread slavery over it." [7]

[7] Nicolay and Hay: Abraham Lincoln, Complete Works, Vol. I.

On February 4, while the Southern leaders were making their farewell speeches in Congress, and while delegates from six cotton states were convening at Montgomery, Alabama, to form a Southern confederacy, a peace convention in which 21 states were represented, met at Washington in response to a proposal (January 19) from Virginia, whose legislature deprecated disunion. The seceding states were not represented. Virginia desired to save the Union and was willing to accept the Crittenden compromise as a constitutional amendment. The subject of future expansion [8] was a prominent feature of the debates and many of the speeches gave the intimation that the South was contemplating national suicide because there was no constitutional amendment regarding future acquisitions of territory. Some Southern delegates, like Reid of North Carolina, were looking forward to the glory of future expansion. Some of the Northern delegates spoke of the evils of expansion, and desired restrictions on future acquisitions. Loomis of Pennsylvania, declaring that new acquisitions would only bring new troubles, said: " We want no more territory north or south." Others, however, were opposed to restrictions for the future on the ground that they were unnecessary and might prove troublesome. Frelinghuysen, of New Jersey, told the Southern delegates that there was no reason for discussing contingencies which might never happen—that they had enough territory for the next two hundred years, and that, before they should need more land possibly even the North would want Cuba and Mexico for trade advantages. In discussing a resolution based on the Crittenden plan, Reverdy Johnson of Maryland, who thought we had sufficient territory and hoped that we would not separate on account of territory we did not have and did not need, desired to insert the word

---

[8] On the influence of the South on expansion, see C. E. Evans (Ed.): Confederate Military History, Vol. I, pp. 59-246, [W. R. Garrett: The South as a factor in the territorial expansion of the United States.]

" present " before " territory " in article 1, stating that a constitutional amendment should not go forth to the world indicating that the United States proposed to acquire new territory in any way. The word " present " was inserted. Afterwards Summer offered an amendment that no territory should be acquired except by discovery or for naval depots and transit routes, without the concurrence of the majority of the senators from each section. The motion was carried, but the proposition failed in the final vote upon the report of the convention.[9] On February 27, the convention, voting by states, recommended to Congress a constitutional amendment which was less favorable to the South than the Crittenden plan but was not satisfactory to the radicals or the Republicans. It advocated the extension of the Missouri compromise line to the Pacific, the establishment, by Congress, of slavery south of that line, and compensation by the United States for fugitive slaves rescued after arrest. A committee of Congress joined in favoring the compromise, but it was too late. On March 4, Crittenden offered the report to the Senate and it received only seven ayes, among whom were Crittenden, Douglas and two Republicans. The radical republicans had been opposed to the peace convention. The House by 113 to 80 and the Senate by 20 to 19 refused to submit the Crittenden compromise to the people, but Congress by a two-thirds vote of each House recommended a constitutional amendment providing that no future amendment should ever give Congress power to interfere with the domestic institutions of the states. This satisfied many in Virginia, North Carolina and Tennessee. Nelson of Tennessee said it would remove the only ground of apprehension to the slave states. But it could not stop secession. Public sentiment changed with the course of events. Virginia

[9] L. E. Chittenden: Report of the Debates and Proceedings of the Secret Sessions of the Conference Convention for proposing amendments to the Constitution of the United States, Feb., 1861. N. Y., 1864.

was at first strongly opposed to disunion, but she was also opposed to coercion in case conciliation failed to bring back seceded states.

A statement of the causes of secession may be found in the farewell speeches of Southern congressmen delivered in January and February and also in the proceedings of the seceding conventions. The predominant tone was that the states seceded because they believed the election of Lincoln meant a blow to the institution of slavery. Toombs, on January 7, in the Senate, said that the South made five demands to cure grievances and prevent secession: (1) Equal right to go to the territories. (2) The same protection for slaves as for other property—leaving each state to protect or prohibit slavery. (3) The delivery of persons committing crimes against slave property and fleeing to other states. (4) The surrender of fugitive slaves. (5) The passage by Congress of laws for the punishment of those aiding or abetting invasion or insurrection in any state.[10] The Mississippi convention said: " Our position is thoroughly identified with the institution of slavery . . . There was no choice left us but submission to the mandates of abolition or a dissolution of the Union." " Your votes," said Jefferson Davis, "refuse to recognize our domestic institution which pre-existed the formation of the Union, our property which was guaranteed by the constitution."[11] In his farewell speech to the Senate, January 21, Mr. Davis said: " Mississippi secedes because she hears the theory that all men are created free and equal made the basis of an attack upon her social institutions."

Mr. Slidell, February 4, in presenting to the Senate an ordinance to dissolve the compact between Louisiana and the United States, stated that the mere election of Lincoln was not the cause of secession, but that it indicated that outside of New Jersey there was a solid North against

[10] P. A. Stovall. Life of Robt. Toombs.
[11] Alfriend: Jefferson Davis, pp. 225-30.

Southern institutions, and he declared that the inauguration of Lincoln with Southern assent would mean slave outbreaks. He spoke of the advantages which the South would have in forming a new nation, and said there was no reason to fear coercion. He was willing to adhere to the old constitution and treaties, pay a portion of the national debt, and leave the navigation of the Mississippi free to the inhabitants of its valley; and he expected foreign nations to acknowledge the *de facto* Southern government and to insist upon communication with Southern ports.[12]

Mr. Benjamin, in his " farewell " of February 5, said: " Of all the causes which justify the action of the Southern states I know none of greater gravity and more alarming magnitude than that now developed of the denial of the right of secession." He declared that the purchase of Louisiana by the United States did not bind the white men of the state by ties that could not be severed. Clingman held that after an honest effort to defeat Lincoln the South was not responsible for his election and was justified in seceding.

The foregoing speeches indicate the presence of a general belief among Southern leaders that the perpetuation of the institution of slavery, or of Southern rights connected with slavery, were endangered by the election of Lincoln. It must be remembered, however, that, until the Southerners withdrew, the Republicans were still the smaller party in both Houses, and that the President had no power to abolish slavery except as a war measure. But the secessionists were correct in their conviction that the Northern moral sense against slavery pointed toward the ultimate doom of the institution, and they made the election of Lincoln a pretext for secession. Did secession and the war then result from the desire to perpetuate slavery? In his speech at Savannah on March 1, 1861, Stephens stated that race servitude was the real cornerstone upon which the Confederacy was based. But, years after the close of the war, when the people, drawn

---

[12] Cong. Globe, Feb. 4, 1861.

together by mutual interests, were again being fused into a durable nationality, Jefferson Davis said: " To whatever extent the question of slavery may have served as an occasion, it was far from being a cause of the war."

Davis held that slavery was only an incident in a group of causes—that the South did not secede on account of the Northern attitude toward slavery, but rather from the fear of what a sectional party might do when once in power.[13]

In the farewell speeches one sees no reference to many causes which had contributed to embitter feeling on the subject of slavery: the lack of communication, the economic, educational, social and political differences which arose from different systems of labor, and the influence of climate and soil in producing them. The Southern states being agricultural communities, were led to the general introduction of slavery, and this in turn kept them agricultural while the North was developing into a country of diversified interests and of denser population than the South. The North had outgrown the economic conditions of 1776, and material interests had been changed by the growth of manufacturing and commercial towns in the North and West. Helper, in his pamphlet of 1859, on the Impending Crisis, said that if slavery could be abolished manufacturing might become an industry in the South; and that the social position of the non-slaveholding whites, consisting of about two-thirds of the voters, would soon compare with the mechanics and farmers of the North.

With the conditions of soil and climate which made slavery more profitable in the South and secured greater immigration to the North; with the differences in institutions which resulted from slavery; with railroads of different gauge and inconvenient connections; sometimes in an atmosphere of misunderstanding where neighbor was ignorant of neighbor, and where some of the opposing politicians learned nothing and forgot nothing—compromise failed, passions controlled,

[13] J. Davis: Rise and Fall of the Confederate Government, 1881.

the spirit of secession spread, and war was precipitated. Southern leaders, feeling that the social and industrial system of the South was insecure, preferred to appeal to the prenational principles of confederation and to repudiate the idea of nationality.[14]

The secession movement had continued under the management of the political leaders and on February 4, 1861, delegates met at Montgomery to organize a government. Conservatives like Stephens were still opposed to secession as a "remedy against anticipated aggressions." Stephens finally decided to accept a place in the provisional government, though he wrote that when he considered the "ambitious . . . men at the head of the movement, who necessarily control[led] at least for the present" he had apprehension and mistrust for the future. Some who joined the movement hoped for something to occur to prevent permanent dissolution, and expected to obtain better terms for slavery by a temporary withdrawal from the Union; others dreamed of a peaceful dissolution, for many in the North were opposed to coercion. There was a strong Southern opposition to secession, especially in Georgia, Virginia, North Carolina and Louisiana. Yet the movement did not lack the substantial support of the majority of the people after it was once begun, though in Georgia especially there was at first a majority of the white people who opposed it. It was only by impassioned persuasion, or by argument of temporary expediency, that the leaders in some parts obtained popular support for their project. Perhaps the United States constitution could never have been carried in 1788 if its ratification had been voted upon by the whole people at the polls, and it has been said that secession would have failed if it had depended upon the popular vote.

[14] Papers rel. to the ratification of the ordinances of secession.

INDEX